BOOK 1 – ETHICAL AND PROFESSIONAL STANDARDS AND QUANTITATIVE METHODS

LEVEL 2 BOOK 1: ETHICAL AND PROFESSIONAL STANDARDS AND QUANTITATIVE METHODS

©2008 Kaplan Schweser. All rights reserved.

Published in September 2008 by Kaplan Schweser.

Printed in the United States of America.

ISBN: 1-60373-229-2 / 978-1-60373-229-1

PPN: 45545CFA

WELCOME TO THE 2009 SCHWESERNOTES™

Thank you for trusting Kaplan Schweser to help you reach your goals. We are all very pleased to be able to help you prepare for the Level 2 CFA Exam. In this introduction, I want to explain the resources included with the SchweserNotes™, suggest how you can best use Schweser materials to prepare for the exam, and direct you toward other educational resources you will find helpful as you study for the exam.

Besides the SchweserNotes themselves, there are many educational resources available at Schweser.com. Just log in using the individual username and password that you received when you purchased the SchweserNotes, and go to Online Access Home. All purchasers of our 2009 Level 2 SchweserNotes™ Pack receive the following:

SchweserNotes™

Five volumes that include complete coverage of all 18 Study Sessions and all Learning Outcome Statements (LOS) with examples, Concept Checkers (multiple-choice questions for every reading), and Challenge Problems for many readings to help you master the material and check your progress. At the end of each topic area, we include a self-test. Self-test questions are created to be exam-like in format and difficulty in order for you to evaluate how well your study of each topic has prepared you for the actual exam.

Practice Exams Volume 1

Three full (120-question, 6-hour) Level 2 practice exams to help you prepare for the exam itself as well as to better target your final review efforts.

Schweser Library

We have created reference videos that are available to all SchweserNotes purchasers. Each Schweser Library volume is approximately 30 to 60 minutes in length. Topics include: "Introduction to Item Sets," "Hypothesis Testing," "Foreign Exchange Basics," "Ratio Analysis," and "Forward Contracts."

Online Schweser Study Planner

Use your Online Access to tell us when you will start and what days of the week you can study. The online Schweser Study Planner will create a study plan just for you, breaking each study session into daily and weekly tasks to keep you on track and help you monitor your progress through the curriculum.

If you received SchweserNotes in a Study Solution package, you will also receive access to our Instructor-led Office Hours. Office Hours allow you to get your questions about the curriculum answered in real time and see others' questions (and instructor answers). Office Hours is a text-based live interactive online chat with our team of Level 2 experts. Archives of previous Office Hours sessions are sorted by topic and are posted shortly after each session.

The Level 2 CFA exam is a formidable challenge (71 readings and nearly 500 Learning Outcome Statements), and you must devote considerable time and effort to be properly prepared. There is no shortcut! You must learn the material, know the terminology and techniques, understand the concepts, and be able to answer (70% of) 120 questions quickly and correctly. Fifteen to 20 hours per week for 20 weeks is probably a good estimate of the study time required on average, but some candidates will need more or less time, depending on their individual backgrounds and experience.

To help you master this material and be well prepared for the CFA Exam, we offer several other educational resources, including:

Live Weekly Classroom Programs
We offer weekly classroom programs in several large cities. Please check at Schweser.com for locations, dates, and availability.

16-Week Online Classes
Our 16-Week Online Classes are available in New York Time (6:30-9:30 pm) or London Time (6:00-9:00 pm). The schedule for the 16-Week Online Classes (3-hour sessions) is as follows:

Class #	Class #
1) Exam Intro, Ethics, & Quant SS 1, 2, 3	9) Equity SS 10, 11
2) Quantitative Methods SS 3	10) Equity SS 12
3) Economics SS 4	11) Alternative Assets SS 13
4) Economics & Corporate Finance SS 4, 8	12) Fixed Income SS 14
5) Corporate Finance SS 9	13) Fixed Income SS 15
6) Financial Statement Analysis SS 5	14) Derivatives SS 16, 17
7) Financial Statement Analysis SS 6	15) Derivatives & Portfolio Management SS 17, 18
8) Financial Statement Analysis SS 7	16) Portfolio Management SS 18

Archived classes are available for viewing at any time throughout the season. Candidates enrolled in the 16-Week Online Classes also have access to another 15+ hours of video instruction in the online Schweser Library, downloadable slide files for all slides presented in class, workshop problems and solutions, and a special e-mail address where they can send questions to the instructor at any time.

Intensive Review
Schweser Seminars are an excellent tool for you to learn how to focus your time, evaluate the intent of the learning outcome statements (LOS), and review the curriculum. CFA® curriculum experts lead our Seminars to help pinpoint your strengths and weaknesses, and to provide the knowledge you need for success on exam day. Visit Schweser.com for a complete listing of Schweser Seminars.

Practice Questions
In order to retain what you learn, it is important that you quiz yourself often. We offer CD, download, and online versions of the SchweserPro™ QBank, which contains thousands of Level 2 practice questions, item sets, and explanations. Quizzes are available for each LOS, reading, or Study Session. Build your own exams using the topics and the number of questions you select.

Practice Exams

In addition to the practice exams included with the SchweserNotes Pack, we also offer six other Level 2 practice exams. Practice Exams Volume 2 contains three full 120-question (6-hour) exams, and three more are available as offered in our 2-Day Mock Exam and Problem Solving Workshop. These are important tools for gaining the speed and confidence you will need to pass the exam. Each book contains the answers with full explanations for self-grading and evaluation. By entering your answers at Schweser.com, you can use our Performance Tracker to find out how you have performed compared to other Schweser Level 2 candidates.

How to Succeed

There are no shortcuts; depend on the fact that CFA Institute will test you in a way that will reveal how well you know the Level 2 curriculum. You should begin early and stick to your study plan. You should first read the SchweserNotes and complete the Concept Checkers and Challenge Problems for each reading. You should prepare for and attend a live class, an online class, or a study group each week. You should take quizzes often using SchweserPro Qbank and go back to review previous readings and Study Sessions as well. At the end of each topic area you should take the self-test to check your progress. You should finish the overall curriculum at least two weeks (preferably four weeks) before the Level 2 exam so that you have sufficient time for Practice Exams and for further review of those topics that you have not yet mastered.

Best regards,

Brent Lekvin

Brent Lekvin, PhD, CFA
VP and Level 2 Manager

Kaplan Schweser

READINGS AND LEARNING OUTCOME STATEMENTS

READINGS

The following material is a review of the Ethical and Professional Standards and Quantitative Methods principles designed to address the learning outcome statements set forth by CFA Institute.

STUDY SESSION 1

Reading Assignments

Ethical and Professional Standards and Quantitative Methods, CFA Program Curriculum, Volume 1, Level 2 (CFA Institute, 2008)

STUDY SESSION 2

Reading Assignments

Ethical and Professional Standards and Quantitative Methods, CFA Program Curriculum, Volume 1, Level 2 (CFA Institute, 2008)

STUDY SESSION 3

Reading Assignments

Ethical and Professional Standards and Quantitative Methods, CFA Program Curriculum, Volume 1, Level 2 (CFA Institute, 2008)

LEARNING OUTCOME STATEMENTS (LOS)

The CFA Institute Learning Outcome Statements are listed below. These are repeated in each topic review; however, the order may have been changed in order to get a better fit with the flow of the review.

STUDY SESSION 1

The topical coverage corresponds with the following CFA Institute assigned reading:
1. **Code of Ethics and Standards of Professional Conduct**
   The candidate should be able to:
   a. state the six components of the Code of Ethics and the seven Standards of Professional Conduct. (page 11)
   b. explain the ethical responsibilities required by the Code and Standards. (page 11)

The topical coverage corresponds with the following CFA Institute assigned reading:
2. **"Guidance" for Standards I–VII**
   The candidate should be able to:
   a. demonstrate a thorough knowledge of the Code of Ethics and Standards of Professional Conduct by applying the Code and Standards to specific situations. (page 16)
   b. recommend practices and procedures designed to prevent violations of the Code of Ethics and Standards of Professional Conduct. (page 16)

The topical coverage corresponds with the following CFA Institute assigned reading:
3. **CFA Institute Soft Dollar Standards**
   The candidate should be able to:
   a. define "soft dollar" arrangements and state the general principles of the Soft Dollar Standards. (page 101)
   b. critique company soft dollar practices and policies. (page 102)
   c. determine whether a product or service qualifies as "permissible research" that can be purchased with client brokerage. (page 105)

The topical coverage corresponds with the following CFA Institute assigned reading:
4. **CFA Institute Research Objectivity Standards**
   The candidate should be able to:
   a. explain the objectives of the Research Objectivity Standards. (page 111)
   b. critique company policies and practices related to research objectivity and distinguish between changes required and changes recommended for compliance with the Research Objectivity Standards. (page 112)

STUDY SESSION 2

The topical coverage corresponds with the following CFA Institute assigned reading:

5. **The Glenarm Company**
6. **Preston Partners**
7. **Super Selection**
   For each of the cases, the candidate should be able to:
   a. critique the practices and policies presented. (pages 121, 123, 126)
   b. explain the appropriate action to take in response to conduct that violates the CFA Institute Code of Ethics and Standards of Professional Conduct. (pages 121, 123, 126)

The topical coverage corresponds with the following CFA Institute assigned reading:

8. **Trade Allocation: Fair Dealing and Disclosure**
   The candidate should be able to:
   a. critique trade allocation practices and determine whether there is compliance with the CFA Institute Standards of Professional Conduct addressing fair dealing and client loyalty. (page 129)
   b. discuss appropriate actions to take in response to trade allocation practices that do not adequately respect client interests. (page 130)

The topical coverage corresponds with the following CFA Institute assigned reading:

9. **Changing Investment Objectives**
   The candidate should be able to:
   a. critique the disclosure of investment objectives and basic policies and determine whether they comply with the CFA Institute Standards of Professional Conduct. (page 131)
   b. discuss appropriate actions needed to ensure adequate disclosure of the investment process. (page 132)

The topical coverage corresponds with the following CFA Institute assigned reading:

10. **Prudence in Perspective**
    The candidate should be able to:
    a. explain the basic principles of the new Prudent Investor Rule. (page 133)
    b. explain the general fiduciary standards to which a trustee must adhere. (page 134)
    c. differentiate between the old Prudent Man Rule and the new Prudent Investor Rule. (page 135)
    d. explain the key factors that a trustee should consider when investing and managing trust assets. (page 135)

STUDY SESSION 3

The topical coverage corresponds with the following CFA Institute assigned reading:

11. **Correlation and Regression**

The candidate should be able to:

a. calculate and interpret a sample covariance and a sample correlation coefficient, and interpret a scatter plot. (page 140)

b. explain the limitations to correlation analysis, including outliers and spurious correlation. (page 145)

c. formulate a test of the hypothesis that the population correlation coefficient equals zero, and determine whether the hypothesis is rejected at a given level of significance. (page 145)

d. differentiate between the dependent and independent variables in a linear regression. (page 147)

e. explain the assumptions underlying linear regression and interpret the regression coefficients. (page 148)

f. calculate and interpret the standard error of estimate, the coefficient of determination, and a confidence interval for a regression coefficient. (page 152)

g. formulate a null and alternative hypothesis about a population value of a regression coefficient, select the appropriate test statistic, and determine whether the null hypothesis is rejected at a given level of significance. (page 154)

h. calculate a predicted value for the dependent variable, given an estimated regression model and a value for the independent variable, and calculate and interpret a confidence interval for the predicted value of a dependent variable. (page 155)

i. describe the use of analysis of variance (ANOVA) in regression analysis, interpret ANOVA results, and calculate and interpret an *F*-statistic. (page 157)

j. discuss the limitations of regression analysis. (page 162)

The topical coverage corresponds with the following CFA Institute assigned reading:

12. **Multiple Regression and Issues in Regression Analysis**

The candidate should be able to:

a. formulate a multiple regression equation to describe the relation between a dependent variable and several independent variables, determine the statistical significance of each independent variable, and interpret the estimated coefficients and their *p*-values. (page 176)

b. formulate a null and an alternative hypothesis about the population value of a regression coefficient, calculate the value of the test statistic, determine whether to reject the null hypothesis at a given level of significance, using a one-tailed or two-tailed test, and interpret the result of the test. (page 178)

c. calculate and interpret 1) a confidence interval for the population value of a regression coefficient and 2) a predicted value for the dependent variable, given an estimated regression model and assumed values for the independent variables. (page 182)

d. explain the assumptions of a multiple regression model. (page 184)

e. calculate and interpret the *F*-statistic, and discuss how it is used in regression analysis, define, distinguish between, and interpret the R^2 and adjusted R^2 in multiple regression, and infer how well a regression model explains the dependent variable by analyzing the output of the regression equation and an ANOVA table. (page 184)

f. formulate a multiple regression equation using dummy variables to represent qualitative factors, and interpret the coefficients and regression results. (page 193)

g. discuss the types of heteroskedasticity and the effects of heteroskedasticity and serial correlation on statistical inference. (page 196)

h. describe multicollinearity and discuss its causes and effects in regression analysis. (page 203)

i. discuss the effects of model misspecification on the results of a regression analysis, and explain how to avoid the common forms of misspecification. (page 205)

j. discuss models with qualitative dependent variables. (page 209)

k. interpret the economic meaning of the results of multiple regression analysis, and critique a regression model and its results. (page 210)

The topical coverage corresponds with the following CFA Institute assigned reading:

13. **Time-Series Analysis**
The candidate should be able to:

a. calculate and evaluate the predicted trend value for a time series, modeled as either a linear trend or a log-linear trend, given the estimated trend coefficients. (page 222)

b. discuss the factors that determine whether a linear or a log-linear trend should be used with a particular time series, and evaluate the limitations of trend models. (page 228)

c. explain the requirement for a time series to be covariance stationary, and discuss the significance of a series not being stationary. (page 237)

d. discuss the structure of an autoregressive model of order p, calculate one- and two-period-ahead forecasts given the estimated coefficients, and explain how autocorrelations of the residuals can be used to test whether the autoregressive model fits the time series. (page 229)

e. explain mean reversion, and calculate a mean-reverting level. (page 238)

f. contrast in-sample forecasts and out-of-sample forecasts, and compare the forecasting accuracy of different time-series models based on the root mean squared error criterion. (page 236)

g. discuss the instability of coefficients of time-series models. (page 236)

h. describe the characteristics of random walk processes, and contrast them to covariance stationary processes. (page 239)

i. discuss the implications of unit roots for time-series analysis, explain when unit roots are likely to occur and how to test for them, and demonstrate how a time series with a unit root can be transformed so that it can be analyzed with an autoregressive model. (page 241)

j. discuss the steps of the unit root test for nonstationarity, and explain the relation of the test to autoregressive time series models. (page 241)

k. discuss how to test and correct for seasonality in a time-series model, and calculate and interpret a forecasted value using an AR model with a seasonal lag. (page 232)

l. explain autoregressive conditional heteroskedasticity (ARCH), and discuss how ARCH models can be applied to predict the variance of a time series. (page 247)

m. explain how time-series variables should be analyzed for nonstationarity and/or cointegration before use in a linear regression. (page 245)

n. select and justify the choice of a particular time-series model from a group of models. (page 248)

CFA INSTITUTE CODE OF ETHICS AND STANDARDS OF PROFESSIONAL CONDUCT AND "GUIDANCE" FOR STANDARDS I–VII

Study Session 1

EXAM FOCUS

In addition to reading this review of the ethics material, we strongly recommend that all candidates for the CFA® examination *purchase* their own copy of the *Standards of Practice Handbook* 9th Edition (2005) and read it multiple times. As a registered candidate, it is your responsibility to own an original copy of the *Code and Standards* and to comply with the *Code and Standards*.

 Professor's Note: The 9th edition of the Standards of Practice Handbook *is now in effect. There are significant revisions, restructurings, additions, and deletions to the previous edition that you should be aware of.*

CFA INSTITUTE CODE OF ETHICS AND STANDARDS OF PROFESSIONAL CONDUCT

LOS 1.a: State the six components of the Code of Ethics and the seven Standards of Professional Conduct.

LOS 1.b: Explain the ethical responsibilities required by the Code and Standards.

Code of Ethics

Members of CFA Institute [including Chartered Financial Analyst® (CFA®) charterholders] and candidates for the CFA designation ("Members and Candidates") must:[1]

- Act with integrity, competence, diligence, respect, and in an ethical manner with the public, clients, prospective clients, employers, employees, colleagues in the investment profession, and other participants in the global capital markets.
- Place the integrity of the investment profession and the interests of clients above their own personal interests.

---

1. Copyright 2005, CFA Institute. Reproduced and republished from "The Code of Ethics," from *Standards of Practice Handbook, 9th ed., 2005*, with permission from CFA Institute. All rights reserved.

- Use reasonable care and exercise independent professional judgment when conducting investment analysis, making investment recommendations, taking investment actions, and engaging in other professional activities.
- Practice and encourage others to practice in a professional and ethical manner that will reflect credit on themselves and the profession.
- Promote the integrity of, and uphold the rules governing, capital markets.
- Maintain and improve their professional competence and strive to maintain and improve the competence of other investment professionals.

The Standards of Professional Conduct are organized into seven standards:

I.   Professionalism
II. Integrity of Capital Markets
III. Duties to Clients
IV. Duties to Employers
V.   Investment Analysis, Recommendations, and Action
VI. Conflicts of Interest
VII. Responsibilities as a CFA Institute Member or CFA Candidate

I.   PROFESSIONALISM

A.   **Knowledge of the Law.** Members and Candidates must understand and comply with all applicable laws, rules, and regulations (including the CFA Institute Code of Ethics and Standards of Professional Conduct) of any government, regulatory organization, licensing agency, or professional association governing their professional activities. In the event of conflict, Members and Candidates must comply with the more strict law, rule, or regulation. Members and Candidates must not knowingly participate or assist in any violation of laws, rules, or regulations and must disassociate themselves from any such violation.

B.   **Independence and Objectivity.** Members and Candidates must use reasonable care and judgment to achieve and maintain independence and objectivity in their professional activities. Members and Candidates must not offer, solicit, or accept any gift, benefit, compensation, or consideration that reasonably could be expected to compromise their own or another's independence and objectivity.

C.   **Misrepresentation.** Members and Candidates must not knowingly make any misrepresentations relating to investment analysis, recommendations, actions, or other professional activities.

D.   **Misconduct.** Members and Candidates must not engage in any professional conduct involving dishonesty, fraud, or deceit or commit any act that reflects adversely on their professional reputation, integrity, or competence.

II.   INTEGRITY OF CAPITAL MARKETS

A.   **Material Nonpublic Information.** Members and Candidates who possess material nonpublic information that could affect the value of an investment must not act or cause others to act on the information.

B.   **Market Manipulation.** Members and Candidates must not engage in practices that distort prices or artificially inflate trading volume with the intent to mislead market participants.

III.   DUTIES TO CLIENTS

A.   **Loyalty, Prudence, and Care.** Members and Candidates have a duty of loyalty to their clients and must act with reasonable care and exercise prudent judgment. Members and Candidates must act for the benefit of their clients and place their clients' interests before their employer's or their own interests. In relationships with clients, Members and Candidates must determine applicable fiduciary duty and must comply with such duty to persons and interests to whom it is owed.

B.   **Fair Dealing.** Members and Candidates must deal fairly and objectively with all clients when providing investment analysis, making investment recommendations, taking investment action, or engaging in other professional activities.

C.   **Suitability.**

1. When Members and Candidates are in an advisory relationship with a client, they must:

    a. Make a reasonable inquiry into a client's or prospective clients' investment experience, risk and return objectives, and financial constraints prior to making any investment recommendation or taking investment action and must reassess and update this information regularly.

    b. Determine that an investment is suitable to the client's financial situation and consistent with the client's written objectives, mandates, and constraints before making an investment recommendation or taking investment action.

    c. Judge the suitability of investments in the context of the client's total portfolio.

2. When Members and Candidates are responsible for managing a portfolio to a specific mandate, strategy, or style, they must make only investment recommendations or take investment actions that are consistent with the stated objectives and constraints of the portfolio.

D.   **Performance Presentation.** When communicating investment performance information, Members or Candidates must make reasonable efforts to ensure that it is fair, accurate, and complete.

E.   **Preservation of Confidentiality.** Members and Candidates must keep information about current, former, and prospective clients confidential unless:

1. The information concerns illegal activities on the part of the client or prospective client,

2. Disclosure is required by law, or

3. The client or prospective client permits disclosure of the information.

IV. DUTIES TO EMPLOYERS

A. **Loyalty.** In matters related to their employment, Members and Candidates must act for the benefit of their employer and not deprive their employer of the advantage of their skills and abilities, divulge confidential information, or otherwise cause harm to their employer.

B. **Additional Compensation Arrangements.** Members and Candidates must not accept gifts, benefits, compensation, or consideration that competes with, or might reasonably be expected to create a conflict of interest with, their employer's interest unless they obtain written consent from all parties involved.

C. **Responsibilities of Supervisors.** Members and Candidates must make reasonable efforts to detect and prevent violations of applicable laws, rules, regulations, and the Code and Standards by anyone subject to their supervision or authority.

V. INVESTMENT ANALYSIS, RECOMMENDATIONS, AND ACTION

A. **Diligence and Reasonable Basis.** Members and Candidates must:

1. Exercise diligence, independence, and thoroughness in analyzing investments, making investment recommendations, and taking investment actions.

2. Have a reasonable and adequate basis, supported by appropriate research and investigation, for any investment analysis, recommendation, or action.

B. **Communication with Clients and Prospective Clients.** Members and Candidates must:

1. Disclose to clients and prospective clients the basic format and general principles of the investment processes used to analyze investments, select securities, and construct portfolios and must promptly disclose any changes that might materially affect those processes.

2. Use reasonable judgment in identifying which factors are important to their investment analyses, recommendations, or actions and include those factors in communications with clients and prospective clients.

3. Distinguish between fact and opinion in the presentation of investment analysis and recommendations.

C. **Record Retention.** Members and Candidates must develop and maintain appropriate records to support their investment analysis, recommendations, actions, and other investment related communications with clients and prospective clients.

VI.   CONFLICTS OF INTEREST

A.   **Disclosure of Conflicts.** Members and Candidates must make full and fair disclosure of all matters that could reasonably be expected to impair their independence and objectivity or interfere with respective duties to their clients, prospective clients, and employer. Members and Candidates must ensure that such disclosures are prominent, are delivered in plain language, and communicate the relevant information effectively.

B.   **Priority of Transactions.** Investment transactions for clients and employers must have priority over investment transactions in which a Member or Candidate is the beneficial owner.

C.   **Referral Fees.** Members and Candidates must disclose to their employer, clients, and prospective clients, as appropriate, any compensation, consideration, or benefit received by, or paid to, others for the recommendation of products or services.

VII.   RESPONSIBILITIES AS A CFA INSTITUTE MEMBER OR CFA CANDIDATE

A.   **Conduct as Members and Candidates in the CFA Program.** Members and Candidates must not engage in any conduct that compromises the reputation or integrity of CFA Institute or the CFA designation or the integrity, validity, or security of the CFA examinations.

B.   **Reference to CFA Institute, the CFA Designation, and the CFA Program.** When referring to CFA Institute, CFA Institute membership, the CFA designation, or candidacy in the CFA Program, Members and Candidates must not misrepresent or exaggerate the meaning or implications of membership in CFA Institute, holding the CFA designation, or candidacy in the CFA Program.

STANDARDS OF PROFESSIONAL CONDUCT: GUIDANCE, COMPLIANCE, AND EXAMPLES

LOS 2.a: Demonstrate a thorough knowledge of the Code of Ethics and Standards of Professional Conduct by applying the Code and Standards to specific situations.

LOS 2.b: Recommend practices and procedures designed to prevent violations of the Code of Ethics and Standards of Professional Conduct.

I. PROFESSIONALISM

 Professor's Note: While we use the term "members" in the following discussion, note that all of the standards apply to candidates as well.

I(A) Knowledge of the Law. Members must understand and comply with laws, rules, regulations, and Code and Standards of any authority governing their activities. In the event of a conflict, follow the more strict law, rule, or regulation. Do not knowingly participate or assist in violations, and *dissociate from any known violation.*

Guidance—Code and Standards vs. Local Law

Members must know the laws and regulations relating to their professional activities in all countries in which they conduct business. Members must comply with applicable laws and regulations relating to their professional activity. Do not violate Code or Standards even if the activity is otherwise legal. Always adhere to the most strict rules and requirements (law or CFA Institute Standards) that apply.

Guidance—Participation or Association With Violations by Others

Members should dissociate, or separate themselves, from any ongoing client or employee activity that is illegal or unethical, even if it involves leaving an employer (an extreme case). While a member may confront the involved individual first, he must approach his supervisor or compliance department. Inaction with continued association may be construed as knowing participation.

Recommended Procedures for Compliance—Members

- Members should have procedures to keep up with changes in applicable laws, rules, and regulations.
- Compliance procedures should be reviewed on an ongoing basis to assure that they address current law, CFA Institute Standards, and regulations.

- Members should maintain current reference materials for employees to access in order to keep up to date on laws, rules, and regulations.
- Members should seek advice of counsel or their compliance department when in doubt.
- Members should document any violations when they disassociate themselves from prohibited activity and encourage their employers to bring an end to such activity.
- There is no requirement under the Standards to report violations to governmental authorities, but this may be advisable in some circumstances and required by law in others.

Recommended Procedures for Compliance—Firms

Members should encourage their firms to:

- Develop and/or adopt a code of ethics.
- Make available to employees information that highlights applicable laws and regulations.
- Establish written procedures for reporting suspected violation of laws, regulations, or company policies.

Application of Standard I(A) Knowledge of the Law[2]

Example 1:

Michael Allen works for a brokerage firm and is responsible for an underwriting of securities. A company official gives Allen information indicating that the financial statements Allen filed with the regulator overstate the issuer's earnings. Allen seeks the advice of the brokerage firm's general counsel, who states that it would be difficult for the regulator to prove that Allen has been involved in any wrongdoing.

Comment:

Although it is recommended that members and candidates seek the advice of legal counsel, the reliance on such advice does not absolve a member or candidate from the requirement to comply with the law or regulation. Allen should report this situation to his supervisor, seek an independent legal opinion, and determine whether the regulator should be notified of the error.

Example 2:

Kamisha Washington's firm advertises its past performance record by showing the 10-year return of a composite of its client accounts. However, Washington discovers that the composite omits the performance of accounts that have left the firm during the 10-year period and that this omission has led to an inflated performance figure. Washington is asked to use promotional material that includes the erroneous performance number when soliciting business for the firm.

---

2. Selected Examples and Comments. Copyright 2005, CFA Institute. Reproduced and republished from *Standards of Practice Handbook*, 9th ed., 2005, with permission from CFA Institute. All Rights Reserved.

Comment:

Misrepresenting performance is a violation of the Code and Standards. Although she did not calculate the performance herself, Washington would be assisting in violating this standard if she were to use the inflated performance number when soliciting clients. She must dissociate herself from the activity. She can bring the misleading number to the attention of the person responsible for calculating performance, her supervisor, or the compliance department at her firm. If her firm is unwilling to recalculate performance, she must refrain from using the misleading promotional material and should notify the firm of her reasons. If the firm insists that she use the material, she should consider whether her obligation to dissociate from the activity would require her to seek other employment.

Example 3:

An employee of an investment bank is working on an underwriting and finds out the issuer has altered their financial statements to hide operating losses in one division. These misstated data are included in a preliminary prospectus that has already been released.

Comment:

The employee should report the problem to his supervisors. If the firm doesn't get the misstatement fixed, the employee should dissociate from the underwriting and further, seek legal advice about whether he should undertake additional reporting or other actions.

Example 4:

Laura Jameson is a U.S. citizen, works for an investment adviser based in the United States, and works in a country where investment managers are prohibited from participating in IPOs for their own accounts.

Comment:

Jameson must comply with the strictest requirements among U.S. law (where her firm is based), the CFA Institute Code and Standards, and the laws of the country where she is doing business. In this case that means she must not participate in any IPOs for her personal account.

> **I(B) Independence and Objectivity.** Use reasonable care to exercise independence and objectivity in professional activities. Members and Candidates are not to offer, solicit, or accept any gift, benefit, compensation, or consideration that would compromise either their own or someone else's independence and objectivity.

 Professor's Note: Gifts, benefits, and other consideration are prohibited if given in an attempt to influence Members or Candidates.

Guidance

Do not let the investment process be influenced by any external sources. Modest gifts are permitted. Allocation of shares in oversubscribed IPOs to personal accounts is NOT permitted. Distinguish between gifts from clients and gifts from entities seeking influence to the detriment of the client. Gifts must be disclosed to the member's employer in any case.

Guidance—Investment Banking Relationships

Do not be pressured by sell-side firms to issue favorable research on current or prospective investment banking clients. It is appropriate to have analysts work with investment bankers in "road shows" only when the conflicts are adequately and effectively managed and disclosed. Be sure there are effective "firewalls" between research/investment management and investment banking activities.

Guidance—Public Companies

Analysts should not be pressured to issue favorable research by the companies they follow. Do not confine research to discussions with company management, but rather use a variety of sources, including suppliers, customers, and competitors.

Guidance—Buy-Side Clients

Buy-side clients may try to pressure sell-side analysts. Portfolio managers may have large positions in a particular security, and a rating downgrade may have an effect on the portfolio performance. As a portfolio manager, there is a responsibility to respect and foster intellectual honesty of sell-side research.

Guidance—Issuer-Paid Research

Remember that this type of research is fraught with potential conflicts. Analysts' compensation for preparing such research should be limited, and the preference is for a flat fee, without regard to conclusions or the report's recommendations.

Recommended Procedures for Compliance

- Protect the integrity of opinions—make sure they are unbiased.
- Create a restricted list and distribute only factual information about companies on the list.
- Restrict special cost arrangements—pay for one's own commercial transportation and hotel; limit use of corporate aircraft to cases in which commercial transportation is not available.
- Limit gifts—token items only. Customary, business-related entertainment is okay as long as its purpose is not to influence a member's professional independence or objectivity.
- Restrict employee investments in equity IPOs and private placements.

- Review procedures—have effective supervisory and review procedures.
- Firms should have formal written policies on independence and objectivity of research.

Application of Standard I(B) Independence and Objectivity

Example 1:

Steven Taylor, a mining analyst with Bronson Brokers, is invited by Precision Metals to join a group of his peers in a tour of mining facilities in several western U.S. states. The company arranges for chartered group flights from site to site and for accommodations in Spartan Motels, the only chain with accommodations near the mines, for three nights. Taylor allows Precision Metals to pick up his tab, as do the other analysts, with one exception—John Adams, an employee of a large trust company who insists on following his company's policy and paying for his hotel room himself.

Comment:

The policy of Adams' company complies closely with Standard I(B) by avoiding even the appearance of a conflict of interest, but Taylor and the other analysts were not necessarily violating Standard I(B). In general, when allowing companies to pay for travel and/or accommodations under these circumstances, members and candidates must use their judgment, keeping in mind that such arrangements must not impinge on a member or candidate's independence and objectivity. In this example, the trip was strictly for business and Taylor was not accepting irrelevant or lavish hospitality. The itinerary required chartered flights, for which analysts were not expected to pay. The accommodations were modest. These arrangements are not unusual and did not violate Standard I(B) so long as Taylor's independence and objectivity were not compromised. In the final analysis, members and candidates should consider both whether they can remain objective and whether their integrity might be perceived by their clients to have been compromised.

Example 2:

Walter Fritz is an equity analyst with Hilton Brokerage who covers the mining industry. He has concluded that the stock of Metals & Mining is overpriced at its current level, but he is concerned that a negative research report will hurt the good relationship between Metals & Mining and the investment banking division of his firm. In fact, a senior manager of Hilton Brokerage has just sent him a copy of a proposal his firm has made to Metals & Mining to underwrite a debt offering. Fritz needs to produce a report right away and is concerned about issuing a less-than-favorable rating.

Comment:

Fritz's analysis of Metals & Mining must be objective and based solely on consideration of company fundamentals. Any pressure from other divisions of his firm is inappropriate. This conflict could have been eliminated if, in anticipation of the offering, Hilton Brokerage had placed Metals & Mining on a restricted list for its sales force.

Example 3:

Tom Wayne is the investment manager of the Franklin City Employees Pension Plan. He recently completed a successful search for firms to manage the foreign equity allocation of the plan's diversified portfolio. He followed the plan's standard procedure of seeking presentations from a number of qualified firms and recommended that his board select Penguin Advisors because of its experience, well-defined investment strategy, and performance record, which was compiled and verified in accordance with the CFA Institute Global Investment Performance Standards. Following the plan selection of Penguin, a reporter from the Franklin City Record called to ask if there was any connection between the action and the fact that Penguin was one of the sponsors of an "investment fact-finding trip to Asia" that Wayne made earlier in the year. The trip was one of several conducted by the Pension Investment Academy, which had arranged the itinerary of meetings with economic, government, and corporate officials in major cities in several Asian countries. The Pension Investment Academy obtains support for the cost of these trips from a number of investment managers including Penguin Advisors; the Academy then pays the travel expenses of the various pension plan managers on the trip and provides all meals and accommodations. The president of Penguin Advisors was one of the travelers on the trip.

Comment:

Although Wayne can probably put to good use the knowledge he gained from the trip in selecting portfolio managers and in other areas of managing the pension plan, his recommendation of Penguin Advisors may be tainted by the possible conflict incurred when he participated in a trip paid partly for by Penguin Advisors and when he was in the daily company of the president of Penguin Advisors. To avoid violating Standard I(B), Wayne's basic expenses for travel and accommodations should have been paid by his employer or the pension plan; contact with the president of Penguin Advisors should have been limited to informational or educational events only; and the trip, the organizer, and the sponsor should have been made a matter of public record. Even if his actions were not in violation of Standard I(B), Wayne should have been sensitive to the public perception of the trip when reported in the newspaper and the extent to which the subjective elements of his decision might have been affected by the familiarity that the daily contact of such a trip would encourage. This advantage would probably not be shared by competing firms.

Example 4:

An analyst in the corporate finance department promises a client that her firm will provide full research coverage of the issuing company after the offering.

Comment:

This is not a violation, but she cannot promise favorable research coverage. Research must be objective and independent.

Example 5:

An employee's boss tells him to assume coverage of a stock and maintain a buy rating.

Comment:

Research opinions and recommendations must be objective and independently arrived at. Following the boss' instructions would be a violation if the analyst determined a buy rating is inappropriate.

Example 6:

A money manager receives a gift of significant value from a client as a reward for good performance over the prior period and informs her employer of the gift.

Comment:

No violation here since the gift is from a client and is not based on performance going forward, but the gift must be disclosed to her employer. If the gift were contingent on future performance, the money manager must obtain permission from the employer. The reason for both the disclosure and permission requirements is that the employer must ensure that the money manager does not give advantage to the client giving or offering additional compensation to the detriment of other clients.

Example 7:

An analyst enters into a contract to write a research report on a company, paid for by that company, for a flat fee plus a bonus based on attracting new investors to the security.

Comment:

This is a violation because the compensation structure makes total compensation depend on the conclusions of the report (a favorable report will attract investors and increase compensation). Accepting the job for a flat fee that does not depend on the report's conclusions or its impact on share price is permitted, with proper disclosure of the fact that the report is funded by the subject company.

> **I(C) Misrepresentation.** Do not misrepresent facts regarding investment analysis, recommendations, actions, or other professional activities.

Guidance

Trust is a foundation in the investment profession. Do not make any misrepresentations or give false impressions. This includes oral and electronic communications. Misrepresentations include guaranteeing investment performance and plagiarism. Plagiarism encompasses using someone else's work (reports, forecasts, charts, graphs, and spreadsheet models) without giving them credit.

Recommended Procedures for Compliance

A good way to avoid misrepresentation is for firms to provide employees who deal with clients or prospects a written list of the firm's available services and a description of the firm's qualifications. Employee qualifications should be accurately presented as well.

To avoid plagiarism, maintain records of all materials used to generate reports or other firm products and properly cite sources (quotes and summaries) in work products. Information from recognized financial and statistical reporting services need not be cited.

Application of Standard I(C) Misrepresentations

Example 1:

Allison Rogers is a partner in the firm of Rogers and Black, a small firm offering investment advisory services. She assures a prospective client who has just inherited $1 million that "we can perform all the financial and investment services you need." Rogers and Black is well equipped to provide investment advice but, in fact, cannot provide asset allocation assistance or a full array of financial and investment services.

Comment:

Rogers has violated Standard I(C) by orally misrepresenting the services her firm can perform for the prospective client. She must limit herself to describing the range of investment advisory services Rogers and Black can provide and offer to help the client obtain elsewhere the financial and investment services that her firm cannot provide.

Example 2:

Anthony McGuire is an issuer-paid analyst hired by publicly traded companies to electronically promote their stocks. McGuire creates a Web site that promotes his research efforts as a seemingly independent analyst. McGuire posts a profile and a strong buy recommendation for each company on the Web site indicating that the stock is expected to increase in value. He does not disclose the contractual relationships with the companies he covers on his Web site, in the research reports he issues, or in the statements he makes about the companies on Internet chat rooms.

Comment:

McGuire has violated Standard I(C) because the Internet site and e-mails are misleading to potential investors. Even if the recommendations are valid and supported with thorough research, his omissions regarding the true relationship between himself and the companies he covers constitute a misrepresentation. McGuire has also violated Standard VI(C) by not disclosing the existence of an arrangement with the companies through which he receives compensation in exchange for his services.

Example 3:

Claude Browning, a quantitative analyst for Double Alpha, Inc., returns in great excitement from a seminar. In that seminar, Jack Jorrely, a well-publicized quantitative analyst at a national brokerage firm, discussed one of his new models in great detail, and Browning is intrigued by the new concepts. He proceeds to test this model, making some minor mechanical changes but retaining the concept, until he produces some very positive results. Browning quickly announces to his supervisors at Double Alpha that he has discovered a new model and that clients and prospective clients alike should be informed of this positive finding as ongoing proof of Double Alpha's continuing innovation and ability to add value.

Comment:

Although Browning tested Jorrely's model on his own and even slightly modified it, he must still acknowledge the original source of the idea. Browning can certainly take credit for the final, practical results; he can also support his conclusions with his own test. The credit for the innovative thinking, however, must be awarded to Jorrely.

Example 4:

Gary Ostrowski runs a small, two-person investment management firm. Ostrowski's firm subscribes to a service from a large investment research firm that provides research reports that can be repackaged as in-house research from smaller firms. Ostrowski's firm distributes these reports to clients as its own work.

Comment:

Gary Ostrowski can rely on third-party research that has a reasonable and adequate basis, but he cannot imply that he is the author of the report. Otherwise, Ostrowski would misrepresent the extent of his work in a way that would mislead the firm's clients or prospective clients.

Example 5:

A member makes an error in preparing marketing materials and misstates the amount of assets his firm has under management.

Comment:

The member must attempt to stop distribution of the erroneous material as soon as the error is known. Simply making the error unintentionally is not a violation, but continuing to distribute material known to contain a significant misstatement of fact would be.

Example 6:

The marketing department states in sales literature that an analyst has received an MBA degree, but he has not. The analyst and other members of the firm have distributed this document for years.

Comment:

The analyst has violated the Standards as he should have known of this misrepresentation after having distributed and used the materials over a period of years.

Example 7:

A member describes an interest-only collateralized mortgage obligation as guaranteed by the U.S. government since it is a claim against the cash flows of a pool of guaranteed mortgages, although the payment stream and the market value of the security are not guaranteed.

Comment:

This is a violation because of the misrepresentation.

Example 8:

A member describes a bank CD as "guaranteed."

Comment:

This is not a violation as long as the limits of the guarantee provided by the Federal Deposit Insurance Corporation are not exceeded and the nature of the guarantee is clearly explained to clients.

Example 9:

A member uses definitions he found online for such terms as variance and coefficient of variation in preparing marketing material.

Comment:

Even though these are standard terms, using the work of others word-for-word is plagiarism.

Example 10:

A candidate reads about a research paper in a financial publication and includes the information in a research report, citing the original research report but not the financial publication.

Comment:

To the extent that the candidate used information and interpretation from the financial publication without citing it, the candidate is in violation of the Standard. The candidate should either obtain the report and reference it directly or, if he relies solely on the financial publication, should cite both sources.

> **I(D) Misconduct.** Do not engage in any professional conduct which involves dishonesty, fraud, or deceit. Do not do anything that reflects poorly on one's integrity, good reputation, trustworthiness, or professional competence.

Guidance

CFA Institute discourages unethical behavior in all aspects of members' and candidates' lives. Do not abuse CFA Institute's Professional Conduct Program by seeking enforcement of this Standard to settle personal, political, or other disputes that are not related to professional ethics.

Recommended Procedures for Compliance

Firms are encouraged to adopt these policies and procedures:

- Develop and adopt a code of ethics and make clear that unethical behavior will not be tolerated.
- Give employees a list of potential violations and sanctions, including dismissal.
- Check references of potential employees.

Application of Standard I(D) Misconduct

Example 1:

Simon Sasserman is a trust investment officer at a bank in a small affluent town. He enjoys lunching every day with friends at the country club, where his clients have observed him having numerous drinks. Back at work after lunch, he clearly is intoxicated while making investment decisions. His colleagues make a point of handling any business with Sasserman in the morning because they distrust his judgment after lunch.

Comment:

Sasserman's excessive drinking at lunch and subsequent intoxication at work constitute a violation of Standard I(D) because this conduct has raised questions about his professionalism and competence. His behavior thus reflects poorly on him, his employer, and the investment industry.

Example 2:

Carmen Garcia manages a mutual fund dedicated to socially responsible investing. She is also an environmental activist. As the result of her participation at nonviolent protests, Garcia has been arrested on numerous occasions for trespassing on the property of a large petrochemical plant that is accused of damaging the environment.

Comment:

Generally, Standard I(D) is not meant to cover legal transgressions resulting from acts of civil disobedience in support of personal beliefs because such conduct does not reflect poorly on the member or candidate's professional reputation, integrity, or competence.

Example 3:

A member intentionally includes a receipt that is not his in his expenses for a company trip.

Comment:

Since this act involves deceit and fraud and reflects on the member's integrity and honesty, it is a violation.

Example 4:

A member tells a client that he can get her a good deal on a car through his father-in-law, but instead gets him a poor deal and accepts part of the commission on the car purchase.

Comment:

The member has been dishonest and misrepresented the facts of the situation and has, therefore, violated the Standard.

II. INTEGRITY OF CAPITAL MARKETS

II(A) Material Nonpublic Information. Members and Candidates in possession of nonpublic information that could affect an investment's value must not act or induce someone else to act on the information.

Professor's Note: This Standard prohibits any conduct that will damage the integrity of the markets. It states that Members and Candidates must not act or cause others to act on material nonpublic information until that same information is made public. It does not matter whether the information is obtained in breach of a duty, is misappropriated, or relates to a tender offer.

Guidance

Information is "material" if its disclosure would impact the price of a security or if reasonable investors would want the information before making an investment decision. Ambiguous information, as far as its likely effect on price, may not be considered material. Information is "nonpublic" until it has been made available to the marketplace. An analyst conference call is not public disclosure. Selectively disclosing information by corporations creates the potential for insider-trading violations.

Guidance—Mosaic Theory

There is no violation when a perceptive analyst reaches an investment conclusion about a corporate action or event through an analysis of public information together with items of nonmaterial, nonpublic information.

Recommended Procedures for Compliance

Make reasonable efforts to achieve public dissemination of the information. Encourage firms to adopt procedures to prevent misuse of material nonpublic information. Use a "firewall" within the firm, with elements including:

- Substantial control of relevant interdepartmental communications, through a clearance area such as the compliance or legal department.
- Review employee trades—maintain "watch," "restricted," and "rumor" lists.

- Monitor and restrict proprietary trading while a firm is in possession of material nonpublic information.

Prohibition of all proprietary trading while a firm is in possession of material nonpublic information may be inappropriate because it may send a signal to the market. In these cases, firms should take the contra side of only unsolicited customer trades.

Application of Standard II(A) Material Nonpublic Information

Example 1:

Josephine Walsh is riding an elevator up to her office when she overhears the chief financial officer (CFO) for the Swan Furniture Company tell the president of Swan that he has just calculated the company's earnings for the past quarter and they have unexpectedly and significantly dropped. The CFO adds that this drop will not be released to the public until next week. Walsh immediately calls her broker and tells him to sell her Swan stock.

Comment:

Walsh has sufficient information to determine that the information is both material and nonpublic. By trading on the inside information, she has violated Standard II(A).

Example 2:

Samuel Peter, an analyst with Scotland and Pierce Incorporated, is assisting his firm with a secondary offering for Bright Ideas Lamp Company. Peter participates, via telephone conference call, in a meeting with Scotland and Pierce investment banking employees and Bright Ideas' CEO. Peter is advised that the company's earnings projections for the next year have significantly dropped. Throughout the telephone conference call, several Scotland and Pierce salespeople and portfolio managers walk in and out of Peter's office, where the telephone call is taking place. As a result, they are aware of the drop in projected earnings for Bright Ideas. Before the conference call is concluded, the salespeople trade the stock of the company on behalf of the firm's clients and other firm personnel trade the stock in a firm proprietary account and in employee personal accounts.

Comment:

Peter violated Standard II(A) because he failed to prevent the transfer and misuse of material nonpublic information to others in his firm. Peter's firm should have adopted information barriers to prevent the communication of nonpublic information between departments of the firm. The salespeople and portfolio managers who traded on the information have also violated Standard II(A) by trading on inside information.

Example 3:

Elizabeth Levenson is based in Taipei and covers the Taiwanese market for her firm, which is based in Singapore. She is invited to meet the finance director of a manufacturing company along with the other ten largest shareholders of the company. During the meeting, the finance director states that the company expects its workforce to strike next Friday, which will cripple productivity and distribution. Can Levenson use this information as a basis to change her rating on the company from "buy" to "sell"?

Comment:

Levenson must first determine whether the material information is public. If the company has not made this information public (a small-group forum does not qualify as a method of public dissemination), she cannot use the information according to Standard II(A).

Example 4:

Jagdish Teja is a buy-side analyst covering the furniture industry. Looking for an attractive company to recommend as a buy, he analyzed several furniture makers by studying their financial reports and visiting their operations. He also talked to some designers and retailers to find out which furniture styles are trendy and popular. Although none of the companies that he analyzed turned out to be a clear buy, he discovered that one of them, Swan Furniture Company (SFC), might be in trouble. Swan's extravagant new designs were introduced at substantial costs. Even though these designs initially attracted attention, in the long run, the public is buying more conservative furniture from other makers. Based on that and on P&L analysis, Teja believes that Swan's next-quarter earnings will drop substantially. He then issues a sell recommendation for SFC. Immediately after receiving that recommendation, investment managers start reducing the stock in their portfolios.

Comment:

Information on quarterly earnings figures is material and nonpublic. However, Teja arrived at his conclusion about the earnings drop based on public information and on pieces of nonmaterial nonpublic information (such as opinions of designers and retailers). Therefore, trading based on Teja's correct conclusion is not prohibited by Standard II(A).

Example 5:

A member's dentist, who is an active investor, tells the member that based on his research he believes that Acme, Inc., will be bought out in the near future by a larger firm in the industry. The member investigates and purchases shares of Acme.

Comment:

There is no violation here because the dentist had no inside information but has reached the conclusion on his own. The information here is not material because there is no reason to suspect that an investor would wish to know what the member's dentist thought before investing in shares of Acme.

Example 6:

A member received an advance copy of a stock recommendation that will appear in a widely read national newspaper column the next day, and purchases the stock.

Comment:

A recommendation in a widely read newspaper column will likely cause the stock price to rise, so this is material non-public information. The member has violated the Standard.

Example 7:

A member is having lunch with a portfolio manager from a mutual fund who is known for his stock-picking ability and often influences market prices when his stock purchases and sales are disclosed. The manager tells the member that he is selling all his shares in Able, Inc., the next day. The member shorts the stock.

Comment:

The fact that the fund will sell its shares of Able is material because news of it will likely cause the shares to fall in price. Since this is also not currently public information, the member has violated the Standard by acting on the information.

Example 8:

A broker who is a member receives the sell order for the Able Inc. shares from the portfolio manager in the above example. The broker sells his shares of Able prior to entering the sell order for the fund, but since his personal holdings are small compared to the stock's trading volume, his trade does not affect the price.

Comment:

The broker has acted on material non-public information (the fund's sale of shares) and has violated the Standard.

Professor's Note: The member also violated Standard VI(B) - Priority of Transactions by front-running the client trade with a trade in his own account. Had the member sold his shares after executing the fund trade, he still would be violating Standard II(A) by acting on his knowledge of the fund trade, which would still not be public information at that point.

II(B) Market Manipulation. Do not engage in any practices intended to mislead market participants through distorted prices or artificially inflated trading volume.

Professor's Note: This Standard requires Members and Candidates to uphold market integrity by banning practices that distort security prices or trading volume with the intent to deceive.

Guidance

This Standard applies to transactions that deceive the market by distorting the price-setting mechanism of financial instruments or by securing a controlling position to manipulate the price of a related derivative and/or the asset itself. Spreading false rumors is also prohibited.

Application of Standard II(B) Market Manipulation

Example 1:

Matthew Murphy is an analyst at Divisadero Securities & Co., which has a significant number of hedge funds among its most important brokerage clients. Two trading days before the publication of the quarter-end report, Murphy alerts his sales force that he is about to issue a research report on Wirewolf Semiconductor, which will include his opinion that:

- quarterly revenues are likely to fall short of management's guidance,
- earnings will be as much as 5 cents per share (or more than 10%) below consensus, and
- Wirewolf's highly respected chief financial officer may be about to join another company.

Knowing that Wirewolf had already entered its declared quarter-end "quiet period" before reporting earnings (and thus would be reluctant to respond to rumors, etc.), Murphy times the release of his research report specifically to sensationalize the negative aspects of the message to create significant downward pressure on Wirewolf's stock to the distinct advantage of Divisadero's hedge fund clients. The report's conclusions are based on speculation, not on fact. The next day, the research report is broadcast to all of Divisadero's clients and to the usual newswire services.

Before Wirewolf's investor relations department can assess its damage on the final trading day of the quarter and refute Murphy's report, its stock opens trading sharply lower, allowing Divisadero's clients to cover their short positions at substantial gains.

Comment:

Murphy violated Standard II(B) by trying to create artificial price volatility designed to have material impact on the price of an issuer's stock. Moreover, by lacking an adequate basis for the recommendation, Murphy also violated Standard V(A).

Example 2:

Sergei Gonchar is the chairman of the ACME Futures Exchange, which seeks to launch a new bond futures contract. In order to convince investors, traders, arbitragers, hedgers, and so on, to use its contract, the exchange attempts to demonstrate that it has the best liquidity. To do so, it enters into agreements with members so that they commit to a substantial minimum trading volume on the new contract over a specific period in exchange for substantial reductions on their regular commissions.

Comment:

Formal liquidity on a market is determined by the obligations set on market makers, but the actual liquidity of a market is better estimated by the actual trading volume and bid-ask spreads. Attempts to mislead participants on the actual liquidity of the market constitute a violation of Standard II(B). In this example, investors have been intentionally misled to believe they chose the most liquid instrument for some specific purpose and could eventually see the actual liquidity of the contract dry up suddenly after the term of the agreement if the "pump-priming" strategy fails. If ACME fully discloses its agreement with members to boost transactions over some initial launch period, it does not violate Standard II(B). ACME's intent is not to harm investors but on the contrary to give them a better service. For that purpose, it may engage in a liquidity-pumping strategy, but it must be disclosed.

Example 3:

A member is seeking to sell a large position in a fairly illiquid stock from a fund he manages. He buys and sells shares of the stock between that fund and another he also manages to create an appearance of activity and stock price appreciation so that the sale of the whole position will have less market impact and he will realize a better return for the fund's shareholders.

Comment:

The trading activity is meant to mislead market participants and is, therefore, a violation of the Standard. The fact that his fund shareholders gain by this action does not change the fact that it is a violation.

Example 4:

A member posts false information about a firm on Internet bulletin boards and stock chat facilities in an attempt to cause the firm's stock to increase in price.

Comment:

This is a violation of the Standard.

III. DUTIES TO CLIENTS AND PROSPECTIVE CLIENTS

III(A) Loyalty, Prudence, and Care. Members must always act for the benefit of clients and place clients' interests before their employer's or their own interests. Members must be loyal to clients, use reasonable care, exercise prudent judgment, and determine and comply with their applicable fiduciary duty to clients.

 Professor's Note: This Standard requires that members and candidates understand and comply with their actual fiduciary duty. There is also a minimum level of conduct—reasonable care and prudent judgment must be exercised in all circumstances.

Guidance

Client interests always come first.

- Exercise the prudence, care, skill, and diligence under the circumstances that a person acting in a like capacity and familiar with such matters would use.

- Manage pools of client assets in accordance with the terms of the governing documents, such as trust documents or investment management agreements.
- Make investment decisions in the context of the total portfolio.
- Vote proxies in an informed and responsible manner. Due to cost benefit considerations, it may not be necessary to vote all proxies.
- Client brokerage, or "soft dollars" or "soft commissions" must be used to benefit the client.

Recommended Procedures of Compliance

Submit to clients, at least quarterly, itemized statements showing all securities in custody and all debits, credits, and transactions.

Encourage firms to address these topics when drafting policies and procedures regarding fiduciary duty:

- Follow applicable rules and laws.
- Establish investment objectives of client. Consider suitability of portfolio relative to client's needs and circumstances, the investment's basic characteristics, or the basic characteristics of the total portfolio.
- Diversify.
- Deal fairly with all clients in regards to investment actions.
- Disclose conflicts.
- Disclose compensation arrangements.
- Vote proxies in the best interest of clients and ultimate beneficiaries.
- Maintain confidentiality.
- Seek best execution.
- Place client interests first.

Application of Standard III(A) Loyalty, Prudence, and Care

Example 1:

First Country Bank serves as trustee for the Miller Company's pension plan. Miller is the target of a hostile takeover attempt by Newton, Inc. In attempting to ward off Newton, Miller's managers persuade Julian Wiley, an investment manager at First Country Bank, to purchase Miller common stock in the open market for the employee pension plan. Miller's officials indicate that such action would be favorably received and would probably result in other accounts being placed with the bank. Although Wiley believes the stock to be overvalued and would not ordinarily buy it, he purchases the stock to support Miller's managers, to maintain the company's good favor, and to realize additional new business. The heavy stock purchases cause Miller's market price to rise to such a level that Newton retracts its takeover bid.

Comment:

Standard III(A) requires that a member or candidate, in evaluating a takeover bid, act prudently and solely in the interests of plan participants and beneficiaries. To meet this requirement, a member or candidate must carefully evaluate the long-term prospects of the company against the short-term prospects presented by the takeover offer and by the ability to invest elsewhere. In this instance, Wiley, acting on behalf of his employer, the trustee, clearly violated Standard III(A) by using the profit-sharing plan to perpetuate existing management, perhaps to the detriment of plan participants and the company's shareholders, and to benefit himself. Wiley's responsibilities to the plan participants and beneficiaries should take precedence over any ties to corporate managers and self-interest. A duty exists to examine such a takeover offer on its own merits and to make an independent decision. The guiding principle is the appropriateness of the investment decision to the pension plan, not whether the decision benefits Wiley or the company that hired him.

Example 2:

Emilie Rome is a trust officer for Paget Trust Company. Rome's supervisor is responsible for reviewing Rome's trust account transactions and her monthly reports of personal stock transactions. Rome has been using Nathan Gray, a broker, almost exclusively for trust account brokerage transactions. Where Gray makes a market in stocks, he has been giving Rome a lower price for personal purchases and a higher price for sales than he gives to Rome's trust accounts and other investors.

Comment:

Rome is violating her duty of loyalty to the bank's trust accounts by using Gray for brokerage transactions simply because Gray trades Rome's personal account on favorable terms.

Example 3:

A member uses a broker for client-account trades that has relatively high prices and average research and execution. In return, the broker pays for the rent and other overhead expenses for the member's firm.

Comment:

This is a violation of the Standard since the member used client brokerage for services that do not benefit clients and failed to get the best price and execution for his clients.

Example 4:

In return for receiving account management business from Broker X, a member directs trades to Broker X on the accounts referred to her by Broker X as well as on other accounts as an incentive to Broker X to send her more account business.

Comment:

This is a violation if Broker X does not offer the best price and execution or if the practice of directing trades to Broker X is not disclosed to clients. The obligation to seek best price and execution is always required unless clients provide a written statement that the member is not to seek best price and execution and that they are aware of the impact of this decision on their accounts.

Example 5:

A member does more trades in client accounts than are necessary to accomplish client goals because she desires to increase her commission income.

Comment:

The member is using client assets (brokerage fees) to benefit herself and has violated the Standard.

III(B) Fair Dealing. Members must deal fairly and objectively with all clients and prospects when providing investment analysis, making investment recommendations, taking investment action, or in other professional activities.

Guidance

Do not discriminate against any clients when disseminating recommendations or taking investment action. Fairly does not mean equally. In the normal course of business, there will be differences in the time e-mails, faxes, etc. are received by different clients. Different service levels are okay, but they must not negatively affect or disadvantage any clients. Disclose the different service levels to all clients and prospects, and make premium levels of service available to all who wish to pay for them.

Guidance—Investment Recommendations

Give all clients a fair opportunity to act upon every recommendation. Clients who are unaware of a change in a recommendation should be advised before the order is accepted.

Guidance—Investment Actions

Treat clients fairly in light of their investment objectives and circumstances. Treat both individual and institutional clients in a fair and impartial manner. Members and Candidates should not take advantage of their position in the industry to disadvantage clients (e.g., in the context of IPOs).

Recommended Procedures for Compliance

Encourage firms to establish compliance procedures requiring proper dissemination of investment recommendations and fair treatment of all customers and clients. Consider these points when establishing fair dealing compliance procedures:

- Limit the number of people who are aware that a change in recommendation will be made.
- Shorten the time frame between decision and dissemination.

- Publish personnel guidelines for pre-dissemination—have in place guidelines prohibiting personnel who have prior knowledge of a recommendation from discussing it or taking action on the pending recommendation.
- Simultaneous dissemination.
- Maintain list of clients and holdings—use to ensure that all holders are treated fairly.
- Develop written trade allocation procedures—ensure fairness to clients, timely and efficient order execution, and accuracy of client positions.
- Disclose trade allocation procedures.
- Establish systematic account review—to ensure that no client is given preferred treatment and that investment actions are consistent with the account's objectives.
- Disclose available levels of service.

Application of Standard III(B) Fair Dealing

Example 1:

Bradley Ames, a well-known and respected analyst, follows the computer industry. In the course of his research, he finds that a small, relatively unknown company whose shares are traded over the counter has just signed significant contracts with some of the companies he follows. After a considerable amount of investigation, Ames decides to write a research report on the company and recommend purchase. While the report is being reviewed by the company for factual accuracy, Ames schedules a luncheon with several of his best clients to discuss the company. At the luncheon, he mentions the purchase recommendation scheduled to be sent early the following week to all the firm's clients.

Comment:

Ames violated Standard III(B) by disseminating the purchase recommendation to the clients with whom he had lunch a week before the recommendation was sent to all clients.

Example 2:

Spencer Rivers, president of XYZ Corporation, moves his company's growth-oriented pension fund to a particular bank primarily because of the excellent investment performance achieved by the bank's commingled fund for the prior 5-year period. A few years later, Rivers compares the results of his pension fund with those of the bank's commingled fund. He is startled to learn that, even though the two accounts have the same investment objectives and similar portfolios, his company's pension fund has significantly underperformed the bank's commingled fund. Questioning this result at his next meeting with the pension fund's manager, Rivers is told that, as a matter of policy, when a new security is placed on the recommended list, Morgan Jackson, the pension fund manager, first purchases the security for the commingled account and then purchases it on a pro rata basis for all other pension fund accounts. Similarly, when a sale is recommended, the security is sold first from the commingled account and then sold on a pro rata basis from all other accounts. Rivers also learns that if the bank cannot get enough shares (especially the hot issues) to be meaningful to all the accounts, its policy is to place the new issues only in the commingled account.

Seeing that Rivers is neither satisfied nor pleased by the explanation, Jackson quickly adds that nondiscretionary pension accounts and personal trust accounts have a lower priority on purchase and sale recommendations than discretionary pension fund accounts. Furthermore, Jackson states, the company's pension fund had the opportunity to invest up to 5% in the commingled fund.

Comment:

The bank's policy did not treat all customers fairly, and Jackson violated her duty to her clients by giving priority to the growth-oriented commingled fund over all other funds and to discretionary accounts over nondiscretionary accounts. Jackson must execute orders on a systematic basis that is fair to all clients. In addition, trade allocation procedures should be disclosed to all clients from the beginning. Of course, in this case, disclosure of the bank's policy would not change the fact that the policy is unfair.

Example 3:

A member gets options for his part in an IPO from the subject firm. The IPO is oversubscribed and the member fills his own and other individuals' orders, but has to reduce allocations to his institutional clients.

Comment:

The member has violated the Standard. He must disclose to his employer and to his clients that he has accepted options for putting together the IPO. He should not take any shares of a hot IPO for himself and should have distributed his allocated shares of the IPO to all clients in proportion to their original order amounts.

Example 4:

A member is delayed in allocating some trades to client accounts. When she allocates the trades, she puts some positions that have appreciated in a preferred client's account and puts trades that have not done as well in other client accounts.

Comment:

This is a violation of the Standard. The member should have allocated the trades to specific accounts prior to the trades or should have allocated the trades proportionally to suitable accounts in a timely fashion.

III(C) SUITABILITY

1. When in an advisory relationship with client or prospect, Members and Candidates must:

   a. Make reasonable inquiry into clients' investment experience, risk and return objectives, and constraints prior to making any recommendations or taking investment action. Reassess information and update regularly.

   b. Be sure investments are suitable to a client's financial situation and consistent with client objectives before making recommendation or taking investment action.

   c. Make sure investments are suitable in the context of a client's total portfolio.

2. When managing a portfolio, investment recommendations and actions must be consistent with stated portfolio objectives and constraints.

 Professor's Note: "Regular updates" to client information should be done at least annually. Suitability is based on a total-portfolio perspective.

Guidance

In advisory relationships, be sure to gather client information at the beginning of the relationship, in the form of an investment policy statement (IPS). Consider client's needs and circumstances and thus the risk tolerance. Consider whether or not the use of leverage is suitable for the client.

If a member is responsible for managing a fund to an index or other stated mandate, be sure investments are consistent with the stated mandate.

Recommended Procedures for Compliance

Members should:

- Put the needs and circumstances of each client and the client's investment objectives into a written IPS for each client.
- Consider the type of client and whether there are separate beneficiaries, investor objectives (return and risk), investor constraints (liquidity needs, expected cash flows, time, tax, and regulatory and legal circumstances), and performance measurement benchmarks.
- Review investor's objectives and constraints at least annually to reflect any changes in client circumstances, as well as prior to material changes in recommendations or decisions.

Application of Standard III(C) Suitability

Example 1:

Ann Walters, an investment adviser, suggests to Brian Crosby, a risk-averse client, that covered call options be used in his equity portfolio. The purpose would be to enhance Crosby's income and partially offset any untimely depreciation in value should the stock market or other circumstances affect his holdings unfavorably. Walters educates Crosby about all possible outcomes, including the risk of incurring an added tax liability if a stock rises in price and is called away and, conversely, the risk of his holdings losing protection on the downside if prices drop sharply.

Comment:

When determining suitability of an investment, the primary focus should be on the characteristics of the client's entire portfolio, not on an issue-by-issue analysis. The basic characteristics of the entire portfolio will largely determine whether the investment recommendations are taking client factors into account. Therefore, the most important aspects of a particular investment will be those that will affect the characteristics of the total portfolio. In this case, Walters properly considered the investment in the context of the entire portfolio and thoroughly explained the investment to the client.

Example 2:

Max Gubler, CIO of a property/casualty insurance subsidiary of a large financial conglomerate, wants to better diversify the company's investment portfolio and increase its returns. The company's investment policy statement (IPS) provides for highly liquid investments, such as large caps, governments, and supra-nationals, as well as corporate bonds with a minimum credit rating of AA—and maturity of no more than five years. In a recent presentation, a venture capital group offered very attractive prospective returns on some of their private equity funds providing seed capital. An exit strategy is already contemplated but investors will first have to observe a minimum 3-year lock-up period, with a subsequent laddered exit option for a maximum of one third of shares per year. Gubler does not want to miss this opportunity and after an extensive analysis and optimization of this asset class with the company's current portfolio, he invests 4% in this seed fund, leaving the portfolio's total equity exposure still well below its upper limit.

Comment:

Gubler violates Standards III(A) and III(C). His new investment locks up part of the company's assets for at least three and for up to as many as five years and possibly beyond. Since the IPS requires investments in highly liquid investments and describes accepted asset classes, private equity investments with a lock-up period certainly do not qualify. Even without such lock-up periods, an asset class with only an occasional, and thus implicitly illiquid, market may not be suitable. Although an IPS typically describes objectives and constraints in great detail, the manager must make every effort to understand the client's business and circumstances. Doing so should also enable the manager to recognize, understand, and discuss with the client other factors that may be or may become material in the investment management process.

Example 3:

A member gives a client account a significant allocation to non-dividend paying high risk securities, even though the client has low risk tolerance and modest return objectives.

Comment:

This is a violation of the Standard.

Example 4:

A member puts a security into a fund she manages that does not fit the mandate of the fund and is not a permitted investment according to the fund's disclosures.

Comment:

This, too, is a violation of the Standard.

> **III(D) Performance Presentation.** Presentations of investment performance information must be fair, accurate, and complete.

Guidance

Members must avoid misstating performance or misleading clients/prospects about investment performance of themselves or their firms, should not misrepresent past performance or reasonably expected performance, and should not state or imply the ability to achieve a rate of return similar to that achieved in the past.

Recommended Procedures for Compliance

Encourage firms to adhere to Global Investment Performance Standards. Obligations under this Standard may also be met by:

- Considering the sophistication of the audience to whom a performance presentation is addressed.
- Presenting performance of weighted composite of similar portfolios rather than a single account.
- Including terminated accounts as part of historical performance.
- Including all appropriate disclosures to fully explain results (e.g., model results included, gross or net of fees, etc.).
- Maintaining data and records used to calculate the performance being presented.

Application of Standard III(D) Performance Presentation

Example 1:

Kyle Taylor of Taylor Trust Company, noting the performance of Taylor's common trust fund for the past two years, states in the brochure sent to his potential clients that "You can expect steady 25% annual compound growth of the value of your investments over the year." Taylor Trust's common trust fund did increase at the rate of 25% per annum for the past year which mirrored the increase of the entire market. The fund, however, never averaged that growth for more than one year, and the average rate of growth of all of its trust accounts for five years was 5% per annum.

Comment:

Taylor's brochure is in violation of Standard III(D). Taylor should have disclosed that the 25% growth occurred in only one year. Additionally, Taylor did not include client accounts other than those in the firm's common trust fund. A general claim of firm performance should take into account the performance of all categories of accounts. Finally, by stating that clients can expect a steady 25% annual compound growth rate, Taylor also violated Standard I(C), which prohibits statements of assurances or guarantees regarding an investment.

Example 2:

Aaron McCoy is vice president and managing partner of the equity investment group of Mastermind Financial Advisors, a new business. Mastermind recruited McCoy because he had a proven 6-year track record with G&P Financial. In developing Mastermind's advertising and marketing campaign, McCoy prepared an advertisement that included the equity investment performance he achieved at G&P Financial. The advertisement for Mastermind did not identify the equity performance as being earned while at G&P. The advertisement was distributed to existing clients and prospective clients of Mastermind.

Comment:

McCoy violated Standard III(D) by distributing an advertisement that contained material misrepresentations regarding the historical performance of Mastermind. Standard III(D) requires that members and candidates make every reasonable effort to ensure that performance information is a fair, accurate, and complete representation of an individual or firm's performance. As a general matter, this standard does not prohibit showing past performance of funds managed at a prior firm as part of a performance track record so long as it is accompanied by appropriate disclosures detailing where the performance comes from and the person's specific role in achieving that performance. If McCoy chooses to use his past performance from G&P in Mastermind's advertising, he should make full disclosure as to the source of the historical performance.

Example 3:

A member puts simulated results of an investment strategy in a sales brochure without disclosing that the results are not actual performance numbers.

Comment:

The member has violated the Standard.

Example 4:

In materials for prospective clients, a member uses performance figures for a large-cap growth composite she has created by choosing accounts that have done relatively well and including some accounts with significant mid-cap exposure.

Comment:

This is a violation of the Standard as the member has attempted to mislead clients and has misrepresented her performance.

> **III(E) Preservation of Confidentiality.** All information about current and former clients and prospects must be kept confidential unless it pertains to illegal activities, disclosure is required by law, or the client or prospect gives permission for the information to be disclosed.

 Professor's Note: This Standard covers all client information, not just information concerning matters within the scope of the relationship. Also note that the language specifically includes not only prospects but former clients as well. Confidentiality regarding employer information is covered in Standard IV.

Guidance

If illegal activities by a client are involved, members may have an obligation to report the activities to authorities. The confidentiality Standard extends to former clients as well.

The requirements of this Standard are not intended to prevent Members and Candidates from cooperating with a CFA Institute Professional Conduct Program (PCP) investigation.

Recommended Procedures for Compliance

Members should avoid disclosing information received from a client except to authorized co-workers who are also working for the client.

Application of Standard III(E) Preservation of Confidentiality

Example 1:

Sarah Connor, a financial analyst employed by Johnson Investment Counselors, Inc., provides investment advice to the trustees of City Medical Center. The trustees have given her a number of internal reports concerning City Medical's needs for physical plant renovation and expansion. They have asked Connor to recommend investments that would generate capital appreciation in endowment funds to meet projected capital expenditures. Connor is approached by a local business man, Thomas Kasey, who is considering a substantial contribution either to City Medical Center or to another local hospital. Kasey wants to find out the building plans of both institutions before making a decision, but he does not want to speak to the trustees.

Comment:

The trustees gave Connor the internal reports so she could advise them on how to manage their endowment funds. Because the information in the reports is clearly both confidential and within the scope of the confidential relationship, Standard III(E) requires that Connor refuse to divulge information to Kasey.

Example 2:

David Bradford manages money for a family-owned real estate development corporation. He also manages the individual portfolios of several of the family members and officers of the corporation, including the chief financial officer (CFO). Based on the financial records from the corporation, as well as some questionable practices of the CFO that he has observed, Bradford believes that the CFO is embezzling money from the corporation and putting it into his personal investment account.

Comment:

Bradford should check with his firm's compliance department as well as outside counsel to determine whether applicable securities regulations require reporting the CFO's financial records.

Example 3:

A member has learned from his client that one of his goals is to give more of his portfolio income to charity. The member tells this to a friend who is on the board of a worthy charity and suggests that he should contact the client about a donation.

Comment:

The member has violated the Standard by disclosing information he has learned from the client in the course of their business relationship.

Example 4:

A member learns that a pension account client is violating the law with respect to charges to the pension fund.

Comment:

The member must bring this to the attention of her supervisor and try to end the illegal activity. Failing this, the member should seek legal advice about any disclosure she should make to legal or regulatory authorities and dissociate herself from any continuing association with the pension account.

IV. DUTIES TO EMPLOYERS

IV(A) Loyalty. In matters related to their employment, Members and Candidates must act for the benefit of their employer and not deprive their employer of the advantage of their skills and abilities, divulge confidential information, or otherwise cause harm to their employer.

Professor's Note: Always act in the employer's best interests and do not deprive the employer of any of Member's/Candidate's skills or abilities. Also protect confidential information. The phrase "in matters related to employment" means that Members/Candidates are not required to subordinate important personal and family obligations to their job.

Guidance

Members must not engage in any activities which would injure the firm, deprive it of profit, or deprive it of the advantage of employees' skills and abilities. Always place client interests above interests of employer. There is no requirement that the employee put employer interests ahead of family and other personal obligations; it is expected that employers and employees will discuss such matters and balance these obligations with work obligations.

Guidance—Independent Practice

Independent practice for compensation is allowed if a notification is provided to the employer fully describing all aspects of the services, including compensation, duration, and the nature of the activities *and* if the employer consents to all terms of the proposed independent practice before it begins.

Guidance—Leaving an Employer

Members must continue to act in their employer's best interests until resignation is effective. Activities which may constitute a violation include:

- Misappropriation of trade secrets.
- Misuse of confidential information.
- Soliciting employer's clients prior to leaving.
- Self-dealing.
- Misappropriation of client lists.

Once an employee has left a firm, simple knowledge of names and existence of former clients is generally not confidential. Also there is no prohibition on the use of experience or knowledge gained while with a former employer.

Guidance—Whistleblowing

There may be isolated cases where a duty to one's employer may be violated in order to protect clients or the integrity of the market, and not for personal gain.

Guidance—Nature of Employment

The applicability of this Standard is based on the nature of the employment—employee versus independent contractor. If Members and Candidates are independent contractors, they still have a duty to abide by the terms of the agreement.

Application of Standard IV(A) Loyalty

Example 1:

James Hightower has been employed by Jason Investment Management Corporation for 15 years. He began as an analyst but assumed increasing responsibilities and is now a senior portfolio manager and a member of the firm's investment policy committee. Hightower has decided to leave Jason Investment and start his own investment management business. He has been careful not to tell any of Jason's clients that he is leaving, because he does not want to be accused of breaching his duty to Jason by soliciting Jason's clients before his departure. Hightower is planning to copy and take with him the following documents and information he developed or worked on while at Jason: (1) the client list, with addresses, telephone numbers, and other pertinent client information; (2) client account statements; (3) sample marketing presentations to prospective clients containing Jason's performance record; (4) Jason's recommended list of securities; (5) computer models to determine asset allocations for accounts with different objectives; (6) computer models for stock selection; and (7) personal computer spreadsheets for Hightower's major corporate recommendations which he developed when he was an analyst.

Comment:

Except with the consent of their employer, departing employees may not take employer property, which includes books, records, reports, and other materials, and may not interfere with their employer's business opportunities. Taking any employer records, even those the member or candidate prepared, violates Standard IV(A).

Example 2:

Dennis Elliot has hired Sam Chisolm who previously worked for a competing firm. Chisolm left his former firm after 18 years of employment. When Chisolm begins working for Elliot, he wants to contact his former clients because he knows them well and is certain that many will follow him to his new employer. Is Chisolm in violation of the Standard IV(A) if he contacts his former clients?

Comment:

Because client records are the property of the firm, contacting former clients for any reason through the use of client lists or other information taken from a former employer without permission would be a violation of Standard IV(A). In addition, the nature and extent of the contact with former clients may be governed by the terms of any non-compete agreement signed by the employee and the former employer that covers contact with former clients after employment.

But simple knowledge of the name and existence of former clients is not confidential information, just as skills or experience that an employee obtains while employed is not "confidential" or "privileged" information. The Code and Standards do not impose a prohibition on the use of experience or knowledge gained at one employer from being used at another employer. The Code and Standards also do not prohibit former employees from contacting clients of their previous firm, absent a non-compete agreement. Members and candidates are free to use public information about their former firm after departing to contact former clients without violating Standard IV(A).

In the absence of a non-compete agreement, as long as Chisolm maintains his duty of loyalty to his employer before joining Elliot's firm, and does not take steps to solicit clients until he has left his former firm, and does not make use of material from his former employer without its permission after he has left, he would not be in violation of the Code and Standards.

Example 3:

Several employees are planning to depart their current employer within a few weeks to form a new firm, and have been careful to not engage in any activities that would conflict with their duty to their current employer. They have just learned that one of their employer's clients has undertaken a request for proposal (RFP) to review and possibly hire a new investment consultant. The RFP has been sent to the employer and all of its competitors. The group believes that the new entity to be formed would be qualified to respond to the RFP and eligible for the business. The RFP submission period is likely to conclude before the employees' resignations are effective. Is it permissible for the group of departing employees to respond to the RFP under their anticipated new firm?

Comment:

A group of employees responding to an RFP that their employer is also responding to would lead to direct competition between the employees and the employer. Such conduct would violate Standard IV(A) unless the group of employees received permission from their employer as well as the entity sending out the RFP.

Example 4:

A member solicits clients and prospects of his current employer to open accounts at the new firm he will be joining shortly.

Comment:

It is a violation of the Standard to solicit the firm's clients and prospects while he is still employed by the firm.

Example 5:

Two employees discuss joining with others in an employee-led buyout of their employer's emerging markets investment management business.

Comment:

There is no violation here. Their employer can decide how to respond to any buyout offer. If such a buyout takes place, clients should be informed of the nature of the changes in a timely manner.

Example 6:

A member is writing a research report on a company as a contract worker for Employer A (using Employer A's premises and materials) with the understanding that Employer A does not claim exclusive rights to the outcome of her research. As she is finishing the report, she is offered a full-time job by Employer B and sends Employer B a copy of a draft of her report for publication.

Comment:

She has violated the Standard by not giving Employer A the first rights to act on her research. She must also be careful not to take any materials used in preparing the report from Employer A's premises.

Example 7:

A member helps develop software for a firm while acting as an unpaid intern and takes the software, without permission, with her when she takes a full-time job at another firm.

Comment:

She is considered an employee of the firm and has violated the Standard by taking her employer's property without permission.

Example 8:

A member prepares to leave his employer and open his own firm by registering with the SEC, renting an office, and buying office equipment.

Comment:

As long as these preparations have not interfered with the performance of his current job, there has been no violation. The solicitation of firm clients and prospects prior to leaving his employer would, however, be a violation of the Standard.

Example 9:

A member is a full-time employee of an investment management firm and wants to accept a paid position as town mayor without asking his employer's permission.

Comment:

Since the member serving as mayor does not conflict with his employer's business interests, as long as the time commitment does not preclude performing his expected job functions well, there is no violation.

Example 10:

A member, who has left one employer, uses public sources to get the phone numbers of previous clients and solicits their business for her new employer.

Comment:

As long as there is no agreement in force between the member and his previous employer that prohibits such solicitation, there is no violation of the Standards.

> **IV(B) Additional Compensation Arrangements.** No gifts, benefits, compensation, or consideration are to be accepted which may create a conflict of interest with the employer's interest unless written consent is received from all parties.

 Professor's Note: "Compensation" includes "gifts, benefits, compensation, or consideration."

Guidance

Compensation includes direct and indirect compensation from a client and other benefits received from third parties. Written consent from a member's employer includes e-mail communication.

Recommended Procedures for Compliance

Make an immediate written report to employer detailing proposed compensation and services, if additional to that provided by employer.

Application of Standard IV(B) Additional Compensation Arrangements

Example 1:

Geoff Whitman, a portfolio analyst for Adams Trust Company, manages the account of Carol Cochran, a client. Whitman is paid a salary by his employer, and Cochran pays the trust company a standard fee based on the market value of assets in her portfolio. Cochran proposes to Whitman that "any year that my portfolio achieves at least a 15% return before taxes, you and your wife can fly to Monaco at my expense and use my condominium during the third week of January. Whitman does not inform his employer of the arrangement and vacations in Monaco the following January as Cochran's guest.

Comment:

Whitman violated Standard IV(B) by failing to inform his employer in writing of this supplemental, contingent compensation arrangement. The nature of the arrangement could have resulted in partiality to Cochran's account, which could have detracted from Whitman's performance with respect to other accounts he handles for Adams Trust. Whitman must obtain the consent of his employer to accept such a supplemental benefit.

Example 2:

A member is on the board of directors of a company whose shares he purchases for client accounts. As a member of the board he receives the company's product at no charge.

Comment:

Since receiving the company's product constitutes compensation for his service, he is in violation of the Standard if he does not disclose this additional compensation to his employer.

> **IV(C) Responsibilities of Supervisors.** All Members and Candidates must make reasonable efforts to detect and prevent violations of laws, rules, regulations, and the Code and Standards by any person under their supervision or authority.

 Professor's Note: The focus is on establishing and implementing reasonable compliance procedures in order to meet this Standard.

Guidance

Members must take steps to prevent employees from violating laws, rules, regulations, or the Code and Standards and make reasonable efforts to detect violations.

Guidance—Compliance Procedures

Understand that an adequate compliance system must meet industry standards, regulatory requirements, and the requirements of the Code and Standards. Members with supervisory responsibilities have an obligation to bring an inadequate compliance system to the attention of firm's management and recommend corrective action. While investigating a possible breach of compliance procedures, it is appropriate to limit the suspected employee's activities.

Recommended Procedures for Compliance

A member should recommend that his employer adopt a code of ethics. Employers should not commingle compliance procedures with the firm's code of ethics—this can dilute the goal of reinforcing one's ethical obligations. Members should encourage employers to provide their code of ethics to clients.

Adequate compliance procedures should:

- Be clearly written.
- Be easy to understand.
- Designate a compliance officer with authority clearly defined.
- Have a system of checks and balances.
- Outline the scope of procedures.
- Outline what conduct is permitted.
- Contain procedures for reporting violations and sanctions.

Once the compliance program is instituted, the supervisor should:

- Distribute it to the proper personnel.
- Update it as needed.
- Continually educate staff regarding procedures.
- Issue reminders as necessary.
- Require professional conduct evaluations.
- Review employee actions to monitor compliance and identify violations.
- Enforce procedures once a violation occurs.

If there is a violation, respond promptly and conduct a thorough investigation while placing limitations on the wrongdoer's activities.

Application of Standard IV(C) Responsibilities of Supervisors

Example 1:

Jane Mattock, senior vice president and head of the research department of H&V, Inc., a regional brokerage firm, has decided to change her recommendation for Timber Products from buy to sell. In line with H&V's procedures, she orally advises certain other H&V executives of her proposed actions before the report is prepared for publication. As a result of his conversation with Mattock, Dieter Frampton, one of the executives of H&V accountable to Mattock, immediately sells Timber's stock from his own account and from certain discretionary client accounts. In addition, other personnel inform certain institutional customers of the changed recommendation before it is printed and disseminated to all H&V customers who have received previous Timber reports.

Comment:

Mattock failed to supervise reasonably and adequately the actions of those accountable to her. She did not prevent or establish reasonable procedures designed to prevent dissemination of or trading on the information by those who knew of her changed recommendation. She must ensure that her firm has procedures for reviewing or recording trading in the stock of any corporation that has been the subject of an unpublished change in recommendation. Adequate procedures would have informed the subordinates of their duties and detected sales by Frampton and selected customers.

Example 2:

Deion Miller is the research director for Jamestown Investment Programs. The portfolio managers have become critical of Miller and his staff because the Jamestown portfolios do not include any stock that has been the subject of a merger or tender offer. Georgia Ginn, a member of Miller's staff, tells Miller that she has been studying a local company, Excelsior, Inc., and recommends its purchase. Ginn adds that the company has been widely rumored to be the subject of a merger study by a well-known conglomerate and discussions between them are under way. At Miller's request, Ginn prepares a memo recommending the stock. Miller passes along Ginn's memo to the portfolio managers prior to leaving for vacation, noting that he has not reviewed the memo. As a result of the memo, the portfolio managers buy Excelsior stock immediately. The day Miller returns to the office, Miller learns that Ginn's only sources for the report were her brother, who is an acquisitions analyst with Acme Industries and the "well-known conglomerate" and that the merger discussions were planned but not held.

Comment:

Miller violated Standard IV(C) by not exercising reasonable supervision when he disseminated the memo without checking to ensure that Ginn had a reasonable and adequate basis for her recommendations and that Ginn was not relying on material nonpublic information.

Example 3:

A member responsible for compliance by the firm's trading desk notices a high level of trading activity in a stock that is not on the firm's recommended list. Most of this trading is being done by a trainee and the member does not investigate this trading.

Comment:

This is a violation of the member's responsibilities as supervisor. She must take steps to monitor the activities of traders in training as well as investigate the reason for the heavy trading of the security by her firm's trading desk.

V. INVESTMENT ANALYSIS, RECOMMENDATIONS, AND ACTION

V(A) Diligence and Reasonable Basis

1. When analyzing investments, making recommendations, and taking investment actions use diligence, independence, and thoroughness.

2. Investment analysis, recommendations, and actions should have a reasonable and adequate basis, supported by research and investigation.

Guidance

The application of this Standard depends on the investment philosophy adhered to, members' and candidates' roles in the investment decision-making process, and the resources and support provided by employers. These factors dictate the degree of diligence, thoroughness of research, and the proper level of investigation required.

Guidance—Using Secondary Research or Third-Party Research

See that the research is sound. Examples of criteria to use to evaluate:

- Review assumptions used.
- How rigorous was the analysis?
- How timely is the research?
- Evaluate objectivity and independence of the recommendations.

Guidance—Group Research and Decision Making

Even if a member does not agree with the independent and objective view of the group, he does not necessarily have to decline to be identified with the report, as long as there is a reasonable and adequate basis.

Recommended Procedures for Compliance

Members should encourage their firms to consider these policies and procedures supporting this Standard:

- Have a policy requiring that research reports and recommendations have a basis that can be substantiated as reasonable and adequate.
- Have detailed, written guidance for proper research and due diligence.
- Have measurable criteria for judging the quality of research.

Application of Standard V(A) Diligence and Reasonable Basis

Example 1:

Helen Hawke manages the corporate finance department of Sarkozi Securities, Ltd. The firm is anticipating that the government will soon close a tax loophole that currently allows oil and gas exploration companies to pass on drilling expenses to holders of a certain class of shares. Because market demand for this tax-advantaged class of stock is currently high, Sarkozi convinces several companies to undertake new equity financings at once before the loophole closes. Time is of the essence, but Sarkozi lacks sufficient resources to conduct adequate research on all the prospective issuing companies. Hawke decides to estimate the IPO prices based on the relative size of each company and to justify the pricing later when her staff has time.

Comment:

Sarkozi should have taken on only the work that it could adequately handle. By categorizing the issuers as to general size, Hawke has bypassed researching all the other relevant aspects that should be considered when pricing new issues and thus has not performed sufficient due diligence. Such an omission can result in investors purchasing shares at prices that have no actual basis. Hawke has violated Standard V(A).

Example 2:

Evelyn Mastakis is a junior analyst asked by her firm to write a research report predicting the expected interest rate for residential mortgages over the next six months. Mastakis submits her report to the fixed-income investment committee of her firm for review, as required by firm procedures. Although some committee members support Mastakis's conclusion, the majority of the committee disagrees with her conclusion and the report is significantly changed to indicate that interest rates are likely to increase more than originally predicted by Mastakis.

Comment:

The results of research are not always clear, and different people may have different opinions based on the same factual evidence. In this case, the majority of the committee may have valid reasons for issuing a report that differs from the analyst's original research. The firm can issue a report different from the original report of the analyst as long as there is a reasonable or adequate basis for its conclusions. Generally, analysts must write research reports that reflect their own opinion and can ask the firm not to put their name on reports that ultimately differ from that opinion. When the work is a group effort, however, not all members of the team may agree with all aspects of the report. Ultimately, members and candidates can ask to have their names removed from the report, but if they are satisfied that the process has produced results or conclusions that have a reasonable or adequate basis, members or candidates do not have to dissociate from the report even when they do not agree with its contents. The member or candidate should document the difference of opinion and any request to remove his or her name from the report.

Example 3:

A member makes a presentation for an offering his firm is underwriting, using maximum production levels as his estimate in order to justify the price of the shares he is recommending for purchase.

Comment:

Using the maximum possible production without acknowledging that this is not the expected level of production (or without presenting a range of possible outcomes and their relative probabilities) does not provide a reasonable basis for the purchase recommendation and is a violation of the Standard.

Example 4:

A member posts buy recommendations in an internet chat room based on "conventional wisdom" and what the public is currently buying.

Comment:

A recommendation that is not based on independent and diligent research into the subject company is a violation of the Standard.

Example 5:

A member is a principal in a small investment firm that bases its securities recommendations on third-party research that it purchases.

Comment:

This is not a violation as long as the member's firm periodically checks the purchased research to determine that it has met and still meets the criteria of objectivity and reasonableness required by the Standard.

V(B) Communication With Clients and Prospective Clients

1. Disclose to clients and prospects basic format and general principles of investment processes used to analyze and select securities and construct portfolios. Promptly disclose any process changes.

2. Use reasonable judgment in identifying relevant factors important to investment analyses, recommendations, or actions, and include factors when communicating with clients and prospects.

3. Investment analyses and recommendations should clearly differentiate facts from opinions.

Guidance

Proper communication with clients is critical to provide quality financial services. Members must distinguish between opinions and facts and always include the basic characteristics of the security being analyzed in a research report.

Members must illustrate to clients and prospects the investment decision-making process utilized. The suitability of each investment is important in the context of the entire portfolio.

All means of communication are included here, not just research reports.

Recommended Procedures for Compliance

Selection of relevant factors in a report can be a judgment call, so be sure to maintain records indicating the nature of the research, and be able to supply additional information if it is requested by the client or other users of the report.

Application of Standard V(B) Communication with Clients and Prospective Clients

Example 1:

Sarah Williamson, director of marketing for Country Technicians, Inc., is convinced that she has found the perfect formula for increasing Country Technician's income and diversifying its product base. Williamson plans to build on Country Technician's reputation as a leading money manager by marketing an exclusive and expensive investment advice letter to high-net-worth individuals. One hitch in the plan is the complexity of Country Technician's investment system—a combination of technical trading rules (based on historical price and volume fluctuations) and portfolio-construction rules designed to minimize risk. To simplify the newsletter, she decides to include only each week's top-five buy and sell recommendations and to leave out details of the valuation models and the portfolio-structuring scheme.

Comment:

Williamson's plans for the newsletter violate Standard V(B) because she does not intend to include all the relevant factors behind the investment advice. Williamson need not describe the investment system in detail in order to implement the advice effectively, but clients must be informed of Country Technician's basic process and logic. Without understanding the basis for a recommendation, clients cannot possibly understand its limitations or its inherent risks.

Example 2:

Richard Dox is a mining analyst for East Bank Securities. He has just finished his report on Boisy Bay Minerals. Included in his report is his own assessment of the geological extent of mineral reserves likely to be found on the company's land. Dox completed this calculation based on the core samples from the company's latest drilling. According to Dox's calculations, the company has in excess of 500,000 ounces of gold on the property. Dox concludes his research report as follows: "Based on the fact that the company has 500,000 ounces of gold to be mined, I recommend a strong BUY."

Comment:

If Dox issues the report as written, he will violate Standard V(B). His calculation of the total gold reserves for the property is an opinion, not a fact. Opinion must be distinguished from fact in research reports.

Example 3:

May & Associates is an aggressive growth manager that has represented itself since its inception as a specialist at investing in small-capitalization domestic stocks. One of May's selection criteria is a maximum capitalization of $250 million for any given company. After a string of successful years of superior relative performance, May expanded its client base significantly, to the point at which assets under management now exceed $3 billion. For liquidity purposes, May's chief investment officer (CIO) decides to lift the maximum permissible market-cap ceiling to $500 million and change the firm's sales and marketing literature accordingly to inform prospective clients and third-party consultants.

Comment:

Although May's CIO is correct about informing potentially interested parties as to the change in investment process, he must also notify May's existing clients. Among the latter group might be a number of clients who not only retained May as a small-cap manager but also retained mid-cap and large-cap specialists in a multiple-manager approach. Such clients could regard May's change of criteria as a style change that could distort their overall asset allocations.

Example 4:

Rather than lifting the ceiling for its universe from $250 million to $500 million, May & Associates extends its small-cap universe to include a number of non-U.S. companies.

Comment:

Standard V(B) requires that May's CIO advise May's clients of this change because the firm may have been retained by some clients specifically for its prowess at investing in domestic small-cap stocks. Other variations requiring client notification include introducing derivatives to emulate a certain market sector or relaxing various other constraints, such as portfolio beta. In all such cases, members and candidates must disclose changes to all interested parties.

Example 5:

A member sends a report to his investment management firm's clients describing a strategy his firm offers in terms of the high returns it will generate in the event interest rate volatility decreases. The report does not provide details of the strategy because they are deemed proprietary. The report does not consider the possible returns if interest rate volatility actually increases.

Comment:

This is a violation on two counts. The basic nature of the strategy must be disclosed including the extent to which leverage is used to generate the high returns when volatility falls. Further, the report must include how the strategy will perform if volatility rises as well as if it falls.

Example 6:

A member's firm changes from its old equity selection model which is based on price-sales ratios to a new model based on several factors including future earnings growth rates, but does not inform clients of this change.

Comment:

This is a violation because members must inform their clients of any significant change in their investment process. Here, the introduction of forecast data on earnings growth can be viewed as a significant change since the old single-variable model was based on reported rather than forecast data.

Example 7:

A member's firm, in response to poor results relative to its stated benchmark, decides to structure portfolios to passively track the benchmark and does not inform clients.

Comment:

This is a significant change in the investment process and must be communicated to clients.

Example 8:

At a firm where individual portfolio managers have been responsible for security selection, a new policy is implemented whereby only stocks on an approved list constructed by the firm's senior managers may be purchased in client accounts. A member who is a portfolio manager does not inform his clients.

Comment:

This is a violation of the Standard because it represents a significant change in the investment process.

 Professor's Note: Remember, the argument that clients "won't care" about a process change can be turned around to "there's no reason NOT to disclose the change."

> **V(C) Record Retention.** Maintain all records supporting analysis, recommendations, actions, and all other investment-related communications with clients and prospects.

Guidance

Members must maintain research records that support the reasons for the analyst's conclusions and any investment actions taken. Such records are the property of the firm. If no other regulatory standards are in place, CFA Institute recommends at least a 7-year holding period.

Recommended Procedures for Compliance

This record-keeping requirement generally is the firm's responsibility.

Application of Standard V(C) Record Retention

Example 1:

One of Nikolas Lindstrom's clients is upset by the negative investment returns in his equity portfolio. The investment policy statement for the client requires that the portfolio manager follow a benchmark-oriented approach. The benchmark for the client included a 35% investment allocation in the technology sector, which the client acknowledged was appropriate. Over the past three years, the portion put into the segment of technology stocks suffered severe losses. The client complains to the investment manager that so much money was allocated to this sector.

Comment:

For Lindstrom, it is important to have appropriate records to show that over the past three years the percentage of technology stocks in the benchmark index was 35%. Therefore, the amount of money invested in the technology sector was appropriate according to the investment policy statement. Lindstrom should also have the investment policy statement for the client stating that the benchmark was appropriate for the client's investment objectives. He should also have records indicating that the investment had been explained appropriately to the client and that the investment policy statement was updated on a regular basis.

Example 2:

A member bases his research reports on interviews, his own analysis, and industry reports from third parties on his industry and related industries.

Comment:

The member must keep records of all the information that went into the research on which his reports and recommendations are based.

Example 3:

A member mails investment research and promotional materials to prospects. If the prospects fail to become customers within one year, their names and information concerning documents sent them are purged from the firm's database.

Comment:

This communication is investment-related, so the recipient name and other relevant information should be retained for at least seven years for future reference.

VI. CONFLICTS OF INTEREST

VI(A) Disclosure of Conflicts. Members and Candidates must make full and fair disclosure of all matters which may impair their independence or objectivity or interfere with their duties to employer, clients and prospects. Disclosures must be prominent, in plain language, and effectively communicate the information.

 Professor's Note: Emphasis in this Standard is on meaningful disclosure— prominent and in plain language.

Guidance

Members must fully disclose to clients, prospects, and their employers all actual and potential conflicts of interest in order to protect investors and employers. These disclosures must be clearly stated.

Guidance—Disclosure to Clients

The requirement that all potential areas of conflict be disclosed allows clients and prospects to judge motives and potential biases for themselves. Disclosure of broker/dealer market-making activities would be included here. Board service is another area of potential conflict.

The most common conflict which requires disclosure is actual ownership of stock in companies that the member recommends or that clients hold.

Guidance—Disclosure of Conflicts to Employers

Members must give the employer enough information to judge the impact of the conflict. Take reasonable steps to avoid conflicts, and report them promptly if they occur.

Recommended Procedures of Compliance

Any special compensation arrangements, bonus programs, commissions, and incentives should be disclosed.

Application of Standard VI(A) Disclosure of Conflicts

Example 1:

Hunter Weiss is a research analyst with Farmington Company, a broker and investment banking firm. Farmington's merger and acquisition department has represented Vimco, a conglomerate, in all of its acquisitions for 20 years. From time to time, Farmington officers sit on the boards of directors of various Vimco subsidiaries. Weiss is writing a research report on Vimco.

Comment:

Weiss must disclose in his research report Farmington's special relationship with Vimco. Broker/dealer management of and participation in public offerings must be disclosed in research reports. Because the position of underwriter to a company presents a special past and potential future relationship with a company that is the subject of investment advice, it threatens the independence and objectivity of the report and must be disclosed.

Example 2:

Samantha Dyson, a portfolio manager for Thomas Investment Counsel, Inc., specializes in managing defined-benefit pension plan accounts, all of which are in the accumulative phase and have long-term investment objectives. A year ago, Dyson's employer, in an attempt to motivate and retain key investment professionals, introduced a bonus compensation system that rewards portfolio managers on the basis of quarterly performance relative to their peers and certain benchmark indexes. Dyson changes her investment strategy and purchases several high-beta stocks for client portfolios in an attempt to improve short-term performance. These purchases are seemingly contrary to the client investment policy statement. Now, an officer of Griffin Corporation, one of Dyson's pension fund clients, asks why Griffin Corporation's portfolio seems to be dominated by high-beta stocks of companies that often appear among the most actively traded issues. No change in objective or strategy has been recommended by Dyson during the year.

Comment:

Dyson violated Standard VI(A) by failing to inform her clients of the changes in her compensation arrangement with her employer that created a conflict of interest. Firms may pay employees on the basis of performance, but pressure by Thomas Investment Counsel to achieve short-term performance goals is in basic conflict with the objectives of Dyson's accounts.

Example 3:

Bruce Smith covers East European equities for Marlborough investments, an investment management firm with a strong presence in emerging markets. While on a business trip to Russia, Smith learns that investing in Russian equity directly is difficult but that equity-linked notes that replicate the performance of the underlying Russian equity can be purchased from a New York-based investment bank. Believing that his firm would not be interested in such a security, Smith purchases a note linked to a Russian telecommunications company for his own account without informing Marlborough. A month later, Smith decides that the firm should consider investing in Russian equities using equity-linked notes, and he prepares a write-up on the market that concludes with a recommendation to purchase several of the notes. One note recommended is linked to the same Russian telecom company that Smith holds in his personal account.

Comment:

Smith violated Standard VI(A) by failing to disclose his ownership of the note linked to the Russian telecom company. Smith is required by the standard to disclose the investment opportunity to his employer and look to his company's policies on personal trading to determine whether it was proper for him to purchase the note for his own account. By purchasing the note, Smith may or may not have impaired his ability to make an unbiased and objective assessment of the appropriateness of the derivative instrument for his firm, but Smith's failure to disclose the purchase to his employer impaired his employer's ability to render an opinion regarding whether the ownership of a security constituted a conflict of interest that might have affected future recommendations. Once he recommended the notes to his firm, Smith compounded his problems by not disclosing that he owned the notes in his personal account—a clear conflict of interest.

Example 4:

An investment management partnership sells a significant stake to a firm that is publicly traded. The partnership has added the firm's stock to its recommended list and approved its commercial paper for cash management accounts.

Comment:

Members are required to disclose such a change in firm ownership to all clients. Further, any transactions in client accounts involving the securities of the public firm, and any recommendations concerning the public firm's securities, must include a disclosure of the business relation between it and the partnership.

Example 5:

A member provides clients with research about a company's stock, and his wife inherits a significant amount of stock in the company.

Comment:

The member must disclose this potential conflict to his employer and in any subsequent reports or recommendations he authors. His employer may prudently choose to reassign the stock.

Example 6:

A member's investment banking firm receives a significant number of options as partial compensation for bringing a firm public. The member will profit personally from a portion of these options as well.

Comment:

In any research report on the public firm's securities the member must disclose the fact that these options exist and include their number and the expiration date(s). Since he will profit personally from these, he must also disclose the extent of his participation in these options.

Example 7:

A member accepts an offer from a stock promoter who will provide additional compensation when the member sells Acme stock to his clients. He does not inform his clients or his employer.

Comment:

The member is in violation of the Standard because he must disclose this additional compensation to those clients to whom he recommends the stock and to his employer. Both have a right to determine for themselves the extent to which this additional compensation might affect the member's objectivity.

Example 8:

A member who is a portfolio manager for a small investment management firm serving individuals accepts a job as a trustee of an endowment fund that has over €1.5 billion in assets and does not disclose this to her employer.

Comment:

This is a significant position that may require a substantial portion of the member's time and may involve decisions on security selection and trading. The member is in violation of the Standard by not disclosing this involvement to her employer and by not discussing it with her employer before accepting the position.

> **VI(B) Priority of Transactions.** Investment transactions for clients and employers must have priority over those in which a Member or Candidate is a beneficial owner.

 Professor's Note: Transactions for clients and employers always have priority over personal transactions.

Guidance

Client transactions take priority over personal transactions and over transactions made on behalf of the member's firm. Personal transactions include situations where the member is a "beneficial owner." Personal transactions may be undertaken only after clients and the member's employer have had an adequate opportunity to act on a recommendation. Note that family-member accounts that are client accounts should be treated just like any client account; they should not be disadvantaged.

Recommended Procedures for Compliance

All firms should have in place basic procedures that address conflicts created by personal investing. The following areas should be included:

- Limited participation in equity IPOs. Members can avoid these conflicts by not participating in IPOs.
- Restrictions on private placements. Strict limits should be placed on employee acquisition of these securities and proper supervisory procedures should be in place. Participation in these investments raises conflict of interest issues, similar to IPOs.
- Establish blackout/restricted periods. Employees involved in investment decision-making should have blackout periods prior to trading for clients—no "front running" (i.e., purchase or sale of securities in advance of anticipated client or employer purchases and sales). The size of the firm and the type of security should help dictate how severe the blackout requirement should be.
- Reporting requirements. Supervisors should establish reporting procedures, including duplicate trade confirmations, disclosure of personal holdings/beneficial ownership positions, and pre-clearance procedures.

- Disclosure of policies. When requested, members must fully disclose to investors their firm's personal trading policies.

Application of Standard VI(B) Priority of Transactions

Example 1:

Erin Toffler, a portfolio manager at Esposito Investments, manages the retirement account established with the firm by her parents. Whenever IPOs become available, she first allocates shares to all her other clients for whom the investment is appropriate; only then does she place any remaining portion in her parents' account, if the issue is appropriate for them. She has adopted this procedure so that no one can accuse her of favoring her parents.

Comment:

Toffler has breached her duty to her parents by treating them differently from her other accounts simply because of the family relationship. As fee-paying clients of Esposito Investments, Toffler's parents are entitled to the same treatment as any other client of the firm. If Toffler has beneficial ownership in the account, however, and Esposito Investments has preclearance and reporting requirements for personal transactions, she may have to preclear the trades and report the transactions to Esposito.

Example 2:

A brokerage's insurance analyst, Denise Wilson, makes a closed-circuit report to her firm's branches around the country. During the broadcast, she includes negative comments about a major company within the industry. The following day, Wilson's report is printed and distributed to the sales force and public customers. The report recommends that both short-term traders and intermediate investors take profits by selling that company's stocks. Several minutes after the broadcast, Ellen Riley, head of the firm's trading department, closes out a long call position in the stock. Shortly thereafter, Riley establishes a sizable "put" position in the stock. Riley claims she took this action to facilitate anticipated sales by institutional clients.

Comment:

Riley expected that both the stock and option markets would respond to the "sell" recommendation, but she did not give customers an opportunity to buy or sell in the options market before the firm itself did. By taking action before the report was disseminated, Riley's firm could have depressed the price of the "calls" and increased the price of the "puts." The firm could have avoided a conflict of interest if it had waited to trade for its own account until its clients had an opportunity to receive and assimilate Wilson's recommendations. As it is, Riley's actions violated Standard VI(B).

Example 3:

A member who is a research analyst does not recommend a stock to his employer because he wants to purchase it quickly for his personal account.

Comment:

He has violated the priority of transactions by withholding this information from his employer and seeking to profit personally at his employer's expense. The member has likely violated his duty to his employer under Standard IV(A) - Loyalty as well.

Example 4:

A member who manages a fund gets hot IPO shares for her husband's account from syndicate firms even when the fund is unable to get shares.

Comment:

The member has violated the Standard by this action. She must act in the interest of the shareholders of the fund and place allocated shares there first. She must also inform her employer of her participation in these offerings through her beneficial interest in her husband's account(s).

Example 5:

A member allows an employee to continue his duties without having signed a required report of his personal trading activity over the last three months. The employee, a CFA candidate, has been purchasing securities for his own account just before firm buy recommendations have been released.

Comment:

The employee has violated the Standard. The member has also violated Standard IV(C)—Responsibilities of Supervisors by allowing the employee to continue in his regular duties.

Example 6:

A member reveals a sell rating on some securities in a broadcast to all of her firm's brokers. The changed rating is sent to clients the next day. Shortly after revealing the change to her firm's brokers and prior to dissemination to clients, she buys puts on the stock for her firm's account.

Comment:

The member did not give clients adequate opportunity to act on the change in recommendation before buying the puts for her firm's account.

VI(C) Referral Fees. Members and Candidates must disclose to their employers, clients, and prospects any compensation consideration or benefit received by, or paid to, others for recommendations of products and services.

Guidance

Members must inform employers, clients, and prospects of any benefit received for referrals of customers and clients, allowing them to evaluate the full cost of the service as well as any potential impartiality. All types of consideration must be disclosed.

Application of Standard VI(C) Referral Fees

Example 1:

Brady Securities, Inc., a broker/dealer, has established a referral arrangement with Lewis Brothers, Ltd., an investment counseling firm. Under this arrangement, Brady Securities refers all prospective tax-exempt accounts, including pension, profit-sharing, and endowment accounts, to Lewis Brothers. In return, Lewis Brothers makes available to Brady Securities on a regular basis the security recommendations and reports of its research staff, which registered representatives of Brady Securities use in serving customers. In addition, Lewis Brothers conducts monthly economic and market reviews for Brady Securities personnel and directs all stock commission business generated by referral account to Brady Securities. Willard White, a partner in Lewis Brothers, calculates that the incremental costs involved in functioning as the research department of Brady Securities amount to $20,000 annually. Referrals from Brady Securities last year resulted in fee income of $200,000, and directing all stock trades through Brady Securities resulted in additional costs to Lewis Brothers' clients of $10,000.

Diane Branch, the chief financial officer of Maxwell, Inc., contacts White and says that she is seeking an investment manager for Maxwell's profit-sharing plan. She adds, "My friend Harold Hill at Brady Securities recommended your firm without qualification, and that's good enough for me. Do we have a deal?" White accepts the new account but does not disclose his firm's referral arrangement with Brady Securities.

Comment:

White violated Standard VI(C) by failing to inform the prospective customer of the referral fee payable in services and commissions for an indefinite period to Brady Securities. Such disclosure could have caused Branch to reassess Hill's recommendation and make a more critical evaluation of Lewis Brothers' services.

Example 2:

James Handley works for the Trust Department of Central Trust Bank. He receives compensation for each referral he makes to Central Trust's brokerage and personal financial management department that results in a sale. He refers several of his clients to the personal financial management department but does not disclose the arrangement within Central trust to his clients.

Comment:

Handley has violated Standard V(C) by not disclosing the referral arrangement at Central Trust Bank to his clients. The Standard does not distinguish between referral fees paid by a third party for referring clients to the third party and internal compensation

---

arrangements paid within the firm to attract new business to a subsidiary. Members and candidates must disclose all such referral fees. Therefore, Handley would be required to disclose, at the time of referral, any referral fee agreement in place between Central Trust Bank's departments. The disclosure should include the nature and the value of the benefit and should be made in writing.

Example 3:

Yeshao Wen is a portfolio manager for a bank. He receives additional monetary compensation from his employer when he is successful in assisting in the sales process and generation of assets under management. The assets in question will be invested in proprietary product offerings such as affiliate company mutual funds.

Comment:

Standard VI(C) is meant to address instances where the investment advice provided by a member or candidate appears to be objective and independent but in fact is influenced by an unseen referral arrangement. It is not meant to cover compensation by employers to employees for generating new business when it would be obvious to potential clients that the employees are "referring" potential clients to the services of their employers.

If Wen is selling the bank's investment management services in general, he does not need to disclose to potential clients that he will receive a bonus for finding new clients and acquiring new assets under management for the bank. Potential clients are likely aware that it would be financially beneficial both to the portfolio manager and the manager's firm for the portfolio manager to sell the services of the firm and attract new clients. Therefore, sales efforts attempting to attract new investment management clients need not disclose this fact.

However, in this example, the assets will be managed in "proprietary product offerings" of the manager's company (for example, an in-house mutual fund) and Wen will receive additional compensation for selling firm products. Some sophisticated investors may realize that it would be financially beneficial to the portfolio manager and the manager's firm if the investor buys the product offerings of the firm.

Best practice, however, dictates that the portfolio manager must disclose to clients that they are compensated for referring clients to firm products. Such discloser will meet the purpose of Standard VI(C), which is to allow investors to determine whether there is any partiality on the part of the portfolio manager when making investment advice.

VII. RESPONSIBILITIES AS A CFA INSTITUTE MEMBER OR CFA CANDIDATE

VII(A) Conduct as Members and Candidates in the CFA Program. Members and Candidates must not engage in conduct that compromises the reputation or integrity of CFA Institute or the CFA designation or the integrity, validity, or security of the CFA exams.

Professor's Note: The Standard is intended to cover conduct such as cheating on the CFA exam or otherwise violating rules of CFA Institute or the CFA program. It is not intended to prevent anyone from expressing any opinions or beliefs concerning CFA Institute or the CFA program.

Members must not engage in any activity that undermines the integrity of the CFA charter. This Standard applies to conduct which includes:

- Cheating on the CFA exam or any exam.
- Not following rules and policies of the CFA program.
- Giving confidential information on the CFA program to Candidates or the public.
- Improperly using the designation to further personal and professional goals.
- Misrepresenting information on the Professional Conduct Statement (PCS) or the CFA Institute Professional Development Program.

Members and candidates are not precluded from expressing their opinions regarding the exam program or CFA Institute.

Application of Standard VII(A) Conduct as Members and Candidates in the CFA Program

Example 1:

Ashlie Hocking is writing Level 2 of the CFA examination in London. After completing the exam, she immediately attempts to contact her friend in Sydney, Australia, to tip him off to specific questions on the exam.

Comment:

Hocking has violated Standard VII(A) by attempting to give her friend an unfair advantage, thereby compromising the integrity of the CFA examination process.

Example 2:

Jose Ramirez is an investment-relations consultant for several small companies that are seeking greater exposure to investors. He is also the program chair for the CFA Institute society in the city where he works. To the exclusion of other companies, Ramirez only schedules companies that are his clients to make presentations to the society.

Comment:

Ramirez, by using his volunteer position at CFA Institute to benefit himself and his clients, compromises the reputation and integrity of CFA Institute, and, thus, violates Standard VII(A).

Example 3:

A member who is an exam grader discusses with friends the guideline answer for and relative candidate performance on a specific question he graded on the CFA exam.

Comment:

He has violated his Grader's Agreement and also the Standard by compromising the integrity of the CFA exam.

Example 4:

A candidate does not stop writing when asked to by the proctor at the CFA exam.

Comment:

By taking additional time compared to other candidates this candidate has violated the Standard, compromising the integrity of the exam process.

Example 5:

A member who is a volunteer on a CFA Institute committee tells her clients that what she learns through her committee work will allow her to better serve their interests.

Comment:

She has violated the Standard by using her CFA committee position to benefit herself personally and to any extent her 'inside' knowledge has benefited her clients.

> **VII(B) Reference to CFA Institute, the CFA Designation, and the CFA Program.** Members and Candidates must not misrepresent or exaggerate the meaning or implications of membership in CFA Institute, holding the CFA designation, or candidacy in the program.

Professor's Note: This Standard prohibits Candidates from engaging in any conduct that may "misrepresent or exaggerate the meaning or implications of membership in CFA Institute, holding the CFA designation, or candidacy in the CFA program." Candidates must not reference any "partial" designation since this also misrepresents or exaggerates credentials.

Guidance

Members must not make promotional promises or guarantees tied to the CFA designation. Do not:

- Over-promise individual competence.
- Over-promise investment results in the future (i.e., higher performance, less risk, etc.).

Guidance—CFA Institute Membership

Members must satisfy these requirements to maintain membership:

- Sign PCS annually.
- Pay annual CFA Institute membership dues.

If they fail to do this, they are no longer active members.

Guidance—Using the CFA Designation

Do not misrepresent or exaggerate the meaning of the designation.

Guidance—Referencing Candidacy in the CFA Program

There is no partial designation. It is acceptable to state that a Candidate successfully completed the program in three years, if in fact they did, but claiming superior ability because of this is not permitted.

Guidance—Proper Usage of the CFA Marks

The Chartered Financial Analyst and CFA marks must always be used either after a charterholder's name or as adjectives, but not as nouns, in written and oral communications.

Recommended Procedures for Compliance

Make sure that members' and candidates' firms are aware of the proper references to a member's CFA designation or candidacy, as this is a common error.

Application of Standard VII(B) Reference to CFA Institute, the CFA Designation, and the CFA Program

Example 1:

An advertisement for AZ Investment Advisors states that all the firm's principals are CFA charterholders and all passed the three examinations on their first attempt. The advertisement prominently links this fact to the notion that AZ's mutual funds have achieved superior performance.

Comment:

AZ may state that all principals passed the three examinations on the first try as long as this statement is true and is not linked to performance or does not imply superior ability. Implying that (1) CFA charterholders achieve better investment results and (2) those who pass the exams on the first try may be more successful than those who do not violates Standard VII(B).

Example 2:

Five years after receiving his CFA charter, Louis Vasseur resigns his position as an investment analyst and spends the next two years traveling abroad. Because he is not actively engaged in the investment profession, he does not file a completed Professional Conduct Statement with CFA Institute and does not pay his CFA Institute membership dues. At the conclusion of his travels, Vasseur becomes a self-employed analyst, accepting assignments as an independent contractor. Without reinstating his CFA Institute membership by filing his Professional Conduct Statement and paying his dues, he prints business cards that display "CFA" after his name.

Comment:

Vasseur has violated Standard VII(B) because Vasseur's right to use the CFA designation was suspended when he failed to file his Professional Conduct Statement and stopped paying dues. Therefore, he no longer is able to state or imply that he is an active CFA charterholder. When Vasseur files his Professional Conduct Statement and resumes paying CFA Institute dues to activate his membership, he will be eligible to use the CFA designation upon satisfactory completion of CFA Institute reinstatement procedures.

Example 3:

A member still uses the initials CFA after his name even though his membership has been suspended for not paying dues and for not submitting a personal conduct statement as required.

Comment:

This is a violation of the Standard.

Example 4:

A member puts the CFA logo on his letterhead, his business cards, and the company letterhead.

Comment:

By putting the logo on the company letterhead (rather than the letterhead or business card of an individual who is a CFA charterholder), the member has violated the Standard.

KEY CONCEPTS

LOS 1.a

Members of CFA Institute [including Chartered Financial Analyst® (CFA®) charterholders] and candidates for the CFA designation ("Members and Candidates") must:[3]

- Act with integrity, competence, diligence, respect, and in an ethical manner with the public, clients, prospective clients, employers, employees, colleagues in the investment profession, and other participants in the global capital markets.
- Place the integrity of the investment profession and the interests of clients above their own personal interests.
- Use reasonable care and exercise independent professional judgment when conducting investment analysis, making investment recommendations, taking investment actions, and engaging in other professional activities.
- Practice and encourage others to practice in a professional and ethical manner that will reflect credit on themselves and the profession.
- Promote the integrity of, and uphold the rules governing, capital markets.
- Maintain and improve their professional competence and strive to maintain and improve the competence of other investment professionals.

The Standards of Professional Conduct are organized into seven standards:

I. Professionalism
II. Integrity of Capital Markets
III. Duties to Clients
IV. Duties to Employers
V. Investment Analysis, Recommendations, and Action
VI. Conflicts of Interest
VII. Responsibilities as a CFA Institute Member or CFA Candidate

---

3. Copyright 2005, CFA Institute. Reproduced and republished from "The Code of Ethics," from Standards of Practice Handbook, 9th ed., 2005, with permission from CFA Institute. All rights reserved.

CONCEPT CHECKERS

 Professor's Note: On the actual Level 2 exam, and in all of our self-tests and practice exams, the questions will have 3 choices. However, by including 4 choices here, as is also done in parts of the source curriculum, we are able to test your comprehension of the material more completely.

1. Jamie Hutchins, CFA, is a portfolio manager for CNV Investments, Inc. Over the years, Hutchins has made several poor personal investments that have led to financial distress and personal bankruptcy. Hutchins feels that her business partner, John Smith, is mostly to blame for her situation since "he did not invest enough money in her investment opportunities and caused them to fail." Hutchins reports Smith to CFA Institute claiming Smith violated the Code and Standards relating to misconduct. Which of the following statements is *most accurate*?
   A. Neither Hutchins nor Smith violated the Code and Standards.
   B. By reporting Smith to CFA Institute, Hutchins has misused the Professional Conduct Program, thus violating the Code and Standards.
   C. Hutchins' bankruptcy reflects poorly on her professional reputation and thus violates the Code and Standards.
   D. Smith's lack of investment in Hutchin's opportunities violated the priority of transactions, and he was appropriately reported to CFA Institute.

2. While working on a new underwriting project, Jean Brayman, CFA, has just received information from her client that leads her to believe that the firm's financial statements in the registration statement overstate the firm's financial position. Brayman should:
   A. report her finding to the appropriate governmental regulatory authority.
   B. immediately dissociate herself from the underwriting in writing to the client.
   C. seek advice from her firm's compliance department as to the appropriate action to take.
   D. inform the client of the problem and issue a press release correcting the statements.

3. Karen Jones, CFA, is an outside director for Valley Manufacturing. At a directors' meeting, Jones finds out that Valley Manufacturing has made several contributions to foreign politicians that she suspects were illegal. Jones checks with her firm's legal counsel and determines that the contributions were indeed illegal. At the next board meeting Jones urges the board to disclose the contributions. The board, however, votes not to make a disclosure. Jones should:
   A. protest the board's actions in writing to the executive officer of Valley.
   B. resign from the board and seek legal counsel as to her legal disclosure requirements.
   C. inform her supervisor of her discovery and cease attending meetings until the matter is resolved.
   D. resign from the board, sell any stock she owns in the firm, and issue a press release explaining her actions.

4.   Carrie Carlson, CFA, is a citizen of Emerging Market Country (EMC) with no securities laws governing the use of inside information. Carlson has clients in Emerging Market Country and in Neighboring Country (NC), which has a few poorly defined laws governing the use of inside information. Should Carlson have inside information on a publicly traded security, she:
   A. can inform her clients in EMC, but not NC.
   B. can only trade for her own account when she has inside information.
   C. can use the information for her NC clients to the extent permitted by the laws of NC.
   D. cannot use the information to trade in either EMC or NC.

5.   In order to dispel the myth that emerging market stocks are illiquid investments, Green Brothers, a "long only" emerging market fund manager, has two of its subsidiaries simultaneously buy and sell emerging market stocks. In its marketing literature, Green Brothers cites the overall emerging market volume as evidence of the market's liquidity. As a result of its actions, more investors participate in the emerging markets fund. Which of the following is *most accurate*? Green Brothers:
   A. did not violate the Code and Standards.
   B. violated the Code and Standards by failing to consider the suitability of emerging market investments.
   C. violated the Code and Standards by manipulating the volume in the emerging securities markets.
   D. would not have violated the Code and Standards if the subsidiaries traded only stocks not included in the fund.

6.   Over the past two days, Lorraine Quigley, CFA and manager of a hedge fund, has been purchasing large quantities of Craeger Industrial Products' common stock while at the same time shorting put options on the same stock. Quigley did not notify her clients of the trades although they are aware of the fund's general strategy to generate returns. Which of the following statements is *most accurate*? Quigley:
   A. did not violate the Code and Standards.
   B. violated the Code and Standards by manipulating the prices of publicly traded securities.
   C. violated the Code and Standards by failing to disclose the transactions to clients before they occurred.
   D. violated the Code and Standards by failing to establish a reasonable and adequate basis before making the trades.

7.   Which of the following statements is *least accurate*? A member or candidate:
   A. can be considered to have effectively participated in a violation by having knowledge of the violation and not taking steps to disassociate themselves from the activity.
   B. is held responsible for participating in illegal acts in instances where violation of the law is evident to those who know or should know the law.
   C. when confronted with potentially illegal activities, should consult with her supervisor and her employer's counsel.
   D. must report evidence of legal violations to the appropriate governmental or regulatory organization.

8. Paula Osgood, CFA, is promoting her new money management firm by issuing an advertisement. Which of these items is *least likely* to be in conflict with the professional designation Standard? The advertisement states that:
    A. she passed three exams covering ethics, financial statement analysis, asset valuation, and portfolio management and that she is a member of the local society. Osgood signs the advertisement followed by the letters CFA in oversized and bold strike letters.
    B. she passed three exams totaling over 18 hours within the minimum period of one and a half years. Knowledge tested included ethics, financial statement analysis, asset valuation, and portfolio management. In addition, she is a member of the local society.
    C. because of her extensive CFA training she will be able to achieve better investment results than non-CFA managers since she is one of very few professionals to have been awarded this designation.
    D. she is one of very few professionals to have been awarded this designation and that she is a member of the local society. She signs the advertisement followed by the letters CFA in oversized and bold strike letters.

9. Melvin Byrne, CFA, manages a portfolio for James Martin, a very wealthy client. Martin's portfolio is well diversified with a slight tilt toward capital appreciation. Martin requires very little income from the portfolio. Recently Martin's brother, Cliff, has become a client of Byrne. Byrne proceeds to invest Cliff's portfolio in a similar manner to James' portfolio based on the fact that both brothers have a similar lifestyle and are only two years apart in age. Which of the following statements is *most accurate*? Byrne:
    A. violated the Code and Standards by deviating from his investment mandate related to James' portfolio.
    B. violated the Code and Standards by knowingly creating a conflict of interest between James' and Cliff's portfolio.
    C. violated the Code and Standards by failing to determine Cliff's objectives and constraints prior to investing his portfolio.
    D. did not violate the Code and Standards.

10. In which of the following is the analyst *least likely* to have committed plagiarism?
    A. Julie Long takes performance projections and charts from a company she is researching, combines them with her own analysis, and publishes them under her own name.
    B. Bill Cooper finds a statistical table in the Federal Reserve Bulletin that supports the work he has done in his industry analysis and has his secretary include the table as part of his report without citing the source.
    C. Jan Niedfeldt gets a call from one of her fellow analysts stating that the analyst's research shows that XYZ Company is a buy. Niedfeldt calls up her major clients and tells them that her research shows XYZ is a buy.
    D. To speed up an acquisition project, Jim Zijacek's boss gives him a report from another firm also working on the project and tells Zijacek to print the report on company letterhead, sign it, and mail it out to the stockholders.

11. Jessica Ellis, CFA, manages an international stock portfolio for a group of wealthy investors with similar investment objectives. According to the investment policy statement, the portfolio is to pursue an aggressive growth strategy while maintaining sufficient international diversification. The fund is prohibited from using leverage. Ellis has just received a request from all of the group of investors to purchase for the fund a large position in German bonds which they believe to be significantly undervalued. Which of the following actions should Ellis take to avoid violating the Code and Standards?
    A. Purchase the bonds since it was requested by the clients to whom Ellis has a fiduciary duty.
    B. Inform the investors that she is unable to make the purchase since it is inconsistent with the international stock portfolio's investment mandate.
    C. Purchase the bonds only after receiving a written consent statement signed by each portfolio investor stating that they are aware that the investment is not suitable for the portfolio.
    D. Change the investment policy statement to reflect an investment strategy that would allow the bond purchase and then purchase the undervalued bonds for the portfolio.

12. In a marketing brochure, DNR Asset Managers presents the performance of several composite portfolios managed according to similar investment strategies. In constructing composites, the firm excludes individual portfolios with less than $1 million in assets, excludes terminated portfolios, and includes simulated results. DNR includes the following disclosure in the brochure: "Past performance is no guarantee of future results. Composites exclude portfolios under $1 million in assets and include results from simulated model portfolios with similar strategies." DNR's brochure:
    A. does not violate the Code and Standards.
    B. violates the Code and Standards by failing to include terminated portfolios in the performance presentation.
    C. violates the Code and Standards by excluding portfolios under $1 million from the composite performance presentations.
    D. violates the Code and Standards by including simulated results of model portfolios even with a disclosure in the presentation.

13. Connie Fletcher, CFA, works for a small money management firm that specializes in pension accounts. Recently, a friend asked her to act as an unpaid volunteer manager for the city's street sweep pension fund. As part of the position, the city would grant Fletcher a free parking space in front of her downtown office. Fletcher is considering the offer. Before she accepts she should:
    A. do nothing since this is a volunteer position.
    B. inform her current clients in writing and discuss the offer with her employer.
    C. inform her current clients in writing, get their permission, and discuss the offer with her employer.
    D. disclose the details of the volunteer position to her employer and obtain written permission from her employer.

14. Which of the following statements about an investment supervisor's responsibilities is *least accurate*? A supervisor:
    A. is expected to know what constitutes an adequate compliance system.
    B. should bring an inadequate compliance system to the attention of management and recommend corrective action.
    C. is responsible for instructing those to whom he has delegated authority about methods to detect and prevent violations of the law and standards.
    D. need only report employee violations of the Code and Standards to upper management and provide a written warning to the employee to cease such activities.

15. Robert Blair, CFA, Director of Research, has had an ongoing battle with management about the adequacy of the firm's compliance system. Recently, it has come to Blair's attention that the firm's compliance procedures are inadequate in that they are not being monitored or carefully followed. What should Blair do?
    A. Resign from the firm unless the compliance system is strengthened and followed.
    B. Send his superior a memo outlining the problem. This will discharge his obligation under the Code.
    C. Take no action since his job is supervision and not policy making.
    D. Decline in writing to continue to accept supervisory responsibility until reasonable compliance procedures are adopted.

16. Ahmed Jamal, CFA, head of research for Valley Brokers, decided it was time to change his recommendation on D&R Company from buy to sell. He orally announced his decision during the Monday staff meeting and said his written report would be finished and disseminated to Valley's customers by the middle of next week. As a result of this announcement, Doris Smith, one of Jamal's subordinates, immediately sold her personal shares in D&R, and Martin Temple told his largest institutional customers of the change the following day. Which Standards have *most likely* been violated?
    A. Jamal violated Standard IV(C) Responsibilities of Supervisors; and Smith violated Standard II(A) Material Nonpublic Information.
    B. Jamal violated Standard IV(C) Responsibilities of Supervisors; Smith violated Standard II(A) Material Nonpublic Information; and Temple violated Standard VI(B) Priority of Transactions.
    C. Jamal violated Standard IV(C) Responsibilities of Supervisors; Smith violated Standard VI(B) Priority Transactions; and Temple violated Standard III(B) Fair Dealing.
    D. Smith violated Standard VI(B) Priority of Transactions; and Temple violated Standard III(B) Fair Dealing.

17. Jack Schleifer, CFA, is an analyst for Brown Investment Managers (BIM). Schleifer has recently accepted an invitation to visit the facilities of ChemCo, a producer of chemical compounds used in a variety of industries. ChemCo offers to pay for Schleifer's accommodations in a penthouse suite at a luxury hotel and allow Schleifer to use the firm's private jet to travel to its three facilities located in New York, Hong Kong, and London. In addition, ChemCo offers two tickets to a formal high-society dinner in New York and a small desk clock with the ChemCo logo. Schleifer declines to use ChemCo's corporate jet and to let the firm pay for his accommodations but accepts the clock and the tickets to the dinner (which he discloses to his employer) since he will be able to market his firm's mutual funds to other guests at the dinner. Has Schleifer violated any CFA Institute Standards of Professional Conduct?
    A. Yes.
    B. No, since he is using the gifts accepted to benefit his employer's interests.
    C. No, since the gifts he accepted were fully disclosed in writing to his employer.
    D. No, since the gifts that he accepted were of nominal value and he declined to accept the hotel accommodations and the use of ChemCo's jet.

18. Based on the Standards of Professional Conduct, a financial analyst is required to do all the following **EXCEPT**:
    A. disclose the fact that his firm is the underwriter for securities issued by a company he covers.
    B. report to his employer the receipt of gifts and additional compensation from clients.
    C. pay for chartered transportation and lodging while visiting a company's remotely located facilities.
    D. pay for commercial transportation and lodging while visiting a company's headquarters.

19. Beth Anderson, CFA, is a portfolio manager for several wealthy clients including Reuben Carlyle. Anderson manages Carlyle's personal portfolio of stock and bond investments. Carlyle recently told Anderson that he is under investigation by the IRS for tax evasion related to his business, Carlyle Concrete (CC). After learning about the investigation, Anderson proceeds to inform a friend at a local investment bank so that they may withdraw their proposal to take CC public. Which of the following is *most accurate*? Anderson:
    A. violated the Code and Standards by failing to immediately terminate the client relationship with Carlyle.
    B. violated the Code and Standards by failing to maintain the confidentiality of her client's information.
    C. violated the Code and Standards by failing to detect and report the tax evasion to the proper authorities.
    D. did not violate the Code and Standards since the information she conveyed pertained to illegal activities on the part of her client.

20.   Gail Stefano, CFA, an analyst for a U.S. brokerage firm that serves U.S. investors, researches public utilities in South American emerging markets. Stefano makes the following statement in a recent report: "Based on the fact that the South American utilities sector has seen rapid growth in new service orders, we expect that most companies in the sector will be able to convert the revenue increases into significant profits. We also believe the trend will continue for the next three to five years." The report goes on to describe the major risks of investing in this market, in particular the political and exchange rate instability associated with South American countries. Stefano's report:
   A. has not violated the Code and Standards.
   B. violated the Code and Standards by failing to properly distinguish factual information from opinions.
   C. violated the Code and Standards by recommending an investment which would not be suitable for all of its clients.
   D. violated the Code and Standards by failing to properly identify details related to the operations of South American utilities.

21.   All of the following violate Standard III(B) Fair Dealing, **EXCEPT**:
   A. before disseminating a change in the analyst's buy recommendation, the analyst calls his best clients and tells them about the change.
   B. a firm makes investment recommendations and also manages a mutual fund. The firm routinely begins trading for the fund's account ten minutes before announcing recommendation changes to client accounts.
   C. after releasing the general recommendation to all clients, an analyst calls the firm's largest institutional clients to discuss the recommendation in more detail.
   D. a portfolio manager allocates IPO shares to her brother's fee-based retirement account only after allocating shares to all other accounts.

22.   Which of the following is *least likely* to constitute a violation of Standard VI(B) Priority of Transactions?
   A. Failure by an analyst to make or change a recommendation until he trades for his own account.
   B. An analyst trades for her son's trust account on the same day her firm changes its buy/sell recommendation.
   C. An analyst takes a position in a stock she recommended one week after the recommendation was made public.
   D. An analyst trades for the firm's account before handling client trades.

23. Jamie Olson, CFA, has just started work as a trainee with Neuvo Management Corp., a small regional money management firm started six months ago. She has been told to make a few cold calls and round up some new clients. In which of the following statements is Olson *least likely* to have violated the Standards of Practice?
    A. "Sure, we can perform all the financial and investment services you need. We've consistently outperformed the market indexes and will continue to do so under our current management."
    B. "Sure, we can assist you with all the financial and investment services you need. If we don't provide the service in-house, we have arrangements with other full-service firms that I would be happy to tell you about."
    C. "Believe me, I've been at this game long enough to know what I'm talking about. I personally guarantee this investment. It's a sure winner."
    D. "Our firm has a long history of successful performance for our clients. While we can't guarantee future results, we do believe we will continue to benefit our clients."

24. Mary Herbst, CFA, a pension fund manager at GBH Investments, is reviewing some of FreeTime, Inc.'s pension fund activities over the past years. Which of the following actions related to FreeTime, Inc.'s pension fund is *least likely* to be a breach of her fiduciary duties?
    A. Paying higher-than-average brokerage fees to obtain research materials used in the management of other funds by the investment group.
    B. Trading with selected brokers so that the brokers will recommend GBH's managers to potential clients.
    C. Substantially increasing the risk of the fund in order to minimize FreeTime, Inc.'s future contributions.
    D. Selectively choosing brokers for the quality of research provided for managing FreeTime's pension.

25. Kevin Minter, CFA, is an investment analyst at Bradley & Company, a small money management firm. Minter keeps detailed records and documentation of relevant research pertaining to his investment recommendations. Because of the limited physical and electronic storage space, however, three days after issuing a recommendation, Minter shreds hard copy documentation and deletes all electronic files except for the recommendation itself. There is no regulatory requirement to maintain records for any specified time period. Which of the following statements is *most accurate*? Minter:
    A. has not violated the Code and Standards.
    B. violated the Code and Standards because he did not maintain hard copy and electronic documentation supporting all of his current recommendations.
    C. violated the Code and Standards because he did not maintain hard copy or electronic documentation supporting his recommendations for seven years.
    D. violated the Code and Standards because he did not maintain hard copy and electronic documentation supporting all of his recommendations.

26.   Eugene Nieder, CFA, has just accepted a new job as a quantitative analyst for Paschal Investments, LLP. Nieder developed a complex model while working for his previous employer and plans to recreate the model for Paschal. Nieder did not make copies of the model or any supporting documents since his employer refused to grant him permission to do so. Nieder will recreate the model from memory. Which of the following statements is *most accurate*?
        A. Nieder can recreate the model without violating the Code and Standards as long as he also generates supporting documentation.
        B. Nieder can recreate the model without violating the Code and Standards as long as he obtains permission to do so from his former employer.
        C. Nieder can recreate the model without violating the Code and Standards without documentation if the model is modified from its original form.
        D. Nieder cannot recreate the model without violating the Code and Standards because it is the property of his former employer.

27.   As part of an agreement with Baker Brokerage, Hern Investment Company, a money manager for individual clients, provides monthly emerging market overviews in exchange for prospective client referrals and European equity research from Baker. Clients and prospects of Hern are not made aware of the agreement, but clients unanimously rave about the high quality of the research provided by Baker. As a result of the research, many non-discretionary clients have earned substantial returns on their portfolios. Managers at Hern have also used the research to earn outstanding returns for the firm's discretionary portfolios. Which of the following statements is *most accurate*? Hern:
        A. has not violated the Code and Standards.
        B. has violated the Code and Standards by using third-party research in discretionary accounts.
        C. has violated the Code and Standards by failing to disclose the referrals made by Baker.
        D. has violated the Code and Standards by failing to communicate the basic investment characteristics to discretionary clients.

28. Frist Investments, Inc., has just hired Michael Pulin to manage institutional portfolios, most of which are pension related. Pulin has just taken the Level 3 CFA exam and is awaiting his results. Pulin has over 15 years of investment management experience with individual clients but has never managed an institutional portfolio. Pulin joined the CFA Institute as an affiliate member two years ago and is in good standing with the organization. Which of the following statements would be *most appropriate* for Frist to use in advertising Pulin as a new member of the firm? Pulin:
   A. has many years of investment experience which, along with his participation in the CFA program, will allow him to deliver superior investment performance relative to other managers.
   B. is a CFA Level 3 and passed the first two exams on the first attempt. He is an affiliate member of the CFA Institute. We expect him to become a regular member if he passes the Level 3 examination.
   C. will be a CFA once he passes the Level 3 CFA exam. He has vast amounts of practical experience as well as an enhanced understanding of the investment process as a result of his participation in the CFA program.
   D. is a Level 3 CFA candidate and has many years of excellent performance in the investment management industry. Pulin is an affiliate member of the CFA Institute and will be eligible to become a CFA charterholder and regular member if he passes the Level 3 CFA exam.

29. Before joining Mitsui Ltd. as an analyst covering the electrical equipment manufacturing industry, Pam Servais, CFA, worked for Internet Security Systems (ISS) where she had access to nonpublic information. While at ISS, Servais learned of a severe environmental problem at two firms handling boron-based components. It is common knowledge that seven firms in the industry worldwide use the same boron handling technique. The two firms for which Servais has knowledge announced the problem last week and had immediate stock price declines of 11% and 17%, respectively. The other five firms have not made an announcement. Servais issues a report citing these facts and recommending Mitsui clients sell shares of the remaining five firms. Servais' issuance of this recommendation:
   A. is not a violation of CFA Institute Standards.
   B. is a violation of CFA Institute Standards insofar as she has failed to deal fairly and objectively with all clients.
   C. is a violation of CFA Institute Standards insofar as it fails to distinguish between opinion and fact.
   D. constitutes a violation of the Standard pertaining to the use of material nonpublic information.

30. Zanuatu, an island nation, does not have any regulations precluding the use of nonpublic information. Alfredo Romero has a friend and fellow CFA charterholder there with whom he has shared nonpublic information regarding firms outside of his industry. The information concerns several firms' internal earnings and cash flow projections. The friend may:
    A. trade on the information under the laws of Zanuatu, which govern her behavior.
    B. not trade on the information under CFA Institute Standards, which govern her behavior.
    C. not trade on the information under the laws of Zanuatu, which govern her behavior.
    D. trade on the information under CFA Institute Standards since the firms concerned are outside of Romero's industry.

31. Samantha Donovan, CFA, is an exam proctor for the Level 2 CFA exam. The day before the exam is to be administered, Donovan faxes a copy of one of the questions to two friends, James Smythe and Lynn Yeats, who are Level 2 candidates in the CFA program. Donovan, Smythe, and Yeats had planned the distribution of an exam question months in advance. Smythe used the fax to prepare for the exam. Yeats, however, had second thoughts and threw the fax away without looking at its contents. Which of the following statements is *most accurate*?
    A. Donovan violated the Code and Standards but Yeats did not.
    B. Yeats violated the Code and Standards but Smythe did not.
    C. Donovan violated the Code and Standards but Smythe did not.
    D. Donovan and Yeats both violated the Code and Standards.

32. Julia Green, CFA, has friends from her previous employer who have suggested that she agree to receive nonpublic information anonymously from them via an Internet chat room. In this way, she receives news about an exciting new product being developed by a firm in Singapore that has the potential to double the firm's revenue. The firm has not previously revealed any information regarding the product to the public. According to the Code and Standards, this information is:
    A. not material and may be traded upon.
    B. both material and nonpublic and may not be traded upon in Singapore, but may be traded on elsewhere.
    C. both material and nonpublic and may not be traded upon in any jurisdiction.
    D. public by virtue of its release in the chat room and may be traded upon.

33. Sally Albright, CFA, works full time for Frank & Company, an investment management firm, as a fixed-income security analyst. Albright has been asked by a business contact at KDG Enterprises to accept some analytical work from KDG on a consulting basis. The work would entail investigating potential distressed debt investments in the small-cap market. Albright should:
   A. accept the work as long as she obtains consent to all the terms of the engagement from Frank & Company.
   B. not accept the work as it violates the Code and Standards by creating a conflict of interest.
   C. accept the work so long as she obtains written consent from KDG.
   D. not accept the work since this will likely expose her to material nonpublic information in violation of the Code and Standards.

34. William Bixby, CFA, oversees a mid-cap fund that is required to invest in a minimum of 40 and a maximum of 60 different issues. Bixby uses a quantitative approach to actively manage the assets. In promotional materials, he states that "through our complex quantitative approach, securities are selected that have similar exposures to a number of risk factors that are found in the S&P 500 Index. Thus, the fund is designed to track the performance of the S&P 500 Index but will receive a return premium of between 2% and 4% according to our model's risk-return measures." This statement is:
   A. permissible since the assertion is supported by modern portfolio theory and estimates from the firms' model.
   B. not permissible since Bixby is misrepresenting the services that she and/or her firm are capable of performing.
   C. not permissible since Bixby is misrepresenting the investment performance she and/or her firm can reasonably expect to achieve.
   D. permissible since the statement describes the basic characteristics of the fund's risk and return objectives.

35. Josef Karloff, CFA, acts as liaison between Pinnacle Financial (an investment management firm) and Summit, Inc. (an investment banking boutique specializing in penny stocks). When Summit underwrites an IPO, Karloff routinely has Pinnacle issue vague statements implying that the firm has cash flows, financial resources, and growth prospects that are far better than is the case in reality. This action is:
   A. permissible under CFA Institute Standards.
   B. a violation of the Standard concerning fair dealing.
   C. a violation of the Standard concerning responsibilities of supervisors.
   D. a violation of the Standard concerning professional misconduct.

36. Shane Matthews, CFA, is a principal at Carlson Brothers, a leading regional investment bank specializing in initial public offerings of small to mid-sized biotech firms. Just before many of the IPOs are offered to the general public, Matthews arranges for 10% of the shares of the firm going public to be distributed to management at 75% of the expected IPO price. This action is:
   A. permissible under CFA Institute Standards.
   B. a violation of the Standard concerning professionalism.
   C. a violation of the Standard concerning disclosure of conflicts of interest.
   D. a violation of the Standard concerning suitability.

37.   Will Hunter, CFA, is a portfolio manager at NV Asset Managers in Baltimore, which specializes in managing labor union pension fund accounts. A friend of Hunter's who is an investment banker asks Hunter to purchase shares in their new IPOs in order to support the price long enough for insiders to liquidate their holdings. Hunter realizes that the price of the shares will almost certainly fall dramatically after his buying support ceases. NV management "strongly suggests" that Hunter "not rock the boat" and honor the investment banker's request since NV has had a long-standing relationship with the investment bank. Hunter agrees to make the purchases. Hunter has:
   A.   not violated the Code and Standards.
   B.   violated the Code and Standards by failing to report fair, accurate, and complete data to his clients.
   C.   violated the Code and Standards by attempting to distort natural market forces.
   D.   violated the Code and Standards by failing to place orders in the appropriate transaction priority.

38.   Neiman Investment Co. receives brokerage business from Pick Asset Management in exchange for referring prospective clients to Pick. Pick advises pension clients—in writing at the time the relationship is established—of the nature of its arrangement with Neiman. With regard to this practice, Pick has:
   A.   fully complied with the Code and Standards.
   B.   violated the Code and Standards by failing to preserve the confidentiality of the agreement with Neiman.
   C.   violated the Code and Standards by inappropriately negotiating an agreement that creates a conflict of interest.
   D.   violated the Code and Standards by inappropriately delegating its fiduciary responsibilities to Neiman.

39.   Fred Johnson, CFA, a financial analyst and avid windsurfer, has begun an investment survey of the water sports leisure industry. His brother sells windsurfing gear in Tampa and tells him that Swordfish9 is the "hottest windsurfing rig on the market and will be highly profitable for Swordfish Enterprises." Johnson had never heard of Swordfish previously but after testing the board himself became very excited about the Swordfish9 and issued an investment recommendation of "buy" on Swordfish Enterprises. As a result of issuing the recommendation, Johnson has:
   A.   not violated the Code and Standards.
   B.   violated the Code and Standards by failing to establish a reasonable and adequate basis.
   C.   violated the Code and Standards concerning professionalism by placing recreational interests ahead of his fiduciary duty to his clients.
   D.   violated the Code and Standards by failing to consider the suitability of the investment for his clients.

40. Daniel Lyons, CFA, is an analyst for a French firm that sells investment research to European companies. Lyons' aunt owns 30,000 shares of French National Bank (FNB). She informs Lyons that as a part of her estate planning she has created a trust in his name into which she has placed 2,000 shares of FNB. The trust is structured so that Lyons will not receive control of the assets for two years, at which time his aunt will also gift her current home to Lyons and move into a retirement community. Lyons is due to update his research coverage of FNB next week. Lyons should:
    A. advise his superiors that he is no longer able to issue research recommendations on FNB.
    B. update the report without notification since the shares are held in trust and are beyond his direct control.
    C. disclose the situation to his employer and, if then asked to prepare a report, also disclose the situation in the report.
    D. disclose the situation to his employer and then prepare the report with no disclosure.

ANSWERS – CONCEPT CHECKERS

1. **B** Hutchins' personal bankruptcy may reflect poorly on her professional reputation if it resulted from fraudulent or deceitful business activities. There is no indication of this, however, and the bankruptcy is thus not a violation. Smith has not violated the Code and Standards by refusing to invest with Hutchins in what turned out to be bad investment opportunities. By reporting Smith to CFA Institute for a violation, Hutchins has misused the Professional Conduct Program to settle a dispute unrelated to professional ethics and has thus violated Standard I(D), Misconduct.

2. **C** According to Standard I(A), informing her supervisor or firm's compliance department is appropriate. Dissociating herself would be premature. She should report her suspicions to a supervisory person and attempt to remedy the situation.

3. **B** According to Standard I(A), since she has taken steps to stop the illegal activities and the board has ignored her, Jones must dissociate from the board and seek legal advice as to what other actions would be appropriate in this instance. She may need to inform legal or regulatory authorities of the illegal activities.

4. **D** According to Standard II(A), members and candidates are under no circumstances allowed to use inside information to trade securities. Carlson must abide by the Code and Standards, which is the most strict regulation in the scenario.

5. **C** The intent of Green Brothers' actions is to manipulate market liquidity in order to attract investment to its own funds. The increased trading activity was not based on market fundamentals or an actual trading strategy to benefit investors. It was merely an attempt to mislead market participants in order to increase assets under Green Brothers' management. The action violates Standard II(B) Market Manipulation.

6. **A** Quigley's trades are most likely an attempt to take advantage of an arbitrage opportunity that exists between Craeger's common stock and its put options. She is not manipulating the prices of securities in an attempt to mislead market participants, which would violate Standard II (A). She is pursuing a legitimate investment strategy. Participants in her hedge fund are aware of the fund's investment strategy, and thus Quigley did not violate the Code and Standards by not disclosing this specific set of trades in advance of trading.

7. **D** According to Standard I(A), in some instances reporting a legal violation to governmental or regulatory officials may be appropriate, but this isn't always necessary, and it isn't required under Standard I(A).

8. **B** According to Standard VII(B), any explanation of the designation in print form should be a concise description of the requirements or of CFA Institute. The other statements contain violations of Standard VII(B), in particular the presentation of the letters CFA. Also, she may not imply superior performance as a result of being a CFA charterholder.

9. **C** Standard III(C) requires that before taking investment action, members and candidates must make a reasonable inquiry into a client's or prospect's investment objectives and constraints as well as their prior investment experience. Byrne cannot assume that because the brothers have similar lifestyles and are close in age, they should have similarly managed portfolios. Byrne should have interviewed Cliff directly before investing his portfolio.

10. **B** According to Standard I(C), a recognized statistical reporting service used as a source of factual data need not be cited.

11. **B**   According to Standard III(C), Ellis must consider the suitability of each new investment (as well as the current holdings) in light of the portfolio mandate. Ellis must only make investments that are in accordance with the portfolio's investment policy statement. Therefore, Ellis should not purchase the unsuitable bonds as requested by her clients.

12. **B**   By failing to include terminated portfolios in the performance presentation, the performance will have an inherent upward bias, making results appear better than they truly are. By excluding the terminated portfolios, DNR misleads its potential investors and thus violates Standard III(D) Performance Presentation. Presentation of simulated performance results is permitted as long as the firm provides full and complete disclosure.

13. **D**   According to Standard IV(A), members and candidates are expected to act for the benefit of the employer and not deprive the employer of their skills. Fletcher is performing work similar to the services that her employer provides for a fee. Although the position is a volunteer position, Fletcher will receive compensation in the form of a free parking space. In light of the circumstances, Fletcher must disclose the details of the position and get written permission before accepting the volunteer position.

14. **D**   According to Standard IV(C), reporting the violation and warning the employee to cease activities that violate the law or the Code and Standards are not enough. The supervisor must take steps (such as limiting employee activity or increasing the level of employee monitoring) to prevent further violations while he conducts an investigation.

15. **D**   According to Standard IV(C), because he is aware that the firm's compliance procedures are not being monitored and followed and because he has repeatedly tried to get company management to correct the situation, Blair should decline supervisory responsibility until adequate procedures to detect and prevent violations of laws, regulations, and the Code and Standards are adopted and followed. If he does not do so, he will be in violation of the Code and Standards.

16. **C**   Jamal failed to properly supervise employees and provide adequate procedures and policies to prevent employee violations. Smith should not have traded her own account ahead of client accounts. Temple should not have disclosed the recommendation change selectively but should have informed his clients fairly and objectively. No inside information was used in the question.

17. **A**   Standard I(B) requires that members and candidates reject offers of gifts or compensation that could compromise their independence or objectivity. Schleifer has appropriately rejected the offer of the hotel accommodations and the use of ChemCo's jet. He may accept the desk clock since this gift is of nominal value and is unlikely to compromise his independence and objectivity. Schleifer cannot accept the tickets to the dinner, however. Since it is a formal high-society dinner, the tickets are most likely expensive or hard to come by. Even though he has disclosed the gift to his employer and he plans to use the dinner as a marketing opportunity for his firm, the gift itself may influence Schliefer's future research in favor of ChemCo. Allowing such potential influence is a violation of Standard I(B).

18. **C**   Standard I(B) requires that an analyst maintain his independence and objectivity by having his firm pay for ordinary travel expenses to visit companies that are the subject of research. However, in some cases, such as remotely located facilities, the company may pay for modest accommodations and chartered flights as long as the transportation and lodging is not lavish and is not intended to exert influence over the analyst.

19. B   Anderson must maintain the confidentiality of client information according to Standard III(E). Confidentiality may be broken in instances involving illegal activities on the part of the client, but the client's information shall be relayed to proper authorities. Anderson did not have the right to inform the investment bank of her client's investigation.

20. A   Historical growth can be cited as a fact since it actually happened. Stefano states that her firm expects further growth and profitability which is an opinion. She does not claim that these are facts. In addition, Stefano identifies relevant factors and highlights in particular the most significant risks of investing in South American utilities. She has fully complied with Standard V(B) Communication With Clients and Prospective Clients. Under the Standard, it is not necessary to include every detail about a potential investment in a report. Members and candidates are expected to use their judgment and identify the most important factors to include.

21. C   This is not necessarily a violation. Firms can offer different levels of service to clients as long as this is disclosed to all clients. The largest institutional clients would likely be paying higher fees for a greater level of service. Also note that the analyst's brother's account in answer D should be treated similarly to any other client account.

22. C   One week is likely an acceptable waiting period.

23. B   Standard I(C)—in the other choices, Olson misrepresents the services that she or her firm are capable of performing, her qualifications, her academic or professional credentials, or the firm's credentials. The firm is small and most likely cannot perform all investment services the client may require. The firm cannot guarantee future outperformance of the market indexes. Olson hasn't been in the business for a long time, as she claims, and cannot guarantee the performance of any investment. The firm doesn't have a long history (only six months).

24. D   Standard III(A)—Herbst is acting as a fiduciary for the pension plan beneficiaries. She may pay higher-than-average brokerage fees so long as doing so benefits the pension beneficiaries, not other clients. Trading with selected brokers solely to gain referrals is not likely to be in the pension beneficiaries' best interest since it does not take into account other important factors for selecting brokerage firms. Minimizing contributions benefits the plan sponsor, not the plan beneficiaries to whom the fiduciary duty is owed. Choosing brokers based on quality of services provided is reasonable.

25. C   Minter is required by Standard V(C) to maintain hard copy *or* electronic documentation of the research and data supporting current investment recommendations for more than three days. In cases where there is no regulatory guidance on an appropriate length of time, the Standard recommends keeping documentation for seven years.

26. A   Nieder must not take models or documents from his previous employer without explicit permission to do so [Standard IV(A)]. He is allowed, however, to reproduce the model from memory but must recreate the supporting documentation to maintain compliance with Standard V(C) Record Retention.

27. C   According to Standard VI(C) Referral Fees, Hern must disclose the referral arrangement between itself and Baker so that potential clients can judge the true cost of Hern's services and assess whether there is any partiality inherent in the recommendation of services.

28. **D** Standard VII(B) governs acceptable methods of referencing the CFA Institute, CFA designation, and CFA Program. Candidates may reference their candidacy if they are enrolled for or waiting for the results of a CFA exam. Pulin may also reference his membership status with the CFA Institute as well as his remaining eligibility requirements to become a CFA charterholder.

29. **A** There is no indication that Servais has inside information pertaining to the situation at the five firms in question—only the two firms that have already gone public with the information. It is common knowledge that the other five firms follow the same boron handling procedures. She is, therefore, in compliance with Standard V(A) concerning the use of material nonpublic information in the issuance of the investment recommendation.

30. **B** Even though the laws of Zanuatu would not preclude trading on the information, as a CFA Charterholder the friend is bound by the CFA Institute Code and Standards. Standard II(A) prohibits the use of material nonpublic information, and the friend may not trade the stocks about which she has such information under any circumstances.

31. **D** In this situation, Donovan, Smythe, and Yeats all violated Standard VII(A) Conduct as Members and Candidates in the CFA Program. The Standard prohibits conduct that compromises the integrity, validity, or security of the CFA exams. Donovan clearly breached the exam security. Smythe and Yeats both compromised the integrity of the exams by planning to use the actual exam question to gain an advantage over other candidates. Even though Yeats did not ultimately use the information to study for the exam, she participated in a scheme to cheat on the CFA exam.

32. **C** The furtive release of such information to a limited circle via an internet chat room does not cause the information to be public. The information is also clearly material. Therefore Green is not allowed to trade on the information under Standard II(A).

33. **A** Albright is entitled to accept work for which she receives outside compensation as long as the appropriate consent is obtained. Under Standard IV(A), such consent must be obtained from her employer prior to beginning the work.

34. **C** It is not reasonable for Bixby to expect a 40-to-60 stock mid-cap portfolio to track the entire S&P 500 Index, which is a large-cap index. He should know that there will be periods of wide variance between the performance of the portfolio and the S&P 500 Index. There is no assurance that a premium of 2% to 4% will consistently be obtained. Bixby is in violation of Standard III(D) since he has made an implicit guarantee of the fund's expected performance.

35. **D** Since the statements are vague, we have no direct evidence that a violation of securities law has occurred. However, under Standard I(C), members and candidates are prohibited from engaging in activities involving false or misleading statements. Karloff's action is a clear attempt to deceive the investing public regarding the value of Summit IPOs.

36. **B** Members and candidates are required to maintain knowledge of and comply with the applicable securities laws governing their professional activities. This type of securities fraud would almost certainly be against the law in most jurisdictions. Matthews's actions, therefore, are in violation of Standard I(A), which require knowledge of and adherence to applicable laws. He has also violated Standard I(D), which prohibits professional misconduct involving fraud and other acts that reflect poorly on the professional's reputation.

37. **C**   NV management is asking Hunter to violate Standard II(B), which prohibits taking actions that are designed to distort prices or artificially increase trading volume. The intent of Hunter's actions is to mislead market participants and allow corporate insiders to take advantage of the artificially high prices.

38. **A**   There is no violation of the CFA Institute Standards regarding this matter. The referral arrangement is fully disclosed to clients before they agree to do business with Pick. Therefore clients can fully assess how the agreement will affect their account before hiring Pick as their asset manager.

39. **B**   Johnson has apparently let his recreational passion cloud his judgment. This is not to say that Swordfish Enterprises is not or will not be an excellent investment. However, if he had never heard of the firm previously, issuing an investment recommendation without conducting a thorough financial investigation indicates a failure to exercise diligence and also indicates that he lacks a reasonable and adequate basis for his recommendation. He is in violation of Standard V(A).

40. **C**   Even though the shares are held in trust, this could still be construed as a conflict of interest. Lyons is obligated under Standard VI(A) to inform his employer of the potential conflict. If he is then authorized to issue investment recommendations on the security in question, the existence of a potential conflict must be disclosed in the report.

Professor's Note: We've included the following item sets to give you a head start on practicing exam-like questions. Remember that the Level 2 exam consists of all item set format questions; that is, a vignette presenting the relevant information followed by six multiple choice questions on that topic. In addition to the three full-length practice exams included with the SchweserNotes Pack, we also offer four other full-length Level 2 practice exams. Practice Exams Volume 2 contains three full 120-question (20 item sets, 6-hour) exams, and another complete exam is available online. Each Practice Exams Volume contains answers and explanations for self-grading.

Item Set #1

Lewis Smithers, CFA, is the lead portfolio manager for Fundamental Investments Corp., a money manager serving several hundred wealthy individual investors. He spent his morning reading several articles on Phoenix-based Pineda Canyon Development in real estate industry publications. He concluded that while Pineda is a majority owner of several developers with huge portfolios of mountainside real estate perfect for the development of ski resorts, the company lacks the cash to build the resorts.

While lunching at his club, Smithers ran into Judith Carson, an old college friend he hadn't seen in months. Carson is managing partner of a land-speculation endeavor that owns thousands of acres of prime real estate. During the course of their conversation, Carson asked Smithers to invest in the partnership, which was about to buy a land developer and its acreage near Sassy River.

When Smithers returned to the office after lunch, he found an e-mail from Liam O'Toole, his largest client, who is knowledgeable about and likes to invest in real estate. O'Toole, who in the past did business with money manager Big Ideas International, had read in Big Ideas' prospect newsletter that a large Arizona developer was close to a deal to sell property in the Sassy River Valley. The article did not identify the parties to the transaction but did reveal the acreage of the land and the proposed sale price. O'Toole wanted to know if Smithers had heard about this deal and if he could get O'Toole a piece of it in exchange for a week at O'Toole's condo in St. Thomas.

Smithers suspected Pineda was the seller and Carson's real estate partnership was the buyer. Seeking to verify this, Smithers called Carson and asked if the partnership's big deal involved Pineda Canyon Development. Carson responded by saying she could neither confirm nor deny that a transaction with Pineda or any other specific company was in the works. A couple of days later, however, Smithers observed Carson and two of her business partners having dinner with Pineda executives. Smithers checked public records and discovered that Pineda was the majority shareholder in the only major development company with significant land ownership in the Sassy River Valley. Smithers concluded that Carson's firm was about to purchase the Sassy River developer from Pineda.

That afternoon, Smithers prepared a purchase recommendation for Pineda stock. He cited the expected sale of Sassy River Valley land for enough cash to fund both the construction of several ski resorts and retire some high interest notes. Smithers worked up some revenue and profit numbers, detailed the location of the property, and submitted a report for approval by the company president.

1. In preparing his recommendation to purchase Pineda, Smithers violated:
   A. none of the standards.
   B. Standard III(A) Loyalty, Prudence, and Care with regard to Carson's information.
   C. Standard II(A) Material Nonpublic Information with regard to Carson's statements.

2. Immediately after submitting his purchase recommendation to his boss, Smithers takes three actions. Which of the following actions is *least likely* a violation of the Code and Standards?
   A. Immediately downgrading two ski equipment manufacturers based only on "trends in the industry."
   B. Advising a colleague in Fundamental's bond department of this new information regarding Pineda's debt.
   C. Giving Carson the names and summary financial information of O'Toole and two other clients as possible limited partners.

3. Fundamental's president, Dana Aaronson, is so impressed with Smithers' report that she sends it to the fulfillment department for printing and faxing five minutes after receiving it from Smithers' supervisor, who has read and approved the report. In her handling of the report, *how many* of the following standards has Aaronson violated?
   • I(B) Independence and Objectivity.
   • IV(C) Responsibilities of Supervisors.
   • V(A) Diligence and Reasonable Basis.
   • II(A) Material Nonpublic Information.
   A. One.
   B. Two.
   C. None.

4. With regard to his information-gathering activities and the creation of his report, did Smithers or anyone else violate Standard III(A) Loyalty, Prudence, and Care?
   A. No one violated the Standard.
   B. O'Toole's disclosure of the Big Ideas newsletter to Smithers is a violation of the Standard.
   C. Carson's discussion with Smithers about the partnership's plans is a violation of the Standard.

5. Because O'Toole brought the information about the real estate deal to Smithers' attention, Smithers purchased Pineda stock for O'Toole immediately after submitting his report to management. The purchase was *most likely* to violate:
   A. Standard III(B) regarding fair dealing.
   B. Standard III(C) regarding suitability of investments.
   C. Standard IV(B) regarding additional compensation arrangements.

6. The Pineda report has been dispatched by e-mail, fax, or mail to every client. The purchase will be announced in one day, not enough time to disseminate Smithers' research to clients with no e-mail or fax capability. Fundamental's trading manager, Bill Johnson, is considering various directives regarding the trading of Pineda stock. Which of the following instructions for portfolio managers is *best*?
   A. Make no trades until the written reports are delivered to every client in 48 hours.
   B. Do not execute any pending sell order for Pineda stock until the client has been informed of the rating change.
   C. Purchase Pineda stock for all discretionary portfolios, then call nondiscretionary clients to seek permission to purchase the stock.

Item Set #2

Gerard Cutty, CFA, a technology-stock analyst and money manager at Unique Investments, has been hearing rumors for months that Simpson Semiconductor was near a breakthrough on a next-generation telecommunications microchip. Simpson is best known on the street for its expert design engineers, perennially shaky balance sheet, and extremely volatile stock.

One morning, as he is listening to a recorded *Barron's* interview with Simpson's CEO, who is also a CFA charterholder, he learns that Simpson has struck a licensing agreement with Simak Foundry, a privately held chip fabricator in Malaysia. Then he reads in *The Asian Wall Street Journal* that a Malaysian bank has loaned $500 million to Simak for construction of a new plant.

Cutty owns an apartment in Paris which is leased to Gladys Catcher, CFA. The lease is about to expire and Cutty and Catcher are currently in the process of renegotiating the terms of the lease. Cutty has other potential tenants for the apartment who are willing to pay more than what Catcher is currently paying, so he would like to negotiate a significant increase in the monthly payments.

Catcher works for a Paris public relations firm that handles accounts for a lot of Asian technology companies. Cutty calls Catcher, and after learning that her firm handled the Simak account, he asks what she knows about the Simak loan. Catcher says Simak has inked a deal with a big U.S. firm to make a new kind of microchip. She refuses to identify the firm but does provide some impressive performance numbers for the new chip.

After conducting a detailed patent search using the chip performance figures as a guide, Cutty learns that a Simpson engineer has filed for a series of patents related to the new technology over the past 18 months, and confirms Catcher's information on the performance of the new chip.

Cutty works up some revenue and market-share projections, then concludes that if the new technology works, it could triple the company's profits over the next three years. He writes up a research report on Simpson, detailing the licensing deal, specs on the new chip, and his opinion about the company's growth potential. Cutty then raises his rating on Simpson from neutral to high-risk buy.

Mary Wabb, lead portfolio manager for Unique Investments, calls Cutty into her office after reviewing the analyst's report. Wabb asks Cutty about his sources and methodology, and Cutty explains his thinking process. She then thanks Cutty for his good work and tells him he will receive Unique's World Series tickets this year. After Cutty leaves, Wabb makes minor edits to the report and sends it to the fulfillment department for inclusion in the daily e-mail report and weekly printed report for clients and prospects. Then Wabb instructs the trading desk to purchase Simpson stock for all client accounts after the reports have been issued.

The day after Cutty's report is released, rival analyst Sue Ellen Slusher, CFA, publishes her own analysis of Simpson Semiconductor. She cites Cutty's report specifically, quoting him directly and rebutting his conclusions point by point with her own research, criticizing his lack of thoroughness and questioning his abilities as an analyst and his academic and professional credentials. Specifically, she says that she's a better analyst than he is because "he earned his charter way back in 1986, when the CFA® exam was a lot easier to pass than it is today, but I earned my charter last year." Slusher writes that after talking with executives at Werfel Wafers, she believes Simpson infringed on Werfel's patent and will never reap the profits from the new technology.

7.   In the production of his research report, Cutty violated:
     A. Standard V(A) Diligence and Reasonable Basis.
     B. Standard II(A) Material Nonpublic Information.
     C. None of the standards.

8.   Which of the following statements is *most accurate* regarding potential violations of Standard III(A) Loyalty, Prudence, and Care in this scenario?
     A. Neither Cutty, Catcher, nor Simpson violated the Standard.
     B. Catcher violated the Standard by revealing information about her client, Simak.
     C. Simpson's CEO violated the Standard by discussing his company's licensing agreement.

9.   Which of the following statements, if found in Cutty's report without clarification, would *most likely* violate Standard V(B) Communications With Clients and Prospective Clients?
     A. Simpson's sales have faltered in recent years, but I believe the new technology will bring back the days of 25% revenue growth.
     B. The new technology could boost Simpson's cash flows considerably and provide flexibility to clean up the balance sheet.
     C. After a few phone calls and an analysis of the relevant information from our internal database, I concluded that Simpson's new technology was more than just a rumor.

10.   Which of Wabb's actions *most likely* violated the Code and Standards? Her:
     A. newsletter instructions violated Standard III(B) Fair Dealing.
     B. trading instructions violated Standard III(C) Suitability.
     C. awarding of World Series tickets to Cutty violated Standard IV(B) Additional Compensation Arrangements.

11. Which of the following actions could Cutty have taken while researching his report on Simpson *without* violating CFA Institute Standards of Professional Conduct?
    A. Not saving the results of the patent search.
    B. Ignoring a rival analyst's report on a Simpson competitor with a similar technology.
    C. Using statements from the Standard & Poor's report on Simpson without verifying them.

12. According to CFA Institute Standards of Professional Conduct, Slusher violated:
    A. Standard VII(B) Reference to CFA Institute, the CFA Designation, and the CFA Program because of her criticism of Cutty's credentials.
    B. Standard V(A) Diligence and Reasonable Basis because her conclusions differed from Cutty's.
    C. Standard I(B) Independence and Objectivity because of her criticism of Cutty's research report and conclusions.

Item Set #3

MH Securities is a subsidiary of MH Group, a large Korean conglomerate, and has recently established offices in the United States and Canada. MH plans to target Korean-Americans and Canadians for its services which include selling the firm's research services as well as Korean equities, bonds, and won-denominated certificates of deposit (CD). Chan-Heung Lee, CFA, has been hired to develop, implement, and oversee MH's compliance activities. Since there are very few compliance procedures in place, Lee will have to build the entire compliance framework. His objective is to conform to the CFA Institute Code and Standards. As one of his first steps, Lee decides to interview several MH employees to determine what formal and informal policies and procedures currently exist at the firm. Lee calls meetings with Jamie Jin, Nadine Yu, and Mark Larson, each of whom is a CFA charterholder.

Jamie Jin has recently been hired as an investment officer by MH. Jin informs Lee during their meeting that her previous employer, Rearguard Funds, has agreed to pay her a 25 basis point commission plus an annual bonus for all Rearguard Funds she sells to MH clients. Jin is unsure whether she will even use any Rearguard products with her new clients but agrees to the arrangement in case a client specifically requests a Rearguard product. Since the likelihood of actually receiving any compensation from Rearguard seems remote, Jamie has not previously disclosed the arrangement to MH.

In his meeting with Nadine Yu, an equity analyst at MH, Lee discovers that Yu has recently and abruptly changed her investment recommendation on Korean won-denominated bonds from buy to sell. She has prepared a research report to this effect and provides a copy to Lee in accordance with one of the firm's few existing compliance procedures. Her change of opinion is based upon nonpublic information provided to her in confidence by a friend on the monetary board at the Bank of Korea. While Lee is surprised at the abrupt change in the recommendation, he does not question the rationale and allows the report to be issued. Having received approval for her investment recommendation, Yu simultaneously releases the report to her individual and institutional research service subscribers as well as to MH's portfolio managers.

Lee's final meeting is with a new hire, Mark Larson, who has recently agreed to go to work for MH starting at the beginning of the next month. Lee is meeting with Larson to discuss new clients that Larson is expected to bring to MH. Larson, without providing details, assures Lee that he will have no problem increasing MH's client base. Prior to leaving his current employer, Affinity Advisors, Larson contacts 25 prospects by calling them, using public records and not Affinity's records, on Saturday mornings from his home. Of the prospects, ten individuals had previously been rejected as being too small for Affinity, but they still meet MH standards. The other 15 individuals remained viable prospects for Affinity. After learning of their status with Affinity, Larson suggests that all 25 prospects consider directing their business to him and his new firm, MH.

Lee's meetings with Jin, Yu, and Larson help him formulate compliance procedures. Lee decides that he will develop a written compliance manual which will be distributed to all of the firm's employees. The manual will delineate procedures for reporting violations and sanctions, describe the supervision hierarchy and each supervisor's duties, and outline the steps to monitor and evaluate the compliance program. Lee also designates Jin as the employee with ultimate responsibility for the compliance procedures and their enforcement.

13. Since there are currently no compliance procedures in place, Lee should:
   A. develop procedures that are in accordance with the CFA Institute Code and Standards as compliance situations arise.
   B. implement a comprehensive set of compliance procedures immediately and verify their conformance with the CFA Institute Code and Standards as circumstances dictate.
   C. determine what constitutes adequate compliance procedures under the CFA Institute Code and Standards, then implement such procedures immediately.

14. Prior to her meeting with Lee, did Jin's decision regarding the disclosure of the arrangement with Rearguard Funds violate any CFA Institute Standards of Professional Conduct?
   A. Yes.
   B. No, since she disclosed the arrangement with Rearguard to Lee in their meeting.
   C. No, since prior to the meeting with Lee, MH did not have any compliance procedures requiring such a disclosure.

15. With regard to Yu's recommendation that investors sell Korean bonds, did Lee and Yu violate any CFA Institute Standards of Professional Conduct?

	Lee	Yu
A.	No	No
B.	Yes	Yes
C.	No	Yes

16. With respect to the release of Yu's investment recommendation, did Yu violate any CFA Institute Standards of Professional Conduct?
   A. No.
   B. Yes. Yu should have released the recommendation to the individual clients first.
   C. Yes. Yu should have released the recommendation to the individual and institutional clients first.

17. In soliciting the list of 10 previously rejected prospects and the list of 15 viable prospects, did Larson violate any CFA Institute Standards of Professional Conduct?

	10 previously-rejected prospects	15 viable prospects
A.	No	No
B.	Yes	Yes
C.	No	Yes

18. Does the compliance program developed by Lee after his meetings with MH employees comply with CFA Institute Standards of Professional Conduct?
    A. Yes.
    B. No. Authority to enforce the compliance program should rest with the compliance officer.
    C. No. Assigning supervisory duties takes away the responsibility of all supervisors to detect all violations of the compliance procedures.

SELF-TEST ANSWERS: ETHICAL AND PROFESSIONAL STANDARDS

Item Set #1

1. **A** Smithers has assembled both material public and nonmaterial nonpublic information as the basis for his recommendation. By putting all of the information together, Smithers has utilized the mosaic theory to come to a conclusion of material nonpublic nature without actually using material nonpublic information. Therefore, he did not violate Standard II(A). Carson is not Smithers' client, and Smithers owes Carson no fiduciary responsibility under Standard III(A). Smithers had no reason to believe Carson would misrepresent anything about the situation.

2. **B** Sharing information between the stock and bond divisions within a single company does not violate any fiduciary duties. It is possible that by not sharing the information, Smithers could violate a fiduciary duty to Fundamental's bond-investing clients. Immediately downgrading the ski equipment manufacturers implies the downgrades were issued solely because of a new deal for Pineda, an act that violates Standard V(A) Diligence and Reasonable Basis. Giving client financial information to a competitor would definitely violate III(E), Preservation of Confidentiality.

3. **C** Nothing in Aaronson's conduct implies any violation of the independence and objectivity Standard, nor the Standard regarding use of material nonpublic information. As president of the firm, Aaronson is NOT responsible for making sure that each analyst has a reasonable basis for every recommendation. Aaronson is entitled to rely on reasonable procedures to detect and prevent such violations. Therefore, she has not violated any of the four listed standards.

4. **A** Standard III(A) Loyalty, Prudence, and Care requires members and candidates act for the benefit of their clients and comply with applicable fiduciary duties. O'Toole has no fiduciary duty to Big Ideas and can share the information with anyone he wishes. As managing partner, Carson is presumably authorized to speak for the partnership and attempt to bring in new investors. She has a fiduciary duty to the limited partners, but revealing the purchase plans to Smithers did not violate that duty as the deal had already been struck, and the information would not affect the purchase price. No actions in the scenario reflect a breach of fiduciary duty.

5. **A** O'Toole is an experienced real estate investor, and Pineda is probably a good fit for him. And because O'Toole is Smithers' biggest client, it can be assumed that Smithers has worked with O'Toole extensively and is familiar with his investment needs and preferences. As such, the purchase most likely satisfies Standard III(C) Suitability. Smithers did not violate Standard IV(B) Additional Compensation Arrangements because he did not accept O'Toole's offer, nor did he do what O'Toole asked in return for the condo, which was to get O'Toole a piece of the deal. By favoring O'Toole over other clients, however, Smithers violates the fair dealing Standard and his fiduciary duty to other clients besides O'Toole. Smithers should not have purchased stock in Pineda for O'Toole until the report had been disseminated to all clients with an interest in the investment.

6. **B**   The fair dealing Standard requires brokers to inform clients of any pending rating changes. If the clients still want to sell Pineda, then Fundamental must sell it for them. Purchasing Pineda stock for all discretionary portfolios violates the Standard III(C) Suitability, as the stock may not be suitable for all account holders. Waiting to make buys until everyone has received a mailed report sounds fair, but it violates the firm's fiduciary duty to discretionary clients and those who can be reached by phone, fax, or e-mail before the merger announcement is made. In addition, Standard III(B) Fair Dealing requires fair dissemination of recommendations, not "equal" dissemination, which is not always practical.

Item Set #2

7. **C**   Cutty's use of someone with whom he does personal business as a source could be perceived by some as a conflict of interest. However, there seems to be no ill intent, and Cutty corroborated Catcher's information from an additional source (the patent search). The research reports Standard requires that the analyst use reasonable judgment and distinguish between fact and opinion—Cutty did that. Cutty's broad-based research also satisfies the requirements of the reasonable basis Standard. None of the nonpublic information Cutty picked up was likely to be considered material by itself, and his conclusions about Simpson are an example of the mosaic theory.

8. **A**   Cutty owes no fiduciary duty to Catcher. Simpson's CEO did not reveal material information, but as CEO he likely would not have been violating a fiduciary duty even if he had. Catcher is in public relations, and her job is to discuss her clients' business with third parties. As such, she is authorized to release information—Standard III(A).

9. **C**   While Cutty clearly states that his opinion is based on his own conclusions rather than verifiable facts, he violates Standard V(B) by not providing details about the evaluation process, which was quite complicated. Therefore, choice C is not an adequate description of the process, and a violation of the Standard. Cutty's use of "I believe" and "could" suggest the statements about sales and cash flows are his opinions. Therefore, choices A and B are not violations.

10. **B**   Since Simpson is a risky stock, it is probably not suitable for all clients, and a blanket purchase order violates Standard III(C) Suitability. Wabb's instructions for the fulfillment department meet the requirements of Standard III(B) Fair Dealing, as the Standard does not require that everyone be notified at the same time, only that the dissemination of information is handled fairly. In this case, everyone with e-mail will get the information at the same time, and those without e-mail will get it later, but at the same time as their low-tech peers. The additional compensation Standard applies to compensation that doesn't come from the employer, and the World Series tickets did indeed come from the employer.

11. **C**   Members are in compliance with Standard V(A) Diligence and Reasonable Basis if they depend on the research of others they know to be competent and diligent. S&P qualifies as such a source. Standard V(C) Record Retention requires analysts to maintain records supporting their actions, so Cutty must save the results of the patent search. A rival's report about a competitor with similar technology could have a material effect on Cutty's financial model for Simpson and must be considered.

12. **A**   Slusher's claim that her credentials are superior to Cutty's because she earned her charter more recently is a violation of Standard VII(B) Reference to CFA Institute, the CFA Designation, and the CFA Program. Slusher did not plagiarize Cutty's work because she cited him as the author. Just because Slusher disagrees with, and criticizes, Cutty's well-researched opinion does not mean she lacks basis for her own analysis, or has violated the independence and objectivity standard.

Item Set #3

13. **C** In order to best conform to the CFA Institute Code and Standards, Lee should first define what constitutes adequate standards. According to Standard IV(C) Responsibilities of Supervisors, "'adequate' procedures are those designed to meet industry standards, regulatory requirements, the requirements of the Code and Standards, and the circumstances of the firm." Once this has been done he should implement the procedures immediately.

14. **A** In order to be in compliance with Standard IV(B) Jin must disclose all additional compensation arrangements, in writing, to her employer. It does not matter whether Rearguard actually pays her a commission on the funds or whether the firm previously had such a policy. In addition, the relationship with Rearguard creates a potential conflict of interest between Jin and her clients since she may be tempted to increase her income by recommending Rearguard Funds that are inappropriate for her clients' needs. Standard VI(A) Disclosure of Conflicts, requires disclosure of such conflicts to clients and prospects. There is no indication that Jin has made such a disclosure.

15. **B** Yu is in violation of Standard II(A) Material Nonpublic Information, as she has used material nonpublic information in her investment recommendations. She is forbidden to act upon such information. Lee, the firm's compliance officer, has violated Standard IV(C) Responsibilities of Supervisors, in the discharge of his responsibility as a supervisor. Given the abrupt change in the recommendation, Lee should have attempted to determine if there was a reasonable basis for the dramatic shift in opinion.

16. **A** According to Standard III(B) Fair Dealing, members and candidates must ensure that all clients are treated equitably with regard to investment recommendations and investment actions. Because MH has clients that subscribe to their research service but do not pay for portfolio management services and the firm has clients that pay for discretionary portfolio management, investment recommendations must be communicated to research subscribers and the firm's portfolio managers simultaneously in order to ensure that all clients have equal opportunity to trade on the firm's research without being disadvantaged because of the type of service the client receives.

17. **C** According to Standard IV(A) Loyalty to Employer, Larson must not solicit current or prospective Affinity clients prior to his leaving. Larson is allowed to solicit prospects that have been rejected by Affinity as long as he does so on his own time, does not use Affinity's client lists, and his actions do not impair his performance at work. His solicitation of prospects who are still viable for Affinity is a clear violation of duty to his employer under Standard IV(A).

18. **B** According to Standard IV(C) Responsibilities of Supervisors, the responsibility to implement procedures and the authority to enforce the procedures should both reside with the compliance officer (in this case Lee, rather than Jin, who is an investment officer).

CFA INSTITUTE SOFT DOLLAR STANDARDS

EXAM FOCUS

"Soft dollars" (or "client brokerage") refers to investment research, products and services, and cash credits given to the investment manager by brokers in return for client business. The soft dollar credit is the client's asset because he pays the commission. Fiduciaries owe their clients two basic duties: to act in the clients' best interest and to disclose conflicts of interest. The cardinal rule is that soft dollars are an asset of the client and may not be used for any purpose that does not benefit that client. The Soft Dollar Standards are voluntary, but firms that claim compliance must meet all of the requirements.

LOS 3.a: Define "soft dollar" arrangements and state the general principles of the Soft Dollar Standards.

Soft dollar arrangement refers to the research and other benefits provided to the client or the client's investment manager by the broker for directing the trade to the broker.

SOME DEFINITIONS

- *Soft dollars* refer to commissions generated on both agency and principal trades.
- An *agency trade* is a transaction that involves the payment of a commission.
- A *principal trade* is a transaction that involves a discount or a spread.
- *Soft dollar practices* involve the use of client brokerage by an investment manager to obtain certain products and services to aid the manager in the investment decision making process.
- *Brokerage* refers to the amount given to a broker as payment for execution services.
- *Research* includes both *proprietary* (generated by the broker) and *third-party* research (purchased by the broker). Research must directly assist the investment manager in the investment decision-making process and not in the management of the firm itself. Research that can be used for both the investment management process and management is called *mixed use* research.
- *Client-directed brokerage* is an arrangement under which the client tells the manager to execute trades under its account with a specific broker. In exchange, the client receives a benefit in addition to the execution services.

GENERAL PRINCIPLES OF THE SOFT DOLLAR STANDARDS

The two key principles of the Soft Dollar Standards are:

1. Brokerage is the property of the client.

2. Investment managers have a duty to obtain best execution, minimize transactions costs, and use client brokerage to benefit clients.

CFA Institute Soft Dollar Standards are intended to ensure:

- Complete disclosure of the investment manager's use of soft dollars and client brokerage.
- Consistent presentation of data so all parties can clearly understand brokerage practices.
- Uniform disclosure and record keeping so the client clearly understands how the investment manager is using client brokerage.
- Consistently high ethical industry standards.

The investment manager should consider that:

- The manager is a fiduciary and as such must disclose all details relating to benefits received through a client's brokerage.
- Third-party and proprietary research are to be treated similarly when examining soft dollar arrangements since the research received is paid for with client brokerage.
- Any research purchased with client brokerage must directly assist the investment manager in the investment process and not in the overall management of the firm.
- If there is ever any question as to whether the research assists in the investment process, it should be paid for with investment manager assets.

LOS 3.b: Critique company soft dollar practices and policies.

CFA INSTITUTE SOFT DOLLAR STANDARDS—REQUIREMENTS AND RECOMMENDATIONS

I. General

Required:

- Soft dollar practices must benefit the client and must place the clients' interests above the investment manager's interests.
- Allocation of client brokerage should not be based on the amount of client referrals the investment manager receives from a broker.
- Regarding mutual funds, the investment manager's client is the fund. The fund's board should set policies regarding broker selection.

II. Relationships With Clients

Required:

- Disclose to the client that the manager may participate in soft dollar arrangements involving the client's account prior to participating in such arrangements.

Recommended:

- It is permissible to use client brokerage from agency trades to obtain research which may not directly benefit the client. Over time, however, the client should receive a benefit from the research.
- As long as no fiduciary regulations apply, it is permissible to use client brokerage obtained from principal trades to benefit other client accounts, as long as this is disclosed to the client and prior consent is received.

III. Selection of Brokers

Proper broker selection is a key area where the investment manager can add value for the client. Failure to obtain best execution will hurt performance.

Required:

- Consider trade execution capabilities when selecting brokers.

Recommended:

- When evaluating best execution, consider the broker's financial responsibility, responsiveness, brokerage rate or spread involved, and range of services provided.

IV. Evaluation of Research

Required:

To be able to use client brokerage to pay for research, these criteria must be followed:

- Research must meet the definition. Research is defined as services and products provided by a broker whose primary use directly assists the investment manager in the investment decision making process, and not in the management of the firm.
- Research must benefit the client.
- The basis for the determination must be documented.
- In the case of principal trades not subject to other fiduciary regulations, the research may benefit other client accounts, as long as disclosure is made to the client and prior permission is received.
- If the criteria regarding client brokerage associated with principal trades is not met, the investment manager must pay for the research.
- In the case of mixed use research, make a reasonable allocation of the cost of the research based on its expected usage. Only portions that are used by the investment manager in the investment decision making process can be paid with client brokerage. Mixed use research allocation must be reevaluated annually.

V. Client-Directed Brokerage

Brokerage is an asset of the client, so the practice of client-directed brokerage does not violate the investment manager's duty.

Required:

- Do not use brokerage from another client to pay for products or services purchased under any client directed brokerage agreement.

Recommended:

- The investment manager should disclose the duty to seek best execution.
- Disclose to the client that the arrangement may adversely affect the manager's ability to obtain best execution and receive adequate research for the client.
- The investment manager should structure the arrangements so that they do not require the commitment of a certain portion of client brokerage to a single broker. The arrangement should ensure that commissions are negotiated and that there is an emphasis on best execution.

VI. Disclosure

Required:

- Investment managers must disclose in plain language their soft dollar policies. Principal trades must be addressed.
- Investment managers must disclose the types of research received through proprietary or third party research, the extent of its use, and whether an affiliated broker is involved.
- To claim compliance with Soft Dollar Standards, the client must receive a statement that soft dollar practices conform to these standards, and the statement must be provided at least annually.
- Investment managers must disclose in writing that more information concerning soft dollar arrangements is available on request.
- Additional information provided upon request may include a description of what the firm obtained through its soft dollar arrangements, the brokers who provided services, and total commissions generated for the client's account.

Recommended:

- As requested by the client, provide a description of the product or service obtained through client brokerage generated by the client's account.
- Provide the total amount of brokerage paid from all accounts over which the investment manager has discretion.

VII. Record Keeping

Required:

The investment manager must maintain records that:

- Meet legal and regulatory requirements.
- Are needed to supply timely information to clients consistent with the disclosure requirements.
- Document any arrangements that obligate the investment manager to generate a specific amount of brokerage.
- Document arrangements with clients regarding soft dollar or client-directed brokerage.
- Document any broker arrangements.
- Document the basis for allocations when using client brokerage for mixed use services and products.
- Show how services and products obtained via soft dollars assist the investment manager in the investment decision making process.
- Show compliance with the CFA Institute Soft Dollar Standards, and identify the personnel responsible.
- Include copies of client disclosures and authorizations.

LOS 3.c: Determine whether a product or service qualifies as "permissible research" that can be purchased with client brokerage.

PERMISSIBLE RESEARCH GUIDANCE

CFA Institute Soft Dollar Standards set forth a 3-level analysis to assist the investment manager in the determination of whether a product or service is permissible research that can be purchased with client brokerage.

Level 1 – Define the Product/Service: Define it in detail, including multiple components. *For example, a computer work station may be classified as a qualifying product, but the electricity to run the equipment would not.*

Level 2 – Determine Usage: Determine the primary use of the product or service. *For example, does the Bloomberg service received directly assist in the investment decision-making process, or is it there just to provide an "overall benefit to the firm"?*

Level 3 – Mixed Use Analysis: This step must be completed only if the product or service is classified as "research" based on the Level 1 and Level 2 analysis above. This Level 3 analysis is the investment manager's allocation of the portion of the product or service which directly assists in the investment decision-making process. *For example, if the Bloomberg service is used 50% of the time to "determine market and industry trends as part of the investment manager's investment decision-making process," then half of the expense can be paid from client brokerage.*

KEY CONCEPTS

LOS 3.a

Brokerage is the property of the client. Investment managers have a duty to obtain best execution, minimize transactions costs, and use client brokerage to benefit clients.

Soft Dollars refer to commissions generated on both agency (payment of a commission) and principal trades (discount or a spread).

Soft dollar practices involve the use of client brokerage by an investment manager to obtain certain products and services to aid the manager in the investment decision making process.

Research includes both proprietary (generated by the broker) and third-party research (purchased by the broker). Research must directly assist the investment manager in the investment decision-making process and not in the management of the firm itself. Research that can be used for both the investment management process and management is called mixed use research.

The Soft Dollar Standards are intended to ensure the following:
- Complete disclosure of the investment manager's use of soft dollars and client brokerage.
- Consistent presentation of data so all parties can clearly understand brokerage practices.
- Uniform disclosure and record keeping so the client clearly understands how the investment manager is using client brokerage.
- Consistently high ethical industry standards.

The investment manager should consider that:
- The manager is a fiduciary and as such must disclose all details relating to benefits received through a client's brokerage.
- Third-party and proprietary research are to be treated similarly when examining soft dollar arrangements since the research received is paid for with client brokerage.
- Any research purchased with client brokerage must directly assist the investment manager in the investment process and not in the overall management of the firm.
- If there is ever any question as to whether the research assists in the investment process, it should be paid for with investment manager assets.

LOS 3.b

Client-directed brokerage is permissible provided that the manager does not use brokerage from another client to pay for products or services purchased under any client directed brokerage agreement.

Disclosure requirements address clarity, discussion of principal trades, types/sources of research, annual updates, and additional information on request.

Record-keeping requirements address the following:
*   Legal / regulatory items, timeliness, and broker arrangements.
*   Obligations to generate a specific amount of brokerage.
*   Mixed use services / products, and client-specific disclosures/ authorizations / arrangements (including soft dollar or client-directed brokerage).
*   Connection among services / products and the investment process.
*   Record of compliance with the CFA Institute Soft Dollar Standards and the personnel responsible.

LOS 3.c

The CFA Institute's 3-level analysis guides the determination of whether a product or service can be purchased with client brokerage. The three levels are:
*   Define the Product/Service.
*   Determine (Primary) Usage.
*   Mixed Use Analysis.

CONCEPT CHECKERS

1. In regards to CFA Institute Soft Dollar Standards, broker selection is a key area of the investment manager's ability to add value to client portfolios. Which of the following is a requirement in selecting and evaluating brokers? The investment manager must consider:
    A. the broker's financial responsibility.
    B. if the broker is capable of providing best execution.
    C. the range of services provided or offered.

2. CFA Institute Soft Dollar Standards focus heavily on whether a product or service constitutes "research" that can be paid for with soft dollars (client brokerage) and whether that same product or service provides lawful and proper assistance to the investment manager in carrying out his investment decision making responsibilities. Which of the following statements regarding permissible or allowable "research" is *most accurate*?
    A. The product or service should directly assist the investment manager in his investment decision-making process and in the management of the investment firm.
    B. Determining what is permissible "research" is subject to specific rules.
    C. CFA Institute recommends performing a three level analysis to assist the investment manager in deciding whether a product or service is "research."

3. Which of these disclosures is recommended but not required under CFA Institute Soft Dollar Standards?
    A. More information concerning the firm's soft dollar standards is available upon request.
    B. The total amount of brokerage paid from all accounts over which the investment manager has discretion.
    C. A statement provided annually to the client that soft dollar practices of the firm conform to CFA Institute Soft Dollar Standards.

4. Western Investment Inc. manages investment accounts for individual investors and employee benefit plans subject to ERISA. In addition the firm manages an institutional hedge fund and a money market fund registered with the SEC as an investment company. Western has claimed compliance with the CFA Institute Soft Dollar Standards. The firm executes trades with a number of broker-dealers, who provide various products and services for the firm's use in exchange for client brokerage.

    Among the products and services provided by one of the broker-dealers is:
    *   Office equipment, including desks, photocopiers, and fax machines.
    *   A subscription to the Bloomberg service, which is used only to provide clients visiting the office with access to security prices and other financial information.

    Is Western in compliance with the Soft Dollar Standards based on its treatment of the office equipment and Bloomberg service?
    A. Both are permitted.
    B. One is permitted, the other is not permitted.
    C. Neither is permitted.

5. Soft dollar practices most precisely refers to:
    A. commissions generated on agency trades.
    B. firms which are in compliance with the CFA Institute's Soft Dollar Standards.
    C. a manager's use of client brokerage to obtain certain products and services to aid the manager in the investment decision making process.

6. An investment firm which is currently in compliance with the CFA Institute's Soft Dollar Standards performs an analysis to determine whether recent services provided by a new broker can be purchased with client brokerage. Which of the following is the firm *least likely* to do as part of this analysis?
    A. Create detailed definitions of the multiple components of the service.
    B. Determine the service use by research / non-research.
    C. Disclose the types of research received through proprietary or third party research.

Answers – Concept Checkers

1. **B** The other choices are all recommendations but not requirements. Best execution is the most critical consideration.

2. **C** Choice A is incorrect because aid in management of the overall firm is not permissible. Choice B is incorrect because determining what is permissible research is not subject to specific and identifiable rules.

3. **B** It is not required under the Soft Dollar Standards to disclose the amount of brokerage paid from all accounts. The other disclosures are required.

4. **C** The office equipment does not satisfy the Soft Dollar Standards definition of research because it does not aid directly in the investment decision-making process. The Bloomberg service also does not satisfy the Soft Dollar Standards because of the way the firm uses the services: it is provided as a service to clients and does not directly assist the investment manager in the investment decision-making process.

5. **C** Soft dollar practices refer to a manager's use of client brokerage to obtain certain products and services to aid the manager in the investment decision making process. Soft dollars refer to commissions generated on agency trades and principal trades. There is no official term to describe firms which are in compliance with the CFA Institute's Soft Dollar Standards.

6. **C** The CFA Institute's 3-level analysis guides the determination of whether a product or service can be purchased with client brokerage. The three levels are:
   - Define the Product/Service
   - Determine (Primary) Usage
   - Mixed Use Analysis

The following is a review of the Ethical and Professional Standards principles designed to address the learning outcome statements set forth by CFA Institute®. This topic is also covered in:

CFA INSTITUTE RESEARCH OBJECTIVITY STANDARDS

EXAM FOCUS

The objectives of CFA Institute's Research Objectivity Standards are to provide specific, measurable standards for managing and disclosing conflicts of interest that may interfere with an analyst's ability to conduct independent research and make objective recommendations.

These standards are intended to be a universal guide for all investment firms by providing ethical standards and practices regarding full and fair disclosure of any conflicts or potential conflicts relating to the firm's research. The goal is objectivity and independence.

LOS 4.a: Explain the objectives of the Research Objectivity Standards.

OBJECTIVES OF RESEARCH OBJECTIVITY STANDARDS

When designing policies and procedures for a firm, strive to achieve these objectives while implementing the CFA Institute Research Objectivity Standards:

A. Prepare research, make recommendations, take investment actions, and develop policies, procedures, and disclosures that put client interests before employees' and the firm's interests.

B. Facilitate full, fair, meaningful, and specific disclosures to clients and prospects of possible and actual conflicts of interest of the firm and its employees.

C. Promote the use of effective policies and procedures that minimize possible conflicts that may adversely affect independence and objectivity of research.

D. Support self-regulation by adhering to specific, measurable standards to promote objective and independent research.

E. Provide a work environment conducive to ethical behavior and adherence to the *Code and Standards*.

LOS 4.b: Critique company policies and practices related to research objectivity and distinguish between changes required and changes recommended for compliance with the Research Objectivity Standards.

IMPORTANT DEFINITIONS

Covered employee. A firm employee who:

- Conducts research, writes research reports, and/or makes investment recommendations.
- Takes investment action on the client's behalf or is involved in the decision-making process.
- May benefit, either personally or professionally, from her ability to influence research reports or investment recommendations.

Immediate family. Anyone who lives with (i.e., has the same principal residence as) the analyst or manager.

Investment manager. Any employee who conducts investment research and/or takes investment action for client accounts or the firm's accounts, *whether or not the person has the title of "investment manager."*

Public appearance. Any forum in which the analyst or manager makes investment recommendations or offers opinions, including seminars, public speaking engagements, interactive electronic forums, and any kind of media interview.

Research analyst. Any employee who is primarily responsible for any part of the process of developing a research report, *whether or not the person has the title of "research analyst."*

Subject company. Company whose securities are covered by a research report or recommendation.

REQUIREMENTS AND RECOMMENDED COMPLIANCE PROCEDURES

1.0 Research Objectivity Policy

Requirements:

The firm must have:

- A formal written independence and objectivity of research policy that it distributes to clients, prospective clients, and employees.
- Supervisory procedures in place to make sure employees comply with the policy.
- A senior officer who attests annually to clients and prospective clients that the firm has complied with the policy.

Recommended Compliance Procedures:

- Identify and describe covered employees—those conducting and writing research and making recommendations, including anyone who would benefit from his ability to influence the recommendations.
- Specify whether covered employees are subject to a code of ethics and standards of professional conduct. Fully disclose any conflicts of interest.
- Any policy should clearly identify the factors on which research analysts' compensation is based.
- Policy should also include terms regarding how research reports may be purchased by clients.

2.0 Public Appearances

Requirements:

Covered employees who make public appearances to discuss research or investment recommendations must disclose any personal and firm conflicts of interest.

Recommended Compliance Procedures:

- Be sure that the audience can make informed judgments and that they consider the investment in the context of their entire portfolio.
- Covered employees making public appearances should always be prepared to disclose all conflicts.
- Firms should require covered employees to disclose all investment banking relationships or whether the analyst has participated in marketing activities for the subject company.
- All supporting research reports should be provided at a reasonable cost. (Note: The Standards don't define "reasonable.")

3.0 Reasonable and Adequate Basis

Requirements:

Research reports and investment recommendations must have a reasonable and adequate basis. Either a single employee or a committee must be charged with reviewing and approving all research reports and investment recommendations.

Recommended Compliance Procedures:

- Firms must provide guidance on what constitutes reasonable and adequate basis for a specific recommendation.
- Offer to provide supporting data to clients, and disclose the current market price of the security.

4.0 Investment Banking

Requirements:

Firms with investment banking operations must have in place policies and procedures that:

- Separate research analysts from the investment banking department.
- Make sure analysts don't report to, and are not supervised by, investment banking personnel.
- Prevent the investment banking department from reviewing, revising, or approving research reports and investment recommendations.

Recommended Compliance Procedures:

- Firms must prohibit any communication between research and investment banking or corporate finance prior to the publication of a research report.
- Investment banking/corporate finance personnel may review reports only to verify factual information or to identify possible conflicts.
- Firms should have quiet periods for IPOs and secondary offerings of sufficient length to ensure that research reports and recommendations are not based on inside information obtained by the analyst through investment banking/corporate finance sources.
- It is recommended that analysts not be allowed to participate in marketing "road shows."

5.0 Research Analyst Compensation

Requirements:

Compensation for research analysts should be directly related to the quality of the research and recommendations provided by the analyst and not directly linked to investment banking or corporate finance activities.

Recommended Compliance Procedures:

- Compensation systems should be based on measurable criteria consistently applied to all research analysts.
- Ideally there should be no link between analyst compensation and investment banking and corporate finance activities, but firms should disclose to what extent analyst compensation depends upon investment banking revenues.

6.0 Relationships With Subject Companies

Requirements:

Analysts must not allow the subject company, prior to publication, to see any part of the research report that might signal the analyst's recommendation or rating, or make any promises concerning a specific recommendation or rating.

Recommended Compliance Procedures:

- Firms should have policies and procedures governing analysts' relationship with subject companies, specifically relating to material gifts, company-sponsored trips, etc.
- There should be efforts made to check facts contained in the research report before publication.
- The compliance and legal departments should receive a report draft before it is shared with the subject company. Any subsequent changes should be carefully documented.

7.0 Personal Investments and Trading

Requirements:

The firm must institute policies and procedures that:

- Address the personal trading of covered employees.
- Ensure covered employees do not share information with anyone who could use that information to trade ahead (i.e., front running) of client trades.
- Ensure covered employees and immediate family members can't trade ahead of client trades.
- Prohibit covered employees and immediate family members from trading contrary to the firm's recommendations, except under cases of extreme financial hardship.
- Prohibit covered employees and immediate family members from participating in IPOs of subject companies or companies in the industry the employee covers.

Recommended Compliance Procedures:

- Always place interests of clients ahead of personal and firm interests.
- Obtain approval from the compliance and legal departments in advance of trading on any securities of subject companies in the industries assigned to the analyst.
- Firms should have procedures in place to prevent employees from trading ahead of investing client trades. Restricted periods should be in place at least 30 calendar days before and 5 calendar days after recommendations are made via research reports.
- It is permissible to allow the analyst to sell contrary to their recommendation in the case of extreme financial hardship.
- Firms should require covered employees to provide the compliance and legal departments with a complete list of personal holdings, including securities in which they have a beneficial interest.

8.0 Timeliness of Research Reports and Recommendations

Requirements:

Regularly issue research reports on subject companies on a timely basis.

Recommended Compliance Procedures:

- Firms should require regular updates to research and recommendations. Quarterly updates are preferred.
- If coverage of a company is discontinued, the analyst should issue a "final" research report.

9.0 Compliance and Enforcement

Requirements:

Firms must enforce their policies and compliance procedures, assess disciplinary sanctions on employees who violate the policies, monitor the effectiveness of the compliance procedures, and maintain records of any internal audits of the policies.

Recommended Compliance Procedures:

- Firms should distribute to clients a list of activities which are violations and include disciplinary sanctions for such violations.

10.0 Disclosure

Requirements:

The firm must disclose conflicts of interests related to covered employees or the firm as a whole.

Recommended Compliance Procedures:

- Disclosures should be complete, prominent, and easy to understand.
- Investment banking/corporate finance relationships should be disclosed.
- All conflicts of interest must be disclosed, including whether the firm makes a market in the subject company's security, whether it has managed a recent IPO or secondary offering, and whether any ownership position or covered employee's family is affiliated in any way with the subject company. Any material gifts from the subject company should also be disclosed.
- Disclose any statistical or quantitative basis for recommendations and ratings.
- Disclose valuation methods used to determine specific price targets and include any risk factors.

11.0 Rating System

Requirements:

The firm must have a rating system that investors find useful for investment decisions and provides investors with information they can use to determine the suitability of specific investments for their own portfolio.

Recommended Compliance Procedures:

- Firms should avoid one-dimensional rating systems since they do not give investors enough information to make informed decisions.
- Rating systems should include the recommendation and rating categories, time horizon categories, and risk categories.
- Absolute (buy, hold, sell, etc.) or relative (market outperform, underperform, etc.) recommendation categories are permitted.
- A complete description of the firm's rating system should be provided to clients upon request.

KEY CONCEPTS

LOS 4.a

When designing policies and procedures for a firm, strive to achieve these objectives while implementing the CFA Institute Research Objectivity Standards:

- Prepare research, make recommendations, take investment actions, and develop policies, procedures, and disclosures that put client interests before employees' and the firm's interests.
- Facilitate full, fair, meaningful, and specific disclosures to clients and prospects of possible and actual conflicts of interest of the firm and its employees.
- Promote the use of effective policies and procedures that minimize possible conflicts that may adversely affect independence and objectivity of research.
- Support self-regulation by adhering to specific, measurable standards to promote objective and independent research.
- Provide a work environment conducive to ethical behavior and adherence to the Code and Standards.

LOS 4.b

Requirements and Recommended Compliance Procedures generally concern the following matters:
1. Research Objectivity Policy
2. Public Appearances
3. Reasonable and Adequate Basis
4. Investment Banking
5. Research Analyst Compensation
6. Relationships with Subject Companies
7. Personal Investments and Trading
8. Timeliness of Research Reports and Recommendations
9. Compliance and Enforcement
10. Disclosure
11. Rating System

CONCEPT CHECKERS

1. Which of the following is *least likely* an objective for proper implementation of the Research Objectivity Standards?
    A. Prepare research, make recommendations, take investment actions, and develop policies, procedures, and disclosures that place client interests before employees' and firm's interests.
    B. Support the appropriate regulatory agency regulation by adhering to specific, measurable standards to promote objective and independent research.
    C. Facilitate full and meaningful disclosures to clients and prospects of possible and actual conflicts of interest of the firm and its employees.

2. When presenting research and recommendations in a public forum, which of the following would be *least likely* to comply with the Research Objectivity Standards?
    A. Firms should require employees to disclose any investment banking relationships or whether the analyst has participated in marketing activities for the subject firm.
    B. Be sure that the audience can make informed judgments, and provide any supporting research at no cost.
    C. Be sure that investors consider the investment in the context of their entire portfolio.

3. Warren Sun, an analyst with Myers and Bradley Partners, has completed a research report on ROS, Inc. In the report Sun has changed his recommendation from buy to hold. Sun sends the entire report to the compliance department and to ROS for review. ROS management suggests a few minor changes to some of the financial data. Sun provides to the compliance department a justification for these changes, and the compliance department approves the changes in advance of the release of the report.

    Are the following actions taken by Sun consistent with the CFA Institute Research Objectivity Standards?

	Sending the report to the subject company?	Making the changes to the report?
A.	Yes	No
B.	No	Yes
C.	No	No

ANSWERS – CONCEPT CHECKERS

1. **B** Self-regulation is an objective, as opposed to regulation by regulatory agencies. Remember that CFA Institute is a self-regulatory organization.

2. **B** Any supporting research should be provided at a reasonable cost. The rest of the statements are correct.

3. **B** The Research Objectivity Standards prohibit Sun from sending the entire report, including his recommendation, to ROS. He is allowed, however, to send the sections of the report containing facts that can be verified by ROS. He is allowed to change the facts presented in the report in response to feedback from ROS, and he has followed the recommended procedures for making those changes and having them approved by the compliance department.

THE GLENARM COMPANY

EXAM FOCUS

The Glenarm case introduces you to the obligations CFA Institute members and CFA® charterholders and candidates have to their employers. This ethics case will give you a sense of the types of scenarios you are likely to encounter on the Level 2 exam. The particulars of this case are not important in terms of test questions. However, understanding how to analyze a case and having the ability to recommend procedures to bring an illustrative firm into compliance are crucial to your success on the ethics portion of the exam.

LOS 5.a: Critique the practices and policies presented.

LOS 5.b: Explain the appropriate action to take in response to conduct that violates the CFA Institute Code of Ethics and Standards of Professional Conduct.

CASE OUTLINE

The main facts of the Glenarm case are as follows:

- Peter Sherman, CFA, was employed for five years with Pearl Investment Management as an emerging markets analyst. While he was at Pearl, he developed outside consulting positions with several Latin American companies. This outside consulting activity was disclosed to Pearl. Sherman recently switched firms and is now employed by the Glenarm Company.
- Glenarm is a small investment management firm that has been investigated, censured, and fined by the SEC for securities violations. Glenarm's partners are eager to repair the firm's reputation and hoped that hiring a CFA charterholder would help retain current clients and bring in new business.
- Prior to joining the firm, Glenarm asked Sherman to solicit current and prospective Pearl clients. Glenarm offered Sherman a large stake in the first-year investment management fees of any Pearl clients that Sherman could bring to Glenarm.
- While still employed at Pearl, Sherman visited socially with several Pearl clients in an attempt to woo them away from Pearl. He also contacted potential Pearl clients that Pearl has been actively soliciting. He even contacted some clients that Pearl had rejected.
- As he left Pearl, Sherman took the following items with him to his new job:
  - Pearl marketing presentations.
  - Computer stock selection models that he developed.
  - Research materials.

- News articles on firms that he had been following.
- A list of research ideas that were rejected by Pearl.

CASE RESULTS

Standard IV(A) Duties to Employers: Loyalty

Violations of Standard IV(A) include:

- It is acceptable for Sherman to contact prospects that Pearl decided not to pursue, because of a particular size or investment objective, while he is still employed at Pearl.
- Unless the employer consents, departing employees may not misappropriate property. All of the items Sherman took are the property of Pearl, and there is a violation.

Professor's Note: Members and Candidates must always act for the benefit of the employer. By taking confidential information, and soliciting clients and prospects to benefit Glenarm, Sherman has harmed his old employer, Pearl, and is in violation of his duty of loyalty. Sherman must act in the "old" employer's best interest while still employed there.

Actions required to prevent these violations include:

- Sherman should not solicit Pearl's clients or prospects until he leaves Pearl's employment.
- Sherman should not have taken Pearl property.

Standard IV(B) Duties to Employers: Additional Compensation Arrangements.

Violations of Standard IV(B) include:

- Sherman did not disclose his consulting arrangements to Glenarm.

Actions required to prevent these violations include:

- Sherman should disclose his consulting arrangements to Glenarm.

Standard VI(A) Disclosure of Conflicts, and Standard I(B) Independence and Objectivity

Violations of Standards VI(A) and I(B) include:

- The consulting arrangements had the potential to affect Sherman's independence and objectivity.
- Disclosures must be prominent and delivered in plain language.

Actions required to prevent these violations include:

- Sherman must disclose all details about outside compensation to Glenarm and obtain written permission from Glenarm in advance of entering into any such arrangements.

PRESTON PARTNERS

EXAM FOCUS

The Preston Partners case emphasizes the violations that can occur when allocating block trades to clients. This ethics case will give you a sense of the types of scenarios you are likely to encounter on the Level 2 exam. The particulars of this case are not important in terms of test questions. However, understanding how to analyze a case and having the ability to recommend procedures to bring an illustrative firm into compliance are crucial to your success on the ethics portion of the exam.

LOS 6.a: Critique the practices and policies presented.

LOS 6.b: Explain the appropriate action to take in response to conduct that violates the CFA Institute Code of Ethics and Standards of Professional Conduct.

CASE OUTLINE

The following statements summarize the main facts of the Preston Partners case:

- Sheldon Preston, CFA, is president of Preston Partners. Preston Partners is a mid-size investment management firm that specializes in managing large-cap portfolios for individuals and pension funds. CFA Institute's Code and Standards have been adopted as part of Preston's compliance manual.
- Preston wrote the firm's compliance manual but did a cursory job because he was in a hurry. A copy of the manual was provided to all employees upon joining the firm.
- During his daily review of Preston Partner trades, Preston found that Gerald Smithson, CFA, had added the stocks of Utah BioChemical Co. and Norgood PLC to all his clients' portfolios.
- Preston Partners manages Utah BioChemical's pension fund. In addition, the president and CEO of Utah BioChemical, Arne Okapuu, has Smithson manage his personal portfolio. Smithson and Okapuu have had a long-term business relationship.
- Smithson was vacationing in London and had seen Okapuu and the chairman of Norgood talking at a restaurant. Smithson contacted an analyst that he knew in London, Andrew Jones, and requested information on Norgood. Jones's latest research report had placed a "hold" recommendation on Norgood stock.
- Norgood is an aggressive investment and Utah BioChemical is a conservative investment.
- Smithson performed a complete analysis of the biotech industry, Norgood, and Utah BioChemical. Based on his analysis and the fact that he saw Okapuu and Norgood's chairman talking, he deduced that a merger between the two firms was possible.

- Smithson ordered block trades of 50,000 shares for each firm. The firm's compliance manual was vague on the proper allocation of shares from a block trade. Smithson decided to allocate shares based on the size of the client's account, with the largest clients receiving their shares first at the most favorable prices. Also, the needs and constraints of Smithson's clients vary widely.
- Utah BioChemical and Norgood announced that they were merging. The share price of both firms increased by 40%.

CASE RESULTS

In researching and making client investment decisions, Smithson complied with Standard V(A) – Diligence and Reasonable Basis. Furthermore, Smithson did not possess or act on insider information. What he learned was assembled through the "mosaic" theory.

However, Smithson did not comply with portions of the Standards relating to suitability of investments for clients and trade allocations. Preston failed to properly exercise his supervisory responsibility.

Standard III(C) Duties to Clients: Suitability

Violations of Standard III(C) include:

- Smithson should have considered clients' individual risk tolerances, needs, circumstances, and goals; he should have also better matched clients with investments. Norgood is too volatile for many clients' accounts.

Actions required to prevent this violation include:

- Be sure that Smithson's clients have written investment objectives and policy statements.
- For accounts which contain unsuitable investments, the shares should be sold, and Preston Partners should reimburse any loss.

Standard III(B) Duties to Clients: Fair Dealing

Violations of Standard III(B) include:

- The firm had no clear procedures for allocating block trades to client accounts. Large accounts were favored, disadvantaging smaller accounts.

Actions required to prevent this violation include:

- Detailed guidelines covering block trades must be prepared, emphasizing fairness to clients, timely executions, and accuracy.

Standard IV(C) Duties to Employers: Responsibilities of Supervisors

Violations of Standard IV(C) include:

- The senior management at Preston Partners should have made reasonable efforts to identify and prevent violations of applicable laws, rules, and regulations. A compliance program should have been in place.
- Supervisors and managers have the responsibility of training, distributing a policies and procedures manual, and providing refresher courses.

Actions required to prevent these violations include:

- Preston must have proper procedures established that would have prevented violations such as those that occurred.
- A compliance officer should be designated.

SUPER SELECTION

EXAM FOCUS

The Super Selection case emphasizes the fiduciary duty that members have to their clients. This ethics case will give you a sense of the types of scenarios you are likely to encounter on the Level 2 exam. The particulars of this case are not important in terms of test questions. However, understanding how to analyze a case and having the ability to recommend procedures to bring an illustrative firm into compliance are crucial to your success on the ethics portion of the exam.

LOS 7.a: Critique the practices and policies presented.

LOS 7.b: Explain the appropriate action to take in response to conduct that violates the CFA Institute Code of Ethics and Standards of Professional Conduct.

CASE OUTLINE

The main facts of the Super Selection case are as follows:

- Patricia Cuff is the CFO and compliance officer for Super Selection Investment Advisors. Cuff is also a member of CFA Institute. CFA Institute's Standards of Practice have been incorporated into Super Selection's compliance manual.
- Karen Trader is a portfolio manager with Super Selection. She has recently purchased shares of Atlantis Medical Devices (AMD) for all of her clients' portfolios. AMD is a rapidly growing biotech firm.
- Trader's friend, Josey James, is president of AMD. James has been providing advice to Trader regarding the viability of certain biotech firms over the past few years. Trader has taken advantage of this advice for both her personal account and her client's portfolios. In many cases, she has placed personal trades before trading for her clients. Trader's personal brokerage statements had not been submitted to Cuff until recently.
- Several years ago, James asked Trader to serve as an outside director for AMD. She was paid with AMD stock options that at the time had no value. AMD earnings and sales are up and AMD directors recently voted to take the firm public via an initial public offering. AMD also began paying directors $5,000 per year. Trader stands to gain considerably by exercising her stock options.
- By the time the offering was to go public, the initial public offering (IPO) market had soured considerably. James called Trader to ask if she could commit to the purchase of a block of AMD shares for her client accounts. Trader had previously determined that AMD shares were not a good investment for her clients—but she changed her mind on the recommendation of James and purchased a considerable amount of AMD stock for her clients.

CASE RESULTS

Several Code and Standard violations are evident relating to Karen Trader's involvement with an outside firm. Although she is not a CFA charterholder or member, she is bound by the CFA Institute Code and Standards to the extent that they are a part of her own company's compliance procedures.

Standard IV(C) Duties to Employers: Responsibilities of Supervisors

The presumption is that Cuff is the "supervisor" and thus must comply with this standard. Cuff has the responsibility to take steps to prevent violations, and as compliance officer she should see that the firm's compliance procedures are adhered to by employees. Any violations must be addressed.

Actions required to prevent these violations include:

- Cuff must take prompt action to correct violations by reporting the violations to the appropriate members of senior management.
- Cuff is a compliance officer and must monitor Trader's personal trades and impose sanctions when necessary.
- If the senior management does not back up Cuff, other options include disclosing the incident to the Board, to the regulators, and even resigning from the firm.

Standard VI(A) Disclosure of Conflicts

Violations of Standard VI(A) include:

- Trader failed to disclose ownership of AMD stock options and also the compensation she received as a director of AMD.

Actions required to prevent this violation include:

- As a supervisor, Cuff must take action to ensure disclosure and, if necessary, by limiting behavior and imposing sanctions.

Standard V(A) Diligence and Reasonable Basis

Violations of Standard V(A) include:

- Trader determined AMD was not a suitable security for her clients. Trader was pressured by James and reversed positions; thus the AMD stock was purchased.

Actions required to prevent this violation include:

- Trader should have conducted due diligence and thorough research before making an investment decision for clients' accounts. Any change in opinion must have a reasonable basis. Trader must also inform clients of any AMD conflicts such as directorship and stock options.
- The compliance officer, Cuff, should review investment actions taken for clients at least annually.

Standard III(A) Duties to Clients: Loyalty, Prudence and Care

Violations of Standard III(A) include:

- The fiduciary duty to clients was violated. Remember that client interests always come first.

Actions required to prevent this violation include:

- Trader should have taken any investment action for the sole benefit of her clients. Cuff must completely investigate Trader's activities to determine other fiduciary breaches. Following any fiduciary breaches, wrongdoers must have their activities limited.

Standard III(C) Duties to Clients: Suitability

Violations of Standard III(C) include:

- AMD stock was purchased for clients without considering client needs and circumstances.

Actions required to prevent this violation include:

- Trader should have considered clients' needs and circumstances instead of taking actions that benefited her personally.
- The compliance officer should establish at least an annual review to compare suitability of investment actions with investment policy statements.

Standard VI(B) – Priority of Transactions

Violations of Standard VI(B) include:

- Trader violated this Standard by trading personally prior to client trades.

Actions required to prevent this violation include:

- By not reporting trades and brokerage accounts, Trader failed to follow her firm's procedures. The compliance officer needs to fully investigate Trader's transactions and recommend proper sanctions.

The following is a review of the Ethical and Professional Standards principles designed to address the learning outcome statements set forth by CFA Institute®. This topic is also covered in:

TRADE ALLOCATION: FAIR DEALING AND DISCLOSURE

EXAM FOCUS

This topic review provides a brief summary of trade allocation procedures as recently updated by CFA Institute. The CFA Institute Code and Standards speak directly to the issue of trade allocation procedures since allocating trades among clients is an example of taking investment action. Under CFA Institute Standard III(B) Duties to Clients – Fair Dealing, "Members and Candidates must deal fairly and objectively with all clients when providing investment analysis, making investment recommendations, taking investment action, or engaging in other professional activities."

LOS 8.a: Critique trade allocation practices and determine whether there is compliance with the CFA Institute Standards of Professional Conduct addressing fair dealing and client loyalty.

TRADE ALLOCATION PRACTICE CRITIQUE

The allocation of client trades on an *ad hoc* basis lends itself to two fundamental fairness problems:

- The allocation of trades may be based on *compensation arrangements*.
- The allocation of trades may be based on *client relationships* with the firm.

As far as compensation arrangements are concerned, an *ad hoc* allocation procedure gives rise to the temptation to allocate a disproportionate share of profitable trades to performance-based fee accounts. In addition to violating Standard III(B) – Duties to Clients: Fair Dealing, this is a clear violation of Standard III(A) – Duties to Clients: Loyalty, Prudence, and Care (which covers fiduciary duty) since this has the effect of increasing fees paid to the investment adviser at the expense of asset-based fee accounts.

As far as the client relationship with the firm is concerned, an *ad hoc* allocation procedure gives rise to the temptation to allocate a disproportionate share of profitable trades to favored clients. In addition to violating the fair dealing standard, this is again a clear violation of Standard III(A) – Duties to Clients: Loyalty, Prudence, and Care, which states that members owe a duty of loyalty to clients and requires them to put clients' interests above their own. Conflicts of interest should be avoided. Giving certain clients special access to attractive IPOs with the intent to receive future investment banking business or more fees creates a conflict and breaches the duty to clients.

LOS 8.b: Discuss appropriate actions to take in response to trade allocation practices that do not adequately respect client interests.

APPROPRIATE RESPONSE TO INADEQUATE TRADE ALLOCATION PRACTICES

- Get advanced indication of client interest regarding any new issues.
- Distribute new issues by client, not by portfolio manager.
- Have in place a fair and objective method for trade allocation, such as pro rata or a similar system.
- Be fair to clients regarding both execution of trades and price.
- Execute orders in a timely and efficient manner.
- Keep records and periodically review them to ensure that all clients are being treated equitably.

The following is a review of the Ethical and Professional Standards principles designed to address the learning outcome statements set forth by CFA Institute®. This topic is also covered in:

CASE STUDY: CHANGING INVESTMENT OBJECTIVES

Study Session 2

EXAM FOCUS

This topic review provides a brief summary of CFA Institute Standard III(C) Duties to Clients: Suitability. When entering into an advisory relationship with a client, the investment manager must inquire about the client's investing experience and investment objectives and constraints before taking any investment actions or making any recommendations. The actions and recommendations must be suitable to the client's situation and must be judged in the context of the entire portfolio. If the investment manager is managing a portfolio according to a specific style or mandate, the recommendations and investment actions must be consistent with the stated objectives and constraints of the specific portfolio.

LOS 9.a: Critique the disclosure of investment objectives and basic policies and determine whether they comply with the CFA Institute Standards of Professional Conduct.

DISCLOSURE OF INVESTMENT OBJECTIVES CRITIQUE

In the case of pooled client funds such as mutual funds, it is particularly important that the portfolio manager's recommendations and investment actions be consistent with the stated objectives and constraints of the fund. The security selection and portfolio construction processes are typically described in the fund's prospectus. *These processes are the key elements upon which the determination of appropriateness and suitability may be determined*. A material deviation from these processes, in the absence of approval from clients, constitutes a violation of CFA Institute Standard III(C) – Duties to Clients: Suitability. *The investment must fit within the mandate or within the realm of investments that are allowed according to the fund's disclosures.*

LOS 9.b: Discuss appropriate actions needed to ensure adequate disclosure of the investment process.

APPROPRIATE RESPONSE TO INADEQUATE DISCLOSURE PROCEDURES

In order to remain in compliance with CFA Institute Standards, a portfolio manager must:

- Determine the client's financial situation, investment objectives, and level of investing expertise.
- Adequately disclose the basic security selection and portfolio construction processes.
- Conduct regular internal checks for compliance with these processes.
- Stick to the stated investment strategy if managing to a specific mandate or strategy.
- Notify investors and potential investors of any potential change in the security selection and portfolio construction processes and secure documentation of authorization for proposed changes.

©2008 Kaplan Schweser

PRUDENCE IN PERSPECTIVE

EXAM FOCUS

The new Prudent Investor Rule incorporates the principles of portfolio theory (think "diversification"), total return analysis (versus the *old* school of thought that capital preservation was the only concern), and management's ability to delegate investment duties. As you read this topic review, note the many similarities between the new Rule and the CFA Institute Standards of Professional Conduct—you'll find the two sets of principles to be quite consistent. You may see this material tested in conjunction with the portfolio management process material in Study Session 18.

WARM-UP: THE OLD PRUDENT MAN RULE

Until recently, the old *Prudent Man Rule* was the accepted legal statute that applied to fiduciary trust law in the U.S. The Prudent Man Rule originated from Justice Putnam's ruling in the *Harvard College v. Amory* case in 1830. Despite its appealing flexibility, the Prudent Man Rule failed to attain wide acceptance outside of Massachusetts until the 1940s. Prior to that time, most states had adopted "legal list" statutes that described appropriate investments for trustees. After the collapse of the bond markets during the Depression, there was general disaffection with legal lists and a trend toward the Prudent Man Rule.

The Prudent Man Rule states that:

In acquiring, investing, reinvesting, exchanging, retaining, selling, and managing property for the benefit of another, a fiduciary shall exercise the judgment and care, under the circumstances then prevailing, which men of prudence, discretion, and intelligence exercise in the management of their own affairs, not in regard to speculation but in regard to the permanent disposition of their funds, considering the probable income as well as the probable safety of their capital.

THE NEW PRUDENT INVESTOR RULE

LOS 10.a: Explain the basic principles of the new Prudent Investor Rule.

Basic Investment Principles

Because the old Rule severely limited trustees' abilities to manage portfolios to the best of their abilities, the American Law Institute in 1992 offered a definitive commentary called the **Prudent Investor Rule**. The substance of the *new* Rule is to change the mindset that certain types of investments are prohibited. There are five basic principles to the new Prudent Investor Rule:

1. Diversification is expected of portfolio managers as a method of reducing risk.

2. Trustees must base an investment's appropriateness on its risk/return profile: how it contributes to the overall risk of the portfolio.

3. Excessive trading (churning) as well as excessive fees and other transactions costs that are not warranted by the portfolio risk/return objectives should be avoided.

4. Current income for the trust must be balanced against the need for growth.

5. Trustees are allowed to delegate investment authority. In fact, this is a duty if the trustee does not have the required level of expertise.

LOS 10.b: Explain the general fiduciary standards to which a trustee must adhere.

GENERAL FIDUCIARY STANDARDS

A trustee must exercise *care*, *skill*, *caution*, *loyalty*, and *impartiality* when managing trust assets. The loyalty and impartiality standards are carried over from the old Rule to the new Rule. The definitions of care, skill, and caution have changed significantly.

*   *Care* means the trustees must do their homework by gathering pertinent information to use in their investment decisions. This could include seeking advice. A higher level of care is required under the new Rule.
*   *Skill* means that if the trustee does not have the relevant investment knowledge, he or she has a duty to seek out such advice. Note the difference in this standard versus the old Rule. The old Rule forbade such delegation. Also, if you have the necessary skill set, you have a duty to use it. Here again, the requirement for skill is higher. Before, you as a trustee needed to have all the answers.
*   *Caution* must be used to balance the need for current income with the need to guard against inflation. In addition, a *total return* approach to money management should be employed. Principal growth (not just maintaining purchasing power) could indeed be a goal in certain circumstances. Caution under the old Rule *really* meant caution—don't lose any money, which meant don't even think about growth!
*   *Loyalty* requires the trustee to avoid conflicts of interest by always acting exclusively in the best interest of beneficiaries. This standard remains fairly constant under both rules.
*   *Impartiality* requires that the trustee act "in a fair and reasonable manner" when handling the conflicting interests of beneficiaries (i.e., remaindermen interests versus current income beneficiaries). Impartiality standards also carry over from the old Rule to the new Rule.

The adherence to these standards is required of the trustee at the time of the investment decision. For example, the trustees of Enron's pension assets may have believed at the time that they acted according to the aforementioned standards. However, it is clear to see today that the decisions they made were not appropriate. We must not judge decisions ex post facto under the new standards.

THE OLD PRUDENT MAN RULE VS. THE NEW PRUDENT INVESTOR RULE

LOS 10.c: Differentiate between the old Prudent Man Rule and the new Prudent Investor Rule.

The new Prudent Investor Rule makes five key changes to the traditional rules governing investment trust management.

- *Use of total return.* The new Rule measures reasonable portfolio return as total return (income plus capital growth). It also emphasizes that the trustee's duty is to not only preserve the purchasing power of the trust but in certain cases to realize principal growth in excess of inflation.
- *Risk management.* Under the new Rule the trustee has the obligation to assess the risk and return objectives of the trust beneficiaries and manage the trust in a prudent manner consistent with those objectives, rather than to avoid all risk.
- *Evaluation in a portfolio context.* While the new Rule calls for the avoidance of undue speculation and risk, it also encourages trustees to view risk in a portfolio context. For example, stock options are risky when held in isolation but can actually reduce portfolio risk when held as part of a properly structured portfolio. Protective put options are an example of this type of strategy.
- *Security restrictions.* No securities are "off-limits" because of their riskiness when held in isolation. For example, under the old Rule options were not allowed, but under the new Rule they are, as long as the manager takes the portfolio perspective to analyzing risk.
- *Delegation of duty.* The *old* Rule did not permit trustees to delegate investment authority. In fact, investing in mutual funds or even index funds was deemed improper. The *new* Rule goes so far as to say that it may be the *duty* of a trustee (this is stronger language than just authority) to delegate, just as a prudent investor would.

 Professor's Note: These principles are consistent with the guidelines outlined in the topic review of the portfolio management process in Study Session #18, where the LOS ask you to explain the importance of the portfolio perspective and define investment objectives and constraints.

LOS 10.d: Explain the key factors that a trustee should consider when investing and managing trust assets.

The new Prudent Investor Rule includes eight key factors that the trustee should consider when investing and managing trust assets:

- Economic conditions.
- Effects of inflation and deflation.
- Impact of investment decisions on the beneficiary's tax liability.
- How each individual investment contributes to the risk and return of the overall portfolio.
- Expected total return from capital appreciation and income.
- Other resources of the beneficiary.
- The beneficiary's liquidity, income, and capital preservation requirements.
- Whether any assets have a special relationship to the requirements of the beneficiary or the trust.

KEY CONCEPTS

LOS 10.a
The five basic principles of the new Prudent Investor Rule are:
* Diversification is expected of portfolio managers as a method of reducing risk.
* Trustees must base an investment's appropriateness on its risk/return profile in a portfolio context.
* Excessive trading (churning), as well as excessive fees and other transactions costs that are not warranted by the portfolio risk/return objectives, should be avoided.
* Current income for the trust must be balanced against the need for growth.
* Trustees are allowed (and may be required under certain circumstances) to delegate investment authority.

LOS 10.b
The general fiduciary standards that a trustee must adhere to are care, skill, caution, loyalty, and impartiality. The adherence to these standards is required of the trustee at the time of the investment decision.

LOS 10.c
The new Prudent Investor Rule differs from the old Prudent Man Rule in a number of areas:
* Total return is emphasized rather than preservation of purchasing power.
* Risk must be consistent with expected return objectives; under the old Rule risk was avoided.
* The investments are evaluated from a risk-return perspective in a portfolio context, not individually.
* No securities are "off-limits" because they are risky on a stand-alone basis.
* Delegation of duties is encouraged rather than prohibited.

LOS 10.d
Key factors the trustee should consider include general economic conditions (including inflation and deflation), total expected return and the risk-return trade-off of the portfolio, and the unique needs of the beneficiary, including the tax situation, other resources available to the beneficiary, liquidity, income and capital preservation requirements, and unique assets with a special relationship to the beneficiary.

CONCEPT CHECKERS

1. Which of the following statements regarding the old Prudent Man Rule is *most accurate*?
    A. The delegation of investment authority to a third party was acceptable.
    B. Trustees were to consider the safety of invested assets as well as income potential.
    C. Each investment was considered in the context of its contribution to the entire portfolio.

2. Which of the following statements is *least likely* to be a basic principle of the new Prudent Investor Rule?
    A. Current income for the trust must be balanced against the need for growth.
    B. Trustees must base appropriateness of risk on an investment's risk/return profile.
    C. Trustees may not delegate investment authority, except in unusual circumstances.

3. In which way are the old Prudent Man Rule and the new Prudent Investor Rule *similar*? Both rules:
    A. forbid entire classes of securities.
    B. instruct trustees to act in a fair and reasonable manner.
    C. stipulate that a total return approach to money management should be employed.

Use the following information to answer Question 4.

Stanley Bostwick, CFA, is a portfolio manager at Cornerstone Trust Company. He has asked Susan Sarahson, a newly hired analyst and Level 2 CFA candidate, to research the differences between the old Prudent Man Rule and the new Prudent Investor Rule. Sarahson conducts her research, meets with Bostwick, and makes the following statements:

Statement 1: "The old Rule allows the delegation of authority and the new rule doesn't."

Statement 2: "The old Rule considers each investment on its own merits, and the new Rule takes a total portfolio approach."

Statement 3: "The old Rule allows for plain vanilla derivative instruments, and the new Rule allows for more exotic derivative instruments."

4. Bostwick has some familiarity with both rules and, after some further consideration, agrees with Sarahson concerning statements #1 and #2, but disagrees with her concerning statement #3. Which of the following statements is *most accurate*?
    A. He was correct to agree with her concerning statement #1.
    B. He was correct to agree with her concerning statement #2.
    C. He was incorrect to disagree with her concerning statement #3.

5.   The new Prudent Investor Rule includes eight key factors that the trustee should consider when investing and managing trust assets. Which of the following is *least likely* to be one of these eight key factors?
A. Economic conditions.
B. Effect of deflation.
C. Impact of investment decisions on the beneficiary's personal beliefs and ethical principles.

6.   The new Prudent Investor Rule includes eight key factors that the trustee should consider when investing and managing trust assets. Which of the following is *least likely* to be one of these eight key factors?
A. Expected total return from capital appreciation and income.
B. The non-systematic risk present in individual investments.
C. Whether any assets have a special relationship to the requirements of the beneficiary or the trust.

7.   The new Prudent Investor specifies five fiduciary standards that the trustee must adhere to. Which of the following is *least likely* to be one of these factors?
A. Skill.
B. Caution.
C. Feasibility.

ANSWERS – CONCEPT CHECKERS

1. **B** Delegation of authority was not permitted under the old Rule. The trustee was required to consider each investment individually and not in a portfolio context. The old Rule has been replaced by the new Prudent Investor Rule.

2. **C** Trustees are allowed to delegate authority and may, under certain circumstances, be required to delegate authority to perform their fiduciary duty to their clients.

3. **B** Trustees are instructed to act "in a fair and reasonable manner" under the impartiality standards of both rules.

4. **B** Only statement #2 is true, so Bostwick was correct to agree with her concerning that statement. The other statements are false, so Bostwick was not correct to agree with her concerning statement #1, but he was correct to disagree with her concerning statement #3.

   Statement #1 is false because the old Rule did not allow for the delegation of duty; the new Rule requires it if the manager does not have the relevant investment knowledge. Statement #3 is false because the old Rule did not allow the investment in securities deemed "imprudent," like derivative instruments, while the new Rule allows them as part of the total portfolio approach.

5. **C** The impact of investment decisions on the beneficiary's *tax liability* is a factor the new rule requires. It may be reasonable to consider the beneficiary's personal beliefs and ethical principles, but this is *not* part of the Prudent Investor Rule.

6. **B** The key point of the Prudent Investor Rule is to consider risk in a portfolio context, rather than the non-systematic risk present in individual investments.

7. **C** Feasibility is not part of the Prudent Investor Rule. The fiduciary standards are care, skill, caution, loyalty, and impartiality.

The following is a review of the Quantitative Methods principles designed to address the learning outcome statements set forth by CFA Institute®. This topic is also covered in:

CORRELATION AND REGRESSION

EXAM FOCUS

The first half of this topic is a review of correlation analysis and regression analysis with one independent variable, two widely used tools for quantifying the relationship between two variables. In addition to calculating and interpreting correlation coefficients and regression estimates, you are expected to be able to test for the statistical significance of these measures. The second half of this topic review is a continuation of the material. You are more likely to be tested on your understanding of multiple regression with more than one independent variable, which is the subject of the next topic review. However, this topic review provides an excellent introduction to the basic concepts of regression analysis. Mastery of this material will make the multiple regression material much easier to understand.

 Professor's Note: For more details on hypothesis testing and simple linear regression, please see the volumes from the online Schweser Library that you received free with your purchase of 2009 SchweserNotes.

SAMPLE COVARIANCE

LOS 11.a: Calculate and interpret a sample covariance and a sample correlation coefficient, and interpret a scatter plot.

The **covariance** between two random variables is a statistical measure of the degree to which the two variables move together. The covariance captures the linear relationship between one variable and another. A positive covariance indicates that the variables tend to move together; a negative covariance indicates that the variables tend to move in opposite directions.

The **sample covariance** is calculated as:

$$\text{cov}_{XY} = \frac{\sum_{i=1}^{n}(X_i - \overline{X})(Y_i - \overline{Y})}{n-1}$$

where:

n   = sample size
X_i = *i*th observation on variable X
$\overline{X}$ = mean of the variable X observations
Y_i = *i*th observation on variable Y
$\overline{Y}$ = mean of the variable Y observations

The actual value of the covariance is not very meaningful because its measurement is extremely sensitive to the scale of the two variables. Also, the covariance may range from negative to positive infinity, and it is presented in terms of squared units (e.g., percent squared). For these reasons, we take the additional step of calculating the correlation coefficient, which converts the covariance into a measure that is easier to interpret.

SAMPLE CORRELATION COEFFICIENT

The **correlation coefficient**, *r*, is a measure of the strength of the linear relationship (correlation) between two variables. The correlation coefficient has no unit of measurement; it is a "pure" measure of the tendency of two variables to move together.

The **sample correlation coefficient** for two variables, *X* and *Y*, is calculated as:

$$r_{XY} = \frac{\text{covariance of X and Y}}{(\text{sample standard deviation of X})(\text{sample standard deviation of Y})} = \frac{\text{cov}_{XY}}{(s_X)(s_Y)}$$

The correlation coefficient is bounded by positive and negative one (i.e., $-1 \le r \le +1$), where a correlation coefficient of +1 indicates that changes in the variables are perfectly positively correlated (i.e., they go up and down together, in lock-step). In contrast, if the correlation coefficient is −1, the changes in the variables are perfectly negatively correlated.

Figure 1 provides the data for two variables, *X* and *Y*, and shows the calculation of the correlation between *X* and *Y*.

Figure 1: Procedure for Computing Correlation

Obs.	X	Y	$X - \overline{X}$	$(X - \overline{X})^2$	$Y - \overline{Y}$	$(Y - \overline{Y})^2$	$(X - \overline{X})(Y - \overline{Y})$
1	12	50	−1.50	2.25	8.40	70.56	−12.60
2	13	54	−0.50	0.25	12.40	153.76	−6.20
3	10	48	−3.50	12.25	6.40	40.96	−22.40
4	9	47	−4.50	20.25	5.40	29.16	−24.30
5	20	70	6.50	42.25	28.40	806.56	184.60
6	7	20	−6.50	42.25	−21.60	466.56	140.40
7	4	15	−9.50	90.25	−26.60	707.56	252.70
8	22	40	8.50	72.25	−1.60	2.56	−13.60
9	15	35	1.50	2.25	−6.60	43.56	−9.90
10	23	37	9.50	90.25	−4.60	21.16	−43.70
Sum	135	416	0.00	374.50	0.00	2,342.40	445.00

$$\overline{X} = 135 / 10 = 13.5 \qquad\qquad s_X^2 = 374.5 / 9 = 41.611$$

$$\overline{Y} = 416 / 10 = 41.6 \qquad\qquad s_Y^2 = 2{,}342.4 / 9 = 260.267$$

Using the information in Figure 1, the sample correlation coefficient for variables X and Y may be calculated as:

$$r_{XY} = \frac{\dfrac{445}{9}}{\sqrt{41.611}\sqrt{260.267}} = \frac{49.444}{(6.451)(16.133)} = 0.475$$

The interpretation of the possible correlation values is summarized in Figure 2.

Figure 2: Interpretation of Correlation Coefficients

Correlation Coefficient (r)	Interpretation
r = +1	perfect positive correlation
0 < r < +1	a positive linear relationship
r = 0	no linear relationship
−1 < r < 0	a negative linear relationship
r = −1	perfect negative correlation

A scatter plot is a collection of points on a graph where each point represents the values of two variables (i.e., an X/Y pair). Figure 3 shows several scatter plots for the two random variables X and Y and the corresponding interpretation of correlation. As shown, an upward-sweeping scatter plot indicates a positive correlation between the two variables, while a downward sweeping plot implies a negative correlation. Also illustrated in Figure 3 is that as we move from left to right in the rows of scatter plots, the extent of the linear relationship between the two variables deteriorates, and the correlation gets closer to zero. Note that for r = 1 and r = –1 the data points lie exactly on a line, but the slope of that line is not necessarily +1 or –1.

Figure 3: Interpretations of Correlation

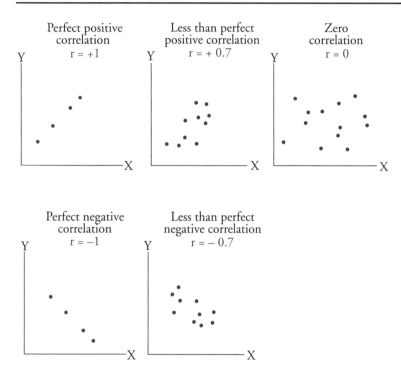

INTERPRETING A SCATTER PLOT

Suppose we wish to graphically represent the data for the returns on Stock A and returns on a market index over the last six months, shown in Figure 4. Figure 5 shows the data graphically with the returns on Stock A on the Y-axis and the returns on the market index on the X-axis. Each point of the scatter plot in Figure 5 represents one month of the six in our sample. The rightmost point in the scatter plot is for the month of March, a 2.0% return on the market index and a 1.8% return on Stock A.

Figure 4: Monthly Returns Data

Month	Return on Stock A	Return on Market Index
Jan	+0.8%	+1.2%
Feb	+0.6%	+0.5%
Mar	+1.8%	+2.0%
Apr	−0.7%	−0.9%
May	+0.3%	+0.2%
June	−0.1%	−0.5%

Figure 5: A Scatter Plot of Returns

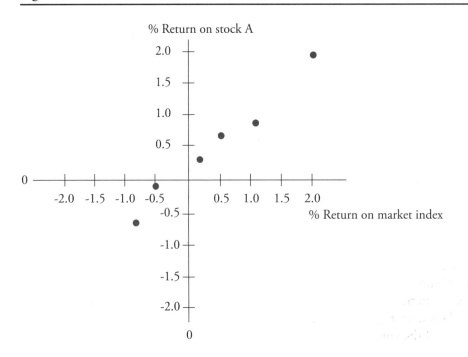

Notice that returns on Stock A appear to be positively correlated with the market index returns.

LIMITATIONS TO CORRELATION ANALYSIS

LOS 11.b: Explain the limitations to correlation analysis, including outliers and spurious correlation.

Limitations to correlation analysis include the impact of outliers, the potential for spurious correlation, and nonlinear relationships.

Outliers

Computed correlation coefficients, as well as other sample statistics, may be affected by outliers. Outliers represent a few extreme values for sample observations. Relative to the rest of the sample data, the value of an outlier may be extraordinarily large or small. Outliers can result in apparent statistical evidence that a significant relationship exists when, in fact, there is none, or that there is no relationship when, in fact, there is a relationship.

Spurious Correlation

Spurious correlation refers to the appearance of a causal linear relationship when, in fact, there is no relation. Certain data items may be highly correlated purely by chance. For example, suppose that you compute the correlation coefficient for historical stock prices and snowfall totals in Minnesota and get a statistically significant relationship—especially for the month of January. Obviously there is no economic explanation for this relationship, so this would be considered a spurious correlation.

Nonlinear Relationships

Correlation measures the *linear* relationship between two variables. That's why in the first panel of Figure 3 that the data points lie perfectly on a straight line when the two variables are perfectly positively correlated. For example, $Y = 6 - 3X$ is a linear relationship. However, two variables could have a *nonlinear* relationship such as $Y = (3X - 6)^2$ and the correlation coefficient would be close to zero. Therefore another limitation of correlation analysis is that it does not capture strong nonlinear relationships between variables.

HYPOTHESIS TESTING OF THE CORRELATION COEFFICIENT

LOS 11.c: Formulate a test of the hypothesis that the population correlation coefficient equals zero, and determine whether the hypothesis is rejected at a given level of significance.

As indicated earlier, the closer the correlation coefficient is to plus or minus one, the stronger the correlation. With the exception of these extremes (i.e., $r = \pm 1.0$), we cannot really speak of the strength of the relationship indicated by the correlation coefficient without a statistical test of significance.

For our purposes, we want *to test whether the correlation between the population of two variables is equal to zero*. Using the lower case Greek letter rho (ρ) to represent the population parameter, the appropriate null and alternative hypotheses can be structured as a two-tailed test as follows:

$$H_0: \rho = 0 \text{ versus } H_a: \rho \neq 0$$

Assuming that the two populations are normally distributed, we can use a *t*-test to determine whether the null hypothesis should be rejected. The test statistic is computed using the sample correlation, *r*, with n – 2 degrees of freedom (*df*):

$$t = \frac{r\sqrt{n-2}}{\sqrt{1-r^2}}$$

To make a decision, the calculated test statistic is compared with the critical *t*-value for the appropriate degrees of freedom and level of significance. Bearing in mind that we are conducting a two-tailed test, the decision rule can be stated as:

$$\text{Reject } H_0 \text{ if } +t_{critical} < t, \text{ or } t < -t_{critical}$$

Example: Test of significance for the correlation coefficient

Using the information from the table in Figure 1, determine if the sample correlation is significant at the 5% level of significance.

Answer:

The hypotheses are structured as $H_0 : \rho = 0$ versus $H_a : \rho \neq 0$.

For the sample data in Figure 1, n = 10 and r = 0.475. Using this information, the test statistic can be computed as:

$$t = \frac{0.475\sqrt{8}}{\sqrt{1-0.475^2}} = \frac{1.3435}{0.88} = 1.527$$

The two-tailed critical *t*-values at a 5% level of significance with df = 10 – 2 = 8 are found in the *t*-table to be ±2.306. (Look in the df = 8 row and match that with the p = 0.05 two-tailed level of significance column.)

Since $-2.306 \leq 1.5267 \leq 2.306$ (i.e., $-t_{critical} \leq t \leq +t_{critical}$), the null cannot be rejected. We conclude that the correlation between variables *X* and *Y* is not significantly different than zero at a 5% significance level.

DEPENDENT AND INDEPENDENT VARIABLES

LOS 11.d: Differentiate between the dependent and independent variables in a linear regression.

The purpose of **simple linear regression** is to explain the variation in a dependent variable in terms of the variation in a single independent variable. Here, the term "variation" is interpreted as the degree to which a variable differs from its mean value. Don't confuse variation with variance—they are related but are not the same.

- The **dependent variable** is the variable whose variation is explained by the independent variable. The dependent variable is also referred to as the *explained variable*, the *endogenous variable*, or the *predicted variable*.
- The **independent variable** is the variable used to explain the variation of the dependent variable. The independent variable is also referred to as the *explanatory variable*, the *exogenous variable*, or the *predicting variable*.

> **Example: Dependent vs. independent variables**
>
> Suppose that you want to predict stock returns with GDP growth. Which variable is the independent variable?
>
> **Answer:**
>
> Since GDP is going to be used as a predictor of stock returns, stock returns are being *explained* by GDP. Hence, stock returns are the dependent (explained) variable, and GDP is the independent (explanatory) variable.

Suppose we want to use excess returns on the S&P 500 (the independent variable) to explain the variation in excess returns on Washington Post (WPO) common stock (the dependent variable). Excess return is defined as the difference between the actual return and the return on 1-month Treasury bills.

We would start by creating a scatter plot with WPO excess returns on the vertical axis and S&P 500 excess returns on the horizontal axis. Monthly excess returns for both variables from June 2004 to May 2007 are plotted in Figure 6. For example, look at the point labeled May 2006. In that month the excess return on the S&P 500 was −7.8% and the excess return on WPO common stock was 1.1%.

Figure 6: Scatter Plot of WPO Excess Returns vs. S&P 500 Index Excess Returns

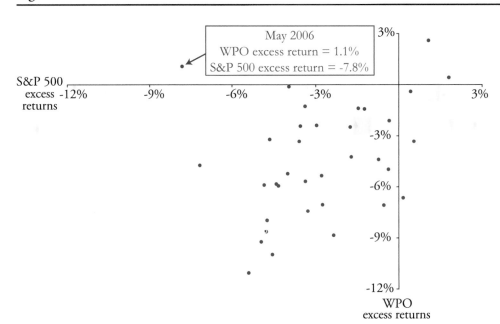

Notice that it appears that the two variables are positively correlated: excess WPO returns tended to be positive (negative) in the same month that S&P 500 excess returns were positive (negative). Note that this is not the case for all the observations, however (including, for example, May 2006). In fact, the correlation between the two is approximately 0.40.

ASSUMPTIONS UNDERLYING LINEAR REGRESSION

LOS 11.e: Explain the assumptions underlying linear regression, and interpret the regression coefficients.

Linear regression requires a number of assumptions. As indicated in the following list, most of the major assumptions pertain to the regression model's residual term (ε).

- A linear relationship exists between the dependent and the independent variable.
- The independent variable is uncorrelated with the residuals.
- The expected value of the residual term is zero ($E(\varepsilon) = 0$).
- The variance of the residual term is constant for all observations $\left(E\left(\varepsilon_i^2\right) = \sigma_\varepsilon^2\right)$.

- The residual term is independently distributed; that is, the residual for one observation is not correlated with that of another observation $\left(E\left(\varepsilon_i\varepsilon_j\right) = 0, j \neq i\right)$.

- The residual term is normally distributed.

SIMPLE LINEAR REGRESSION MODEL

Professor's Note: We'll first calculate the regression coefficients and then interpret them. Note that the LOS does not ask you to calculate regression coefficients; we included that step so you can better understand the interpretation of the coefficients.

The following linear regression model is used to describe the relationship between two variables, X and Y:

$$Y_i = b_0 + b_1 X_i + \varepsilon_i, \; i=1, ..., n$$

where:
Y_i = ith observation of the dependent variable, Y
X_i = ith observation of the independent variable, X
b_0 = regression intercept term
b_1 = regression slope coefficient
ε_i = the residual for the ith observation (also referred to as the disturbance term or error term)

Based on the regression model stated above, the regression process estimates an equation for a line through a scatter plot of the data that "best" explains the observed values for Y in terms of the observed values for X. The linear equation, often called the line of best fit, or regression line, takes the following form:

$$\hat{Y}_i = \hat{b}_0 + \hat{b}_1 X_i, \; i=1, ..., n$$

where:
$\hat{Y}_i$ = the estimated value of Y_i given X_i

$\hat{b}_0$ = the estimated intercept term

$\hat{b}_1$ = the estimated slope coefficient

Professor's Note: The hat "^" above a variable or parameter indicates a predicted value.

The regression line is just one of the many possible lines that can be drawn through the scatter plot of X and Y. In fact, the criteria used to estimate this line forms the very essence of linear regression. The regression line is the line for which the estimates of $\hat{b}_0$ and $\hat{b}_1$ are such that the sum of the squared differences (vertical distances) between the Y-values predicted by the regression equation ($\hat{Y}_i = \hat{b}_0 + \hat{b}_1 X_i$) and actual Y-values, Y_i, is minimized. The sum of the squared vertical distances between the estimated and actual Y-values is referred to as the **sum of squared errors** (SSE).

Thus, the regression line is the line that minimizes the SSE. This explains why simple linear regression is frequently referred to as *ordinary least squares* (OLS) regression, and the values estimated by the estimated regression equation, $\hat{Y}_i$, are called least squares estimates.

The estimated **slope coefficient** ($\hat{b}_1$) for the regression line describes the change in Y for a one unit change in X. It can be positive, negative, or zero, depending on the relationship between the regression variables. The slope term is calculated as:

$$\hat{b}_1 = \frac{\text{cov}_{XY}}{\sigma_X^2}$$

 Professor's Note: For the exam, know that the slope equals covariance divided by variance.

The **intercept** term ($\hat{b}_0$) is the line's intersection with the Y-axis at $X = 0$. It can be positive, negative, or zero. A property of the least squares method is that the intercept term may be expressed as:

$$\hat{b}_0 = \overline{Y} - \hat{b}_1 \overline{X}$$

where:
$\overline{Y}$ = the mean of Y
$\overline{X}$ = the mean of X

The intercept equation highlights the fact that the regression line passes through a point with coordinates equal to the mean of the independent and dependent variables (i.e., the point $\overline{X}, \overline{Y}$).

Example: Computing the slope coefficient and intercept term

Compute the slope coefficient and intercept term for the WPO regression example using the following information:

cov(S&P 500, WPO) = 0.000336 $\overline{\text{S\&P 500}}$ = −2.70%

var(S&P 500)   = 0.000522 $\overline{\text{WPO}}$ = −4.05%

Answer:

The slope coefficient is calculated as $\hat{b}_1$ = 0.000336/0.000522 = 0.64.

The intercept term is:

$$\hat{b}_0 = \overline{\text{WPO}} - \hat{b}_1 \, \overline{\text{S\&P 500}} = -4.05\% - 0.64(-2.70\%) = -2.3\%$$

The estimated regression line that minimizes the SSE in our WPO stock return example is shown in Figure 7.

This regression line has an intercept of −2.3% and a slope of 0.64. The model predicts that if the S&P 500 excess return is −7.8% (what it was in May 2006), then the WPO excess return would be −2.3% + (0.64)(−7.8%) = −7.3%. The residual for May 2006 is

8.4%, which is the difference between the actual WPO return (1.1%) and the predicted return (–7.3%).

Figure 7: Estimated Regression Equation for WPO vs. S&P 500

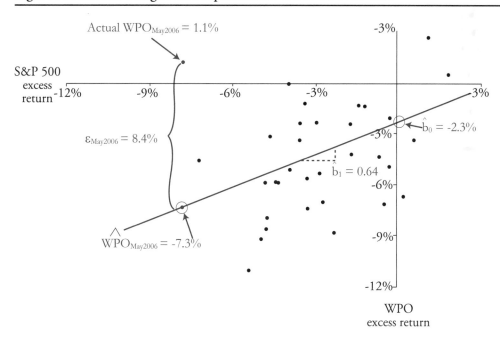

INTERPRETING A REGRESSION COEFFICIENT

The estimated intercept represents the value of the dependent variable at the point of intersection of the regression line and the axis of the dependent variable (usually the vertical axis). In other words, the intercept is an estimate of the dependent variable when the independent variable takes on a value of zero.

We also mentioned earlier that the estimated slope coefficient is interpreted as the change in the dependent variable for a 1-unit change in the independent variable. For example, an estimated slope coefficient of 2 would indicate that the dependent variable will change two units for every 1-unit change in the independent variable.

Example: Interpreting regression coefficients

In the WPO regression example, the estimated slope coefficient was 0.64 and the estimated intercept term was –2.3%. Interpret each coefficient estimate.

Answer:

The slope coefficient of 0.64 can be interpreted to mean that when excess S&P 500 returns increase (decrease) by 1% WPO excess returns increase (decrease) by 0.64%.

The intercept term of –2.3% can be interpreted to mean that when the excess return on the S&P 500 is zero, the return on WPO stock is –2.3%.

Professor's Note: As we will discuss in Study Session 18, the slope coefficient in a regression like this is called the stock's beta, and it measures the relative amount of systematic risk in WPO's returns. Notice that WPO is less risky than average, because its returns tend to increase or decrease by less than the change in the market returns. A stock with a beta of one would have an average level of systematic risk and a stock with a beta greater than one would have more than average systematic risk.

The intercept term in this regression is called the stock's ex-post alpha. It is a measure of excess risk-adjusted returns. A negative ex-post alpha means that WPO underperformed the S&P 500 on a risk-adjusted basis over the time period.

Keep in mind, however, that any conclusions regarding the importance of an independent variable in explaining a dependent variable require determining the statistical significance of the slope coefficient. Simply looking at the magnitude of the slope coefficient does not address the issue of the importance of the variable. A hypothesis test must be conducted, or a confidence interval must be formed, to assess the importance of the variable.

STANDARD ERROR OF ESTIMATE

LOS 11.f: Calculate and interpret the standard error of estimate, the coefficient of determination, and a confidence interval for a regression coefficient.

The **standard error of estimate** (SEE) measures the degree of variability of the actual Y-values relative to the estimated Y-values from a regression equation. The SEE gauges the "fit" of the regression line. *The smaller the standard error, the better the fit.*

The SEE is the standard deviation of the error terms in the regression. As such, SEE is also referred to as the standard error of the residual, or standard error of the regression.

In some regressions, the relationship between the independent and dependent variables is very strong (e.g., the relationship between 10-year Treasury bond yields and mortgage rates). In other cases, the relationship is much weaker (e.g., the relationship between stock returns and inflation). SEE will be low (relative to total variability) if the relationship is very strong and high if the relationship is weak.

COEFFICIENT OF DETERMINATION (R^2)

The **coefficient of determination** (R^2) is defined as the percentage of the total variation in the dependent variable explained by the independent variable. For example, an R^2 of 0.63 indicates that the variation of the independent variable explains 63% of the variation in the dependent variable.

Professor's Note: For simple linear regression (i.e., one independent variable), the coefficient of determination, R^2, may be computed by simply squaring the correlation coefficient, r. In other words, $R^2 = r^2$, for regression with one independent variable. This approach is not appropriate when more than one independent variable is used in the regression, as is the case with the multiple regression techniques presented in the next topic review.

We will show you how to calculate the SEE and the R^2 using an ANOVA table in LOS 11.i.

REGRESSION COEFFICIENT CONFIDENCE INTERVAL

Hypothesis testing for a regression coefficient may use the confidence interval for the coefficient being tested. For instance, a frequently asked question is whether an estimated slope coefficient is statistically different from zero. In other words, the null hypothesis is H_0: $b_1 = 0$ and the alternative hypothesis is H_a: $b_1 \neq 0$. If the confidence interval at the desired level of significance does not include zero, the null is rejected, and the coefficient is said to be statistically different from zero.

The confidence interval for the regression coefficient, b_1, is calculated as:

$$\hat{b}_1 \pm \left(t_c \times s_{\hat{b}_1} \right), \text{ or } \left[\hat{b}_1 - \left(t_c \times s_{\hat{b}_1} \right) < b_1 < \hat{b}_1 + \left(t_c \times s_{\hat{b}_1} \right) \right]$$

In this expression, t_c is the critical two-tailed *t*-value for the selected confidence level with the appropriate number of degrees of freedom, which is equal to the number of sample observations minus 2 (i.e., n – 2).

The standard error of the regression coefficient is denoted as $s_{\hat{b}_1}$. It is a function of the SEE: as SEE rises, $s_{\hat{b}_1}$ also increases, and the confidence interval widens. This makes sense because SEE measures the variability of the data about the regression line, and the more variable the data, the less confidence there is in the regression model to estimate a coefficient.

Professor's Note: It is highly unlikely you will have to calculate $s_{\hat{b}_1}$ on the exam. It is included in the output of all statistical software packages and should be given to you if you need it.

Although the confidence interval for regression parameters looks slightly different than what you've seen at Level 1, it is precisely the same concept. All confidence intervals take the predicted value, then add and subtract the critical test statistic times the variability of the parameter estimate.

Example: Calculating the confidence interval for a regression coefficient

The estimated slope coefficient, b_1, from the WPO regression is 0.64 with a standard error equal to 0.26. Assuming that the sample had 36 observations, calculate the 95% confidence interval for b_1.

Answer:

The confidence interval for b_1 is:

$$\hat{b}_1 \pm \left(t_c \times s_{\hat{b}_1}\right), \text{ or } \left[\hat{b}_1 - \left(t_c \times s_{\hat{b}_1}\right) < b_1 < \hat{b}_1 + \left(t_c \times s_{\hat{b}_1}\right)\right]$$

The critical two-tail t-values are ± 2.03 (from the t-table with n – 2 = 34 degrees of freedom). We can compute the 95% confidence interval as:

$$0.64 \pm (2.03)(0.26) = 0.64 \pm 0.53 = 0.11 \text{ to } 1.17$$

Since this confidence interval does not include zero, we can conclude that the slope coefficient is significantly different from zero.

REGRESSION COEFFICIENT t-TEST

LOS 11.g: Formulate a null and alternative hypothesis about a population value of a regression coefficient, select the appropriate test statistic, and determine whether the null hypothesis is rejected at a given level of significance.

A t-test may also be used to test the hypothesis that the true slope coefficient, b_1, is equal to some hypothesized value. Letting $\hat{b}_1$ be the point estimate for b_1, the appropriate test statistic with n – 2 degrees of freedom is:

$$t_{b_1} = \frac{\hat{b}_1 - b_1}{s_{\hat{b}_1}}$$

The decision rule for tests of significance for regression coefficients is:

Reject H_0 if $t > +t_{critical}$ or $t < -t_{critical}$

Rejection of the null means that the slope coefficient is *different* from the hypothesized value of b_1.

To test whether an independent variable explains the variation in the dependent variable (i.e., it is statistically significant), the hypothesis that is tested is whether the true slope is zero ($b_1 = 0$). The appropriate test structure for the null and alternative hypotheses is:

H_0: $b_1 = 0$ versus H_a: $b_1 \neq 0$

Example: Hypothesis test for significance of regression coefficients

The estimated slope coefficient from the WPO example is 0.64 with a standard error equal to 0.26. Assuming that the sample has 36 observations, determine if the estimated slope coefficient is significantly different than zero at a 5% level of significance.

Answer:

The calculated test statistic is $t = \dfrac{\hat{b}_1 - b_1}{s_{\hat{b}_1}} = \dfrac{0.64 - 0}{0.26} = 2.46$

The critical two-tailed *t*-values are ± 2.03 (from the *t*-table with df = 36 – 2 = 34). Since $t > t_{critical}$ (i.e., 2.46 > 2.03), we reject the null hypothesis and conclude that the slope is different from zero. Note that the *t*-test and the confidence interval lead to the same conclusion to reject the null hypothesis and conclude that the slope coefficient is statistically significant.

PREDICTED VALUE OF THE DEPENDENT VARIABLE

LOS 11.h: Calculate a predicted value for the dependent variable, given an estimated regression model and a value for the independent variable, and calculate and interpret a confidence interval for the predicted value of a dependent variable.

Predicted values are values of the dependent variable based on the estimated regression coefficients and a prediction about the value of the independent variable. They are the values that are *predicted* by the regression equation, given an estimate of the independent variable.

For a simple regression, the predicted (or forecast) value of *Y* is:

$$\hat{Y} = \hat{b}_0 + \hat{b}_1 X_p$$

where:
$\hat{Y}$ = predicted value of the dependent variable
X_p = forecasted value of the independent variable

Example: Predicting the Dependent Variable

Given the WPO regression equation:

$$\widehat{WPO} = -2.3\% + (0.64)\,(\widehat{S\&P\ 500})$$

Calculate the predicted value of WPO excess returns if forecasted S&P 500 excess returns are 10%.

Answer:

The predicted value for WPO excess returns is determined as follows:

$$\widehat{WPO} = -2.3\% + (0.64)(10\%) = 4.1\%$$

CONFIDENCE INTERVALS FOR PREDICTED VALUES

Professor's Note: Just about everything we do in this topic review related to simple linear regression will be repeated in the next topic review on multiple linear regression. However, you are only responsible for being able to calculate a confidence interval for the predicted value in simple linear regression, not multiple regression.

Confidence intervals for the predicted value of a dependent variable are calculated in a manner similar to the confidence interval for the regression coefficients. The equation for the confidence interval for a predicted value of Y is:

$$\hat{Y} \pm \left(t_c \times s_f\right) \Rightarrow \left[\hat{Y} - \left(t_c \times s_f\right) < Y < \hat{Y} + \left(t_c \times s_f\right)\right]$$

where:
t_c = the two-tailed critical *t*-value at the desired level of significance with df = n – 2
s_f = the standard error of the forecast

The challenge with computing a confidence interval for a predicted value is calculating s_f. It's highly unlikely that you will have to calculate the standard error of the forecast (it will probably be provided if you need to compute a confidence interval for the dependent variable). However, if you do need to calculate s_f, it can be done with the following formula for the variance of the forecast:

$$s_f^2 = SEE^2 \left[1 + \frac{1}{n} + \frac{(X - \bar{X})^2}{(n-1)s_x^2}\right]$$

where:
SEE^2 = variance of the residuals = the square of the standard error of estimate
s_x^2 = variance of the independent variable
X = value of the independent variable for which the forecast was made

Professor's Note: This equation implies that the standard error of the forecast is larger than the SEE, but the difference between the two decreases as the number of observations increases, all else equal. If you are asked on the exam to calculate a confidence interval for a predicted value and the sample size is large, you'll get closer to the correct answer by using SEE^2 rather than s_f^2.

Example: Confidence interval for a predicted value

Calculate a 95% prediction interval on the predicted value of WPO from the previous example. Assume the standard error of the forecast is 3.67, and the forecasted value of S&P 500 excess returns is 10%.

Answer:

The predicted value for WPO is:

$$\widehat{WPO} = -2.3\% + (0.64)(10\%) = 4.1\%$$

The 5% two-tailed critical t-value with 34 degrees of freedom is 2.04. The prediction interval at the 95% confidence level is:

$$\widehat{WPO} \pm (t_c \times s_f) \Rightarrow \left[4.1\% \pm (2.04 \times 3.67\%) \right] = 4.1\% \pm 7.5\%$$

or

$$-3.4\% \text{ to } 11.6\%$$

This range can be interpreted as, given a forecasted value for S&P 500 excess returns of 10%, we can be 95% confident that the WPO excess returns will be between −3.4% and 11.6%.

ANALYSIS OF VARIANCE

LOS 11.i: Describe the use of analysis of variance (ANOVA) in regression analysis, interpret ANOVA results, and calculate and interpret an F-statistic.

Analysis of variance (ANOVA) is a statistical procedure for analyzing the total variability of a data set. Let's define some terms before we move on to ANOVA tables.

- **Total sum of squares** (SST) *measures the total variation* in the dependent variable. SST is equal to the sum of the squared differences between the actual Y-values and the mean of Y:

$$SST = \sum_{i=1}^{n} (Y_i - \overline{Y})^2$$

- **Regression sum of squares** (RSS) *measures the variation in the dependent variable explained by the independent variable.* RSS is the sum of the squared distances between the predicted Y-values and the mean of Y.

$$RSS = \sum_{i=1}^{n} (\hat{Y}_i - \overline{Y})^2$$

- **Sum of squared errors** (SSE) *measures the unexplained variation* in the dependent variable. It's also known as the sum of squared residuals or the residual sum of squares. SSE is the sum of the squared vertical distances between the actual Y-values and the predicted Y-values on the regression line.

$$SSE = \sum_{i=1}^{n} (Y_i - \hat{Y}_i)^2$$

 Professor's Note: You don't have to memorize the formulas for the sums of squares. You do need to know what they measure and how you use them to construct an ANOVA table.

Thus, total variation = explained variation + unexplained variation, or:

SST = RSS + SSE

Figure 8 illustrates how the total variation in the dependent variable (SST) is composed of RSS and SSE.

Figure 8: Components of the Total Variation

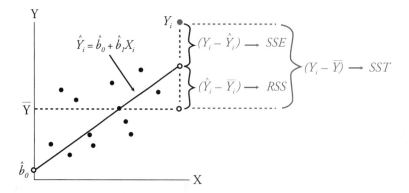

The output of the ANOVA procedure is an ANOVA table, which is a summary of the variation in the dependent variable. ANOVA tables are included in the regression output of many statistical software packages. You can think of the ANOVA table as the source of the data for the computation of many of the regression concepts discussed in this topic review. A generic ANOVA table for a simple linear regression (one independent variable) is presented in Figure 9.

Figure 9: ANOVA Table

Source of Variation	Degrees of Freedom	Sum of Squares	Mean Sum of Squares
Regression (explained)	k = 1	RSS	$\text{MSR} = \dfrac{\text{RSS}}{\text{k}} = \dfrac{\text{RSS}}{1} = \text{RSS}$
Error (unexplained)	n − 2	SSE	$\text{MSE} = \dfrac{\text{SSE}}{\text{n} - 2}$
Total	n − 1	SST	

Professor's Note: k *is the number of slope parameters estimated and* n *is the number of observations. In general, the regression df = k and the error df = (n − k − 1). Since we are limited to simple linear regressions in this topic review (one independent variable) we use k = 1 for the regression df and n − 1 − 1 = n − 2 for the error df.*

The mean regression sum of squares (MSR) and mean squared error (MSE) are simply calculated as the appropriate sum of squares divided by its degrees of freedom.

Calculating R² and SEE ~~Coefficient of Determination~~

The R² and the standard error of estimate (SEE) can also be calculated directly from the ANOVA table as we discussed in LOS 11.f. The R² is the percentage of the total variation in the dependent variable explained by the independent variable:

$$R^2 = \frac{\text{total variation } (\text{SST}) - \text{unexplained variation } (\text{SSE})}{\text{total variation } (\text{SST})}$$

$$= \frac{\text{explained variation } (\text{RSS})}{\text{total variation } (\text{SST})}$$

The SEE is the standard deviation of the regression error terms, and is equal to the square root of the mean squared error (MSE):

$$\text{SEE} = \sqrt{\text{MSE}} = \sqrt{\frac{\text{SSE}}{\text{n} - 2}}$$

Professor's Note: Make sure you recognize the distinction between the sum of squared errors (SSE) and the standard error of estimate (SEE). SSE is the sum of the squared residuals, while SEE is the standard deviation of the residuals.

Example: Using the ANOVA table

Complete the ANOVA table for the WPO regression example and calculate the R^2 and the standard error of estimate (SEE).

Partial ANOVA Table For WPO Regression Example

Source of Variation	Degrees of Freedom	Sum of Squares	Mean Sum of Squares
Regression (explained)	?	0.00756	?
Error (unexplained)	?	0.04064	?
Total	?	?	

Answer:

Recall that the data included three years of monthly return observations, so the total number of observations (n) is 36.

Completed ANOVA Table For WPO Regression Example

Source of Variation	Degrees of Freedom	Sum of Squares	Mean Sum of Squares
Regression (explained)	1	0.0076	0.0076
Error (unexplained)	34	0.0406	0.0012
Total	35	0.0482	

$$R^2 = \frac{\text{explained variation (RSS)}}{\text{total variation (SST)}} = \frac{0.0076}{0.0482} = 0.158$$

$$SEE = \sqrt{MSE} = \sqrt{0.0012} = 0.035$$

THE *F*-STATISTIC

An *F*-test assesses how well a set of independent variables, as a group, explains the variation in the dependent variable. In multiple regression, the *F*-statistic is used to test whether *at least one* independent variable in a set of independent variables explains a significant portion of the variation of the dependent variable. We will discuss the use of the *F*-test in multiple regression with more than one independent variable in the next topic review.

The *F*-statistic is calculated as:

$$F = \frac{MSR}{MSE} = \frac{RSS/k}{SSE/n-k-1}$$

where:
MSR = mean regression sum of squares
MSE = mean squared error

Important: This is always a one-tailed test!

In multiple regression, the *F*-statistic tests *all* independent variables as a group.

The *F*-Statistic With One Independent Variable

For simple linear regression, there is only one independent variable, so the *F*-test tests the same hypothesis as the *t*-test for statistical significance of the slope coefficient:

$$H_0: b_1 = 0 \text{ versus } H_a: b_1 \neq 0$$

To determine whether b_1 is statistically significant using the *F*-test, the calculated *F*-statistic is compared with the critical *F*-value, F_c, at the appropriate level of significance. The degrees of freedom for the numerator and denominator with one independent variable are:

$$df_{numerator} = k = 1$$

$$df_{denominator} = n - k - 1 = n - 2$$

where:
n = number of observations

The decision rule for the *F*-test is:

Decision rule: reject H_0 if $F > F_c$

Rejection of the null hypothesis at a stated level of significance indicates that the independent variable is significantly different than zero, which is interpreted to mean that it makes a significant contribution to the explanation of the dependent variable. In simple linear regression, it tells us the same thing as the *t*-test of the slope coefficient (t_{b_1}). In fact, in simple linear regression with one independent variable, $F = t_{b_1}^2$.

Example: Calculating and interpreting the *F*-statistic

Use the completed ANOVA table from the previous example to calculate and interpret the *F*-statistic. Test the null hypothesis at the 5% significance level that the slope coefficient is equal to 0.

Answer:

$$F = \frac{MSR}{MSE} = \frac{0.0076}{0.0012} = 6.33$$

$$df_{numerator} = k = 1$$

$$df_{denominator} = n - k - 1 = 36 - 1 - 1 = 34$$

The null and alternative hypotheses are: H_0: $b_1 = 0$ versus H_a: $b_1 \neq 0$. The critical F-value for 1 and 34 degrees of freedom at a 5% significance level is approximately 4.1. Remember, it's a one-tail test, so we use the 5% F-table! Therefore we can reject the null hypothesis and conclude that the slope coefficient is significantly different than zero. Recall from the earlier examples that we also rejected the null hypothesis using the t-statistic and that the 95% confidence interval did not include 0. Note that here, $t^2 = 2.46^2 \approx F = 6.33$. The difference is due to rounding of the t-statistic to two decimal places.

 Professor's Note: The bottom line is that the F-test is not as useful when we only have one independent variable because it tells us the same thing as the t-test of the slope coefficient. Make sure you know that fact for the exam, and then concentrate on the application of the F-test in multiple regression.

LOS 11.j: Discuss the limitations of regression analysis.

Limitations of regression analysis include the following:

- Regression relations change over time. This means that the estimation equation based on data from a specific time period may not be relevant for forecasts or predictions in another time period. This is referred to as *parameter instability*.
- Even if the regression model accurately reflects the historical relationship between the two variables, its usefulness in investment analysis will be limited if other market participants are also aware of and act on this evidence.
- If the assumptions of regression analysis are not valid, the interpretation and tests of hypotheses are not valid. For example, the regression assumptions are violated if the data is *heteroskedastic* (non-constant variance of the error terms) or exhibits *autocorrelation* (error terms are not independent). We will discuss these issues in much more detail in the next topic review.

KEY CONCEPTS

LOS 11.a

A scatter plot is a collection of points on a graph where each point represents the values of two variables (i.e., an X/Y pair).

The sample covariance, cov_{XY}, measures the linear relationship between two random variables and is calculated as:

$$\frac{\sum_{i=1}^{N}(X_i - \bar{X})(Y_i - \bar{Y})}{n-1}$$

Sample correlation is a measure of the relationship between two variables:

$$r_{XY} = \frac{cov_{XY}}{(s_X)(s_Y)}, \text{ which takes on values from } -1.0 \text{ to } +1.0$$

LOS 11.b

There are three limitations of correlation analysis.

* Outliers, or values that are unusually large or small, may influence the results of regression and the estimate of the correlation coefficient.
* Spurious correlation means that there may appear to be a relationship between two variables when, in fact, there is none.
* Correlation only measures linear relationships, but not nonlinear ones.

LOS 11.c

A *t*-test is used to determine if a correlation coefficient, *r*, is statistically significant:

$$t = \frac{r\sqrt{n-2}}{\sqrt{1-r^2}}$$

Significance is supported if the test statistic is less than $-t_{critical}$ or greater than $t_{critical}$ with n – 2 degrees of freedom.

LOS 11.d

Linear regression provides an estimate of the linear relationship between an independent variable (the explanatory variable) and a dependent variable (the predicted variable).

The general form of the linear regression model is $Y_i = b_0 + b_1X_i + \varepsilon_i$.

* Y_i and X_i are the *i*th observation of the dependent and independent variable, respectively.
* b_0 = intercept = the value of Y if X is zero.
* b_1 = slope coefficient = the expected change in Y for a one-unit change in X.
* ε_i = residual error for the *i*th observation.

LOS 11.e

Assumptions made with simple linear regression include:

- A linear relationship exists between the dependent and the independent variable.
- The independent variable is uncorrelated with the residuals.
- The expected value of the residual term is zero ($E(\varepsilon) = 0$).
- The variance of the residual term is constant for all observations $\left(E\left(\varepsilon_i^2\right) = \sigma_\varepsilon^2\right)$.
- The residual term is independently distributed; that is, the residual for one observation is not correlated with that of another observation $\left(E\left(\varepsilon_i \varepsilon_j\right) = 0, j \neq i\right)$.

The regression line, $\hat{Y}_i = \hat{b}_0 + \hat{b}_1 X_i$, is the line through the data that minimizes the sum of the squared vertical distances between Y_i and $\hat{Y}_i$ (i.e. minimize $\sum_{i=1}^{n}(Y_i - \hat{Y}_i)^2$, or SSE).

The estimated intercept, $\hat{b}_0$, represents the value of the dependent variable at the point of intersection of the regression line and the axis of the dependent variable (usually the vertical axis). The estimated slope coefficient, $\hat{b}_1$, is interpreted as the change in the dependent variable for a one-unit change in the independent variable.

The estimated slope coefficient ($\hat{b}_1$) is equal to $\dfrac{\text{cov}_{XY}}{\sigma_X^2}$. The intercept term ($\hat{b}_0$) is calculated as: $\hat{b}_0 = \overline{Y} - \hat{b}_1 \overline{X}$

LOS 11.f

The confidence interval for the regression coefficient, b_1, is calculated as:

$$\hat{b}_1 \pm \left(t_c \times s_{\hat{b}_1}\right), \text{ or } \left[\hat{b}_1 - \left(t_c \times s_{\hat{b}_1}\right) < b_1 < \hat{b}_1 + \left(t_c \times s_{\hat{b}_1}\right)\right]$$

LOS 11.g

A t-test with n – 2 degrees of freedom is used to conduct hypothesis tests of the estimated regression parameters.

$$t = \frac{\hat{b}_1 - b_1}{s_{\hat{b}_1}}$$

LOS 11.h

A predicted value of the dependent variable, $\hat{Y}$, is determined by inserting the predicted value of the independent variable, X_p, in the regression equation and calculating $\hat{Y}_p = \hat{b}_0 + \hat{b}_1 X_p$.

The confidence interval for a predicted Y-value is $\left[\hat{Y} - \left(t_c \times s_f\right) < Y < \hat{Y} + \left(t_c \times s_f\right)\right]$, where s_f is the standard error of the forecast.

LOS 11.i
ANOVA Table for Simple Linear Regression (k = 1)

Source of Variation	Degrees of Freedom	Sum of Squares	Mean Sum of Squares
Regression (explained)	k = 1	RSS	$MSR = \dfrac{RSS}{k} = \dfrac{RSS}{1} = RSS$
Error (unexplained)	n − 2	SSE	$MSE = \dfrac{SSE}{n-2}$
Total	n − 1	SST	

The standard error of the estimate in a simple linear regression is calculated as:

$$SEE = \sqrt{\frac{SSE}{n-2}}$$

The coefficient of determination, R^2, is the proportion of the total variation of the dependent variable explained by the regression:

$$R^2 = \frac{RSS}{SST} = \frac{SST - SSE}{SST}$$

In multiple regression (next topic review) the F-test tests the statistical significance of all of the independent variables.

In simple linear regression, because there is only one independent variable (k=1), the F-test tests the same null hypothesis as testing the statistical significance of b_1, using the t-test: $H_0 : b_1 = 0$ vs. $H_u : b_1 \neq 0$. With only one independent variable, F is calculated as:

$$F\text{-stat} = \frac{MSR}{MSE} \text{ with 1 and n} - 2 \text{ degrees of freedom}$$

In fact, in simple linear regression $F = t_{b_1}^{\,2}$.

LOS 11.j
The limitations of regression analysis include the following:
- Parameter instability (especially when dealing with economic and financial variables).
- The limited usefulness of regression models in identifying profitable investment strategies based on publicly available information.
- The possibility of violating the assumptions underlying regression analysis (heteroskedasticity and autocorrelation).

CONCEPT CHECKERS

Use the following data to answer Questions 1 through 3.

An analyst is given the data in the following table for a regression of the annual sales for Company XYZ, a maker of paper products, on paper product industry sales.

Regression Output

Parameters	Coefficient	Standard Error of the Coefficient
Intercept	–94.88	32.97
Slope (industry sales)	0.2796	0.0363

The correlation between company and industry sales is 0.9757. The regression was based on five observations.

1. Which of the following is *closest* to the value and reports the *most likely* interpretation of the R^2 for this regression? The R^2 is:
    A. 0.048, indicating that the variability of industry sales explains about 4.8% of the variability of company sales.
    B. 0.952, indicating that the variability of industry sales explains about 95.2% of the variability of company sales.
    C. 0.952, indicating that the variability of company sales explains about 95.2% of the variability of industry sales.

2. Based on the regression results, XYZ Company's market share of any increase in industry sales is expected to be *closest* to:
    A. 4%.
    B. 28%.
    C. 45%.

3. The analyst determines that the *t*-statistic is 7.72 and that the correlation coefficient is not significant (using 95% confidence). Is the analyst correct?
    A. Yes.
    B. No, because the test statistic is 60.93.
    C. No, because the correlation coefficient is significantly different from zero (using 95% confidence).

$$t = \frac{\sigma\sqrt{n-2}}{\sqrt{1-r^2}} = \frac{.9757\sqrt{3}}{\sqrt{1-.952}} = \frac{1.69}{.21} = 7.72$$

crit
± 3.182

Use the following information to answer Questions 4 and 5.

A study was conducted by the British Department of Transportation to estimate urban travel time between locations in London, England. Data was collected for motorcycles and passenger cars. Simple linear regression was conducted using data sets for both types of vehicles, where Y = urban travel time in minutes and X = distance between locations in kilometers. The following results were obtained:

Regression Results for Travel Times Between Distances in London		
Passenger cars:	$\hat{Y} = 1.85 + 3.86X$	$R^2 = 0.758$
Motorcycles:	$\hat{Y} = 2.50 + 1.93X$	$R^2 = 0.676$

4. The estimated increase in travel time for a motorcycle commuter planning to move 8 km farther from his workplace in London is *closest* to:
    A. 31 minutes.
    B. 15 minutes.
    C. 0.154 hours.

5. Based on the regression results, which model is more reliable?
    A. The passenger car model because 3.86 > 1.93.
    B. The motorcycle model because 1.93 < 3.86.
    C. The passenger car model because 0.758 > 0.676.

6. Which of the following is not a necessary assumption of simple linear regression analysis?
    A. The residuals are normally distributed.
    B. There is a constant variance of the error term.
    C. The dependent variable is uncorrelated with the residuals.

7. Which of the following statements regarding simple linear regression is *most accurate*?
    A. If the units of the independent variable are tons instead of pounds the estimated slope coefficient will be 2,000 times larger.
    B. If the slope of the regression line is +1, the variables are perfectly positively correlated.
    C. If a researcher knows the sum of squared errors, the number of observations, and the standard error of estimate he can calculate the coefficient of determination for the regression.

8. What is the *most appropriate* interpretation of a slope coefficient estimate equal to 10.0?
    A. The predicted value of the dependent variable when the independent variable is zero is 10.0.
    B. For every one unit change in the independent variable the model predicts that the dependent variable will change by 10 units.
    C. For every one unit change in the independent variable the model predicts that the dependent variable will change by 0.1 units.

9. What is the appropriate alternative hypothesis to test the statistical significance of the intercept term in the following regression?

$$Y = a_1 + a_2(X) + \varepsilon$$

A. $H_A: a_1 \neq 0$.
B. $H_A: a_1 > 0$.
C. $H_A: a_2 \neq 0$.

10. Consider the following statement: In a simple linear regression, the appropriate degrees of freedom for the critical t-value used to calculate a confidence interval around both a parameter estimate and a predicted Y-value is the same as the number of observations minus two. The statement is:
A. justified.
B. not justified, because the appropriate of degrees of freedom used to calculate a confidence interval around a parameter estimate is the number of observations.
C. not justified, because the appropriate of degrees of freedom used to calculate a confidence interval around a predicted Y-value is the number of observations.

11. The variation in the dependent variable explained by the independent variable is measured by the:
A. mean squared error.
B. sum of squared errors.
C. regression sum of squares.

CHALLENGE PROBLEMS

Use the following information for Questions 12 through 17.

Bill Coldplay, CFA, is analyzing the performance of the Vanguard Growth Index Fund (VIGRX) over the past three years. The fund employs a passive management investment approach designed to track the performance of the MSCI US Prime Market Growth index, a broadly diversified index of growth stocks of large U.S. companies.

Coldplay estimates a regression using excess monthly returns on VIGRX (exVIGRX) as the dependent variable and excess monthly returns on the S&P 500 index (exS&P) as the independent variable. The data are expressed in decimal terms (e.g., 0.03, not 3%).

$$exVIGRX_t = b_0 + b_1(exS\&P_t) + \varepsilon_t$$

A scatter plot of excess returns for both return series from June 2004 to May 2007 are shown in the following figure.

Analysis of Large Cap Growth Fund

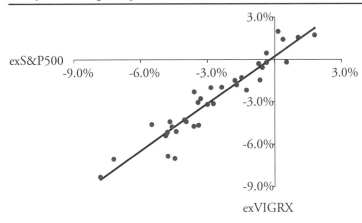

Results from that analysis are presented in the following figures.

Estimated Coefficients

Coefficient	Coefficient Estimate	Standard Error
b_0	0.0023	0.0022
b_1	1.1163	0.0624

Partial ANOVA Table

Source of Variation	Sum of Squares
Regression (explained)	0.0228
Error (unexplained)	0.0024

12. The 90% confidence interval for b_0 is *closest* to:
    A. −0.0014 to +0.0060.
    B. −0.0006 to +0.0052.
    C. +0.0001 to +0.0045.

13. Are the intercept term and the slope coefficient statistically significantly different from zero at the 5% significance level?

	Intercept term significant?	Slope coefficient significant?
A.	Yes	Yes
B.	Yes	No
C.	No	Yes

14. Coldplay would like to test the following hypothesis: H_0: $b_1 \leq 1$ vs. H_1: $b_1 > 1$ at the 1% significance level. The calculated *t*-statistic and the appropriate conclusion are:

	Calculated *t*-statistic	Appropriate conclusion
A.	1.86	Reject H_0
B.	1.86	Fail to reject H_0
C.	2.44	Reject H_0

15. Coldplay forecasts the excess return on the S&P 500 for June 2007 to be 5% and the 95% confidence interval for the predicted value of the excess return on VIGRX for June 2007 to be 3.9% to 7.7%. The standard error of the forecast is *closest* to:
    A. 0.0080.
    B. 0.0093.
    C. 0.0111.

16. The R^2 from the regression is *closest* to:
    A. 0.095.
    B. 0.295.
    C. 0.905.

17. The standard error of estimate (SEE) is *closest* to:
    A. 0.008.
    B. 0.014.
    C. 0.049.

18. Which of the following statements *least* accurately describes a limitation of correlation analysis?
    A. Outliers may influence the results of regression.
    B. Serial correlation means that there may appear to be a relationship between two or more variables when, in fact, there is none.
    C. Correlation only measures linear relationships, but not nonlinear ones.

19. Regression analysis is *least likely* to be limited by:
    A. parameter instability.
    B. insufficient data.
    C. violations of the assumptions underlying regression analysis.

20. Carla Preusser finds that the total assets under management by a popular hedge fund manager, and the number of lizards lying out in the sun in a nearby park, can be modeled as functions of time: $f(x) = t^{1.8}$ and $f(y) = t + 5$ respectively. The correlation between the two models is 0.98. Two potential problems with using the lizards to predict total assets include:

A. spurious correlation and the non-linear relationship in the total assets function.

B. spurious correlation and the non-geometric relationship in the lizard function.

C. outliers and non-linear relationship in the total assets function.

ANSWERS – CONCEPT CHECKERS

1. **B** The R^2 is computed as the correlation squared: $(0.9757)^2 = 0.952$.

   The interpretation of this R^2 is that 95.2% of the variation in Company XYZ's sales is explained by the variation in industry sales. Answer C is incorrect because it is the independent variable (industry sales) that explains the variation in the dependent variable (company sales). This interpretation is based on the economic reasoning used in constructing the regression model.

2. **B** The slope coefficient of 0.2796 indicates that a $1 million increase in industry sales will result in an increase in firm sales of approximately 28% ($279,600) of that amount.

3. **C** The test of significance for the correlation coefficient is evaluated using the following t-statistic:

$$t = \frac{r\sqrt{n-2}}{\sqrt{1-r^2}} = \frac{0.9757\sqrt{3}}{\sqrt{1-0.952}} = \frac{1.69}{0.219} = 7.72$$

   From the t-table, we find that with df = 3 and 95% significance, the two-tailed critical t values are ±3.182 (recall that for the t-test the degrees of freedom = n – 2). Since the computed t is greater than +3.182, the correlation coefficient is significantly different from zero.

4. **B** The slope coefficient is 1.93, indicating that each additional kilometer increases travel time by 1.93 minutes:

   1.93 × 8 = 15.44

5. **C** The higher R^2 for the passenger car model indicates that regression results are more reliable. Distance is a better predictor of travel time for cars. Perhaps the aggressiveness of the driver is a bigger factor in travel time for motorcycles than it is for autos.

6. **C** The model does not assume that the dependent variable is uncorrelated with the residuals. It does assume that the independent variable is uncorrelated with the residuals.

7. **A** If the independent variable is in pounds, the interpretation of the slope coefficient is the change in the dependent variable for a one pound change in the independent variable. If the independent variable is measured in tons (2,000 pounds) the slope coefficient is interpreted as the change in the dependent variable for a 2,000 pound change in the independent variable, which will be 2,000 times larger. The slope of the regression line is not a function of the correlation between the two variables. The researcher would need to know either the regression sum of squares or the total sum of squares, along with the sum of squared errors, in order to calculate the coefficient of determination.

8. **B** The slope coefficient is best interpreted as the predicted change in the dependent variable for a 1-unit change in the independent variable. If the slope coefficient estimate is 10.0 and the independent variable changes by one unit, the dependent variable will change by 10 units. The intercept term is best interpreted as the value of the dependent variable when the independent variable is equal to zero.

9. **A** In this regression, a_1 is the intercept term. To test the statistical significance means to test the null hypothesis that a_1 is equal to zero versus the alternative that it is not equal to zero.

10. **A** In simple linear regression the appropriate degrees of freedom for both confidence intervals is the number of observations in the sample (n) minus two.

11. **C** The regression sum of squares measures the variation in the dependent variable explained by the independent variable (i.e., the explained variation). The sum of squared errors measures the variation in the dependent variable NOT explained by the independent variable. The mean squared error is equal to the sum of squared errors divided by its degrees of freedom.

ANSWERS – CHALLENGE PROBLEMS

12. **A** Note that there are 36 monthly observations from June 2004 to May 2007, so n = 36. The critical two-tailed 10% t-value with 34 (n – 2 = 36 – 2 = 34) degrees of freedom is approximately 1.69. Therefore the 90% confidence interval for b_0 (the intercept term) is 0.0023 +/– (0.0022)(1.69), or –0.0014 to +0.0060.

13. **C** The critical two-tailed 5% t-value with 34 degrees of freedom is approximately 2.03. The calculated t-statistics for the intercept term and slope coefficient are, respectively, 0.0023/0.0022 = 1.05 and 1.1163/0.0624 = 17.9. Therefore the intercept term is not statistically different from zero at the 5% significance level, while the slope coefficient is.

14. **B** Notice that this is a one-tailed test. The critical one-tailed 1% t-value with 34 degrees of freedom is approximately 2.44. The calculated t-statistic for the slope coefficient is (1.1163 – 1)/0.0624 = 1.86. Therefore the slope coefficient is not statistically different from one at the 1% significance level and Coldplay should fail to reject the null hypothesis.

15. **B** This is a tricky question because you are given the confidence interval and its midpoint and asked to solve for the standard error of the forecast (s_f). Remember to also convert the percentages to decimals. The critical two-tailed 5% t-value with 34 degrees of freedom is approximately 2.03. The midpoint, or predicted value is 0.0023 +1.1163 × 0.05 = 0.058. Therefore, 0.058 +/– (2.03)(s_f) is equivalent to 0.039 to 0.077 and solving for s_f yields s_f = 0.0093.

16. **C** SST is equal to the sum of RSS and SSE: 0.0228 + 0.0024 = 0.0252. R^2 = RSS/SST = 0.0228/0.0252 = 0.905.

17. **A** Because n = 36, and the degrees of freedom for the sum of squared errors (SSE) is n – 2 in simple linear regression, the degrees of freedom for SSE is 34 and the mean squared error is SSE/34. The standard error of estimate (SEE) is equal to the square root of the mean squared error:

$$SEE = \sqrt{\frac{0.0024}{34}} = 0.008$$

18. **B** The appearance of a relationship between two variables when there is none is spurious correlation. Outliers may influence the results of regression and the estimate of the correlation coefficient. Correlation only measures linear relationships properly.

19. **B**   The insufficient availability of data is not likely to be much of a limitation for most financial and economic models; usually an abundance of data is available. The other choices are limitations of regression analysis.

20. **A**   There is little to no chance that the relationship between total assets under management and lizards in a park is other than a coincidence. The correlation is spurious. The non-linear relationship in the total assets function makes correlation a poor choice of a measure.

The following is a review of the Quantitative Methods principles designed to address the learning outcome statements set forth by CFA Institute®. This topic is also covered in:

MULTIPLE REGRESSION AND ISSUES IN REGRESSION ANALYSIS

EXAM FOCUS

Multiple regression is the centerpiece of the quantitative methods topic at Level 2. It is a useful analysis tool that shows up throughout the Level 2 curriculum. Multiple regression is especially important for multifactor models in Study Sessions 10 (Equity), and 18 (Portfolio Management). It should be considered as highly probable to appear on the exam: be ready for it and you're on your way to Level 3!

You should know how to use a *t*-test to assess the significance of the individual regression parameters and an *F*-test to assess the effectiveness of the model as a whole in explaining the dependent variable. You should understand the effect that heteroskedasticity, serial correlation, and multicollinearity have on regression results, be able to detect the existence of each of these conditions, and recommend corrective actions. Also be able to identify the common model misspecifications.

Focus on interpretation of the regression equation and the test statistics. Remember that most of the test and descriptive statistics discussed (e.g., *t*-stat, *F*-stat, and R^2) are provided in the output of statistical software. Hence, application and interpretation of these measurements are more likely than actual computations on the exam.

WARM-UP: MULTIPLE REGRESSION BASICS

Multiple regression is regression analysis with more than one independent variable. It is used to quantify the influence of two or more independent variables on a dependent variable. For instance, simple (or univariate) linear regression explains the variation in stock returns in terms of the variation in systematic risk as measured by beta. With multiple regression, stock returns can be regressed against beta and against additional variables, such as firm size, equity, and industry classification, that might influence returns.

The general multiple linear regression model is:

$$Y_i = b_0 + b_1 X_{1i} + b_2 X_{2i} + \ldots + b_k X_{ki} + \varepsilon_i$$

where:
Y_i = *i*th observation of the dependent variable Y, i = 1, 2, …, n
X_j = independent variables, j = 1, 2, …, k
X_{ji} = *i*th observation of the *j*th independent variable
b_0 = intercept term
b_j = slope coefficient for each of the independent variables
ε_i = error term for the *i*th observation
n = number of observations
k = number of independent variables

The multiple regression methodology estimates the intercept and slope coefficients such that the sum of the squared error terms, $\sum_{i=1}^{n} \varepsilon_i^2$, is minimized. The result of this procedure is the following regression equation:

$$\hat{Y}_i = \hat{b}_0 + \hat{b}_1 X_{1i} + \hat{b}_2 X_{2i} + \ldots + \hat{b}_k X_{ki}$$

where the "^" indicates an estimate for the corresponding regression coefficient

The residual, $\hat{\varepsilon}_i$, is the difference between the observed value, Y_i, and the predicted value from the regression, $\hat{Y}_i$:

$$\hat{\varepsilon}_i = Y_i - \hat{Y}_i = Y_i - \left(\hat{b}_0 + \hat{b}_1 X_{1i} + \hat{b}_2 X_{2i} + \ldots + \hat{b}_k X_{ki}\right)$$

MULTIPLE REGRESSION: FORMULATION AND INTERPRETATION

LOS 12.a: Formulate a multiple regression equation to describe the relation between a dependent variable and several independent variables, determine the statistical significance of each independent variable, and interpret the estimated coefficients and their *p*-values.

Professor's Note: Testing the statistical significance of the regression coefficients means conducting a t-test with a null hypothesis that the regression coefficient is equal to zero. Rather than cover that concept here, even though it is mentioned in LOS 12.a, we will cover it in detail in LOS 12.b as part of our general discussion of hypothesis testing. We will also defer a discussion of p-values to LOS 12.b.

Let's illustrate multiple regression using research by Arnott and Asness (2003).[1] As part of their research the authors test the hypothesis that future 10-year real earnings growth in the S&P 500 (EG10) can be explained by the trailing dividend payout ratio of the stocks in the index (PR) and the yield curve slope (YCS). YCS is calculated as the difference between the 10-year T-bond yield and the 3-month T-bill yield at the start of the period. All three variables are measured in percent.

Formulating the Multiple Regression Equation

The authors formulate the following regression equation using annual data from 1946 to 2001 (which results in 46 observations because the last observation is for 1991 and the dependent variable for the 1991 observation is the real earnings growth from 1991 to 2001):

$$EG10 = b_0 + b_1 PR + b_2 YCS + \varepsilon$$

The results of this regression are shown in Figure 1.

---

1. Arnott, Robert D., and Clifford S. Asness. 2003. "Surprise! Higher Dividends = Higher Earnings Growth." *Financial Analysts Journal*, vol. 59, no. 1 (January/February): 70–87.

Figure 1: Coefficient and Standard Error Estimates for Regression of EG10 on PR and YCS

	Coefficient	Standard Error
Intercept	−11.6%	1.657%
PR - slope co.	0.25	0.032
YCS slope	0.14	0.280

Interpreting the Multiple Regression Results

The interpretation of the estimated regression coefficients from a multiple regression is the same as in simple linear regression for the intercept term but significantly different for the slope coefficients:

- The **intercept term** is the value of the dependent variable when the independent variables are all equal to zero.
- Each slope coefficient is the estimated change in the dependent variable for a one-unit change in that independent variable, *holding the other independent variables constant.* That's why the slope coefficients in a multiple regression are sometimes called **partial slope coefficients**.

For example, in the real earnings growth example, we can make these interpretations:

- *Intercept term*: If the dividend payout ratio is zero and the slope of the yield curve is zero, we would expect the subsequent 10-year real earnings growth rate to be −11.6%.
- *PR coefficient*: If the payout ratio increases by 1%, we would expect the subsequent 10-year earnings growth rate to increase by 0.25%, *holding YCS constant.*
- *YCS coefficient*: If the yield curve slope increases by 1%, we would expect the subsequent 10-year earnings growth rate to increase by 0.14%, *holding PR constant.*

Let's discuss the interpretation of the multiple regression slope coefficients in more detail. Suppose we run a regression of the dependent variable Y on a single independent variable $X1$ and get the following result:

$$Y = 2.0 + 4.5X1$$

The appropriate interpretation of the estimated slope coefficient is that if $X1$ increases by 1 unit, we would expect Y to increase by 4.5 units.

Now suppose we add a second independent variable $X2$ to the regression and get the following result:

$$Y = 1.0 + 2.5X1 + 6.0X2$$

Notice that the estimated slope coefficient for $X1$ changed from 4.5 to 2.5 when we added $X2$ to the regression. We would expect this to happen most of the time when a second variable is added to the regression, unless $X2$ is uncorrelated with $X1$, because

---

if $X1$ increases by 1 unit then we would expect $X2$ to change as well. The multiple regression equation captures this relationship between $X1$ and $X2$ when predicting Y.

Now the interpretation of the estimated slope coefficient for $X1$ is that if $X1$ increases by 1 unit, we would expect Y to increase by 2.5 units, *holding X2 constant*.

LOS 12.b: Formulate a null and an alternative hypothesis about the population value of a regression coefficient, calculate the value of the test statistic, determine whether to reject the null hypothesis at a given level of significance, using a one-tailed or two-tailed test, and interpret the result of the test.

Hypothesis Testing of Regression Coefficients

As with simple linear regression, the magnitude of the coefficients in a multiple regression tells us nothing about the importance of the independent variable in explaining the dependent variable. Thus, we must conduct hypothesis testing on the estimated slope coefficients to determine if the independent variables make a significant contribution to explaining the variation in the dependent variable.

The *t*-statistic used to test the significance of the individual coefficients in a multiple regression is calculated using the same formula that is used with simple linear regression:

$$t = \frac{\hat{b}_j - b_j}{s_{\hat{b}_j}} = \frac{\text{estimated regression coefficient} - \text{hypothesized value}}{\text{coefficient standard error of } b_j}$$

The *t*-statistic has $n - k - 1$ degrees of freedom.

 Professor's Note: An easy way to remember the number of degrees of freedom for this test is to recognize that "k" is the number of regression coefficients in the regression, and the "1" is for the intercept term. Therefore the degrees of freedom is the number of observations minus k minus 1.

Determining Statistical Significance

The most common hypothesis test done on the regression coefficients is to test statistical significance, which means testing the null hypothesis that the coefficient is zero versus the alternative that it is not:

"testing statistical significance" $\Rightarrow H_0: b_j = 0$ versus $H_a: b_j \neq 0$

Example: Testing the statistical significance of a regression coefficient

Test the statistical significance of the independent variable PR in the real earnings growth example at the 10% significance level. The results of that regression are reproduced in the following figure.

Coefficient and Standard Error Estimates for Regression of EG10 on PR and YCS

	Coefficient	Standard Error
Intercept	–11.6%	1.657%
PR	0.25	0.032
YCS	0.14	0.280

Answer:

We are testing the following hypothesis:

H_0: PR = 0 versus H_a: PR ≠ 0

The 10% two-tailed critical t-value with $46 - 2 - 1 = 43$ degrees of freedom is approximately 1.68. We should reject the null hypothesis if the t-statistic is greater than 1.68 or less than –1.68.

The t-statistic is:

$$t = \frac{0.25}{0.032} = 7.8$$

Therefore, because the t-statistic of 7.8 is greater than the upper critical t-value of 1.68, we can reject the null hypothesis and conclude that the PR regression coefficient is statistically significantly different from zero at the 10% significance level.

Interpreting p-Values

The p-value is the smallest level of significance for which the null hypothesis can be rejected. An alternative method of doing hypothesis testing of the coefficients is to compare the p-value to the significance level:

*   If the p-value is less than significance level, the null hypothesis can be rejected.
*   If the p-value is greater than the significance level, the null hypothesis cannot be rejected.

Example: Interpreting p-values

Given the following regression results, determine which regression parameters for the independent variables are statistically significantly different from zero at the 1% significance level, assuming the sample size is 60.

t = 2.65

Variable	Coefficient	Standard Error	t-Statistic	p-Value
Intercept	0.40	0.40	1.0	0.3215
X1	8.20	2.05	4.0	0.0002
X2	0.40	0.18	2.2	0.0319
X3	−1.80	0.56	−3.2	0.0022

Answer:

The independent variable is statistically significant if the *p*-value is less than 1%, or 0.01. Therefore *X*1 and *X*3 are statistically significantly different from zero.

Figure 2 shows the results of the *t*-tests for each of the regression coefficients of our 10-year earnings growth example, including the *p*-values.

Figure 2: Regression Results for Regression of EG10 on PR and YCS

we can reject null at

	Coefficient	Standard Error	t-statistic	p-value at
Intercept	−11.6%	1.657%	−7.0	< 0.0001
PR	0.25	0.032	7.8	< 0.0001
YCS	0.14	0.280	0.5	0.62

As we determined in a previous example, we can reject the null hypothesis and conclude that PR is statistically significant. We can also draw the same conclusion for the intercept term because −7.0 is less than the lower critical value of −1.68 (because it is a two-tailed test). However, we fail to reject the null hypothesis for YCS, so we cannot conclude that YCS has a statistically significant effect on the dependent variable, EG10, when PR is also included in the model. The *p*-values tell us exactly the same thing (as they always will): the intercept term and PR are statistically significant at the 10% level because their *p*-values are less than 0.10, while YCS is not statistically significant because its *p*-value is greater than 0.10.

Other Tests of the Regression Coefficients

You should also be prepared to formulate one and two-tailed tests in which the null hypothesis is that the coefficient is equal to some value other than zero, or that it is greater than or less than some value.

Example: Testing regression coefficients (two-tail test)

Using the data from Figure 2, test the null hypothesis that PR is equal to 0.20 versus the alternative that it is not equal to 0.20 using a 5% significance level.

Answer:

We are testing the following hypothesis:

H_0: PR = 0.20 versus H_a: PR $\neq$ 0.20

The 5% two-tailed critical t-value with $46 - 2 - 1 = 43$ degrees of freedom is approximately 2.02. We should reject the null hypothesis if the t-statistic is greater than 2.02 or less than −2.02.

The t-statistic is:

$$t = \frac{0.25 - 0.20}{0.032} = 1.56$$

Therefore, because the t-statistic of 1.56 is between the upper and lower critical t-values of −2.02 and 2.02, we cannot reject the null hypothesis and must conclude that the PR regression coefficient is not statistically significantly different from 0.20 at the 5% significance level.

Example: Testing regression coefficients (one-tailed test)

Using the data from Figure 2, test the null hypothesis that the intercept term is greater than or equal to −10.0% versus the alternative that it is less than −10.0% using a 1% significance level.

Answer:

We are testing the following hypothesis:

H_0: Intercept $\geq$ −10.0% versus H_a: Intercept < −10.0%

The 1% **one**-tailed critical t-value with $46 - 2 - 1 = 43$ degrees of freedom is approximately 2.42. We should reject the null hypothesis if the t-statistic is less than −2.42.

The *t*-statistic is:

$$t = \frac{-11.6\% - (-10.0\%)}{1.657\%} = -0.96$$

Therefore, because the *t*-statistic of –0.96 is not less than –2.42, we cannot reject the null hypothesis.

CONFIDENCE INTERVALS

LOS 12.c: Calculate and interpret 1) a confidence interval for the population value of a regression coefficient and 2) a predicted value for the dependent variable, given an estimated regression model and assumed values for the independent variables.

Confidence Intervals for a Regression Coefficient

The confidence interval for a regression coefficient in multiple regression is calculated and interpreted the same way as it is in simple linear regression. For example, a 95% confidence interval is constructed as follows:

$$\hat{b}_j \pm (t_c \times s_{\hat{b}_j})$$

or

estimated regression coefficient $\pm$ (critical *t*-value)(coefficient standard error)

The critical *t*-value is a two-tailed value with n – k – 1 degrees of freedom and a 5% significance level, where *n* is the number of observations and *k* is the number of independent variables.

Example: Calculating a confidence interval for a regression coefficient

Calculate the 90% confidence interval for the estimated coefficient for the independent variable PR in the real earnings growth example.

Answer:

The critical *t*-value is 1.68, the same as we used in testing the statistical significance at the 10% significance level (which is the same thing as a 90% confidence level). The estimated slope coefficient is 0.25 and the standard error is 0.032. The 90% confidence interval is:

$$0.25 \pm (1.68)(0.032) = 0.25 \pm 0.054 = 0.196 \text{ to } 0.304$$

Professor's Note: Notice that because zero is not contained in the 90% confidence interval, we can conclude that the PR coefficient is statistically significant at the 10% level, the same conclusion we made when using the t-test in LOS 12.b. Constructing a confidence interval and conducting a t-test with a null hypothesis of "equal to zero" will always result in the same conclusion regarding the statistical significance of the regression coefficient.

PREDICTING THE DEPENDENT VARIABLE

We can use the regression equation to make predictions about the dependent variable *based on forecasted values of the independent variables.* The process is similar to forecasting with simple linear regression, only now we need predicted values for more than one independent variable. The predicted value of dependent variable Y is:

$$\hat{Y}_i = \hat{b}_0 + \hat{b}_1 \hat{X}_{1i} + \hat{b}_2 \hat{X}_{2i} + \ldots + \hat{b}_k \hat{X}_{ki}$$

where:

$\hat{Y}_i$ = the predicted value of the dependent variable

$\hat{b}_j$ = the estimated slope coefficient for the jth independent variable

$\hat{X}_{ji}$ = the forecast of the jth independent variable, j = 1, 2, ..., k

Professor's Note: The prediction of the dependent variable uses the estimated intercept and all of the estimated slope coefficients, regardless of whether the estimated coefficients are statistically significantly different from zero. For example, suppose you estimate the following regression equation: $\hat{Y} = 6 + 2X_1 + 4X_2$, and you determine that only the first independent variable (X_1) is statistically significant (i.e., you rejected the null that $b_1 = 0$). To predict Y given forecasts of $X_1 = 0.6$ and $X_2 = 0.8$, you would use the complete model: $\hat{Y} = 6 + (2 \times 0.6) + (4 \times 0.8) = 10.4$. Alternatively, you could drop X2 and reestimate the model using just X1, but remember that the coefficient on X1 will likely change.

Example: Calculating a predicted value for the dependent variable

An analyst would like to use the estimated regression equation from the previous example to calculate the predicted 10-year real earnings growth for the S&P 500, assuming the payout ratio of the index is 50%. He observes that the slope of the yield curve is currently 4%.

Answer:

$$\widehat{EG10} = -11.6\% + 0.25(50\%) + 0.14(4\%) = 1.46\%$$

The model predicts a 1.46% real earnings growth rate for the S&P 500, assuming a 50% payout ratio, when the slope of the yield curve is 4%.

MULTIPLE REGRESSION ASSUMPTIONS

LOS 12.d: Explain the assumptions of a multiple regression model.

As with simple linear regression, most of the assumptions made with the multiple regression pertain to ε, the model's error term:

- A linear relationship exists between the dependent and independent variables. In other words, the model on the first page of this topic review correctly describes the relationship.
- The independent variables are not random, and there is no exact linear relation between any two or more independent variables.
- The expected value of the error term, conditional on the independent variable, is zero [i.e., $E(\varepsilon | X_1, X_2, ... X_k) = 0$].
- The variance of the error terms is constant for all observations [i.e., $E(\varepsilon_i^2) = \sigma_\varepsilon^2$].
- The error term for one observation is not correlated with that of another observation [i.e., $E(\varepsilon_i \varepsilon_j) = 0, j \neq i$].
- The error term is normally distributed.

ANALYSIS OF MULTIPLE REGRESSION MODEL

LOS 12.e: Calculate and interpret the *F*-statistic, and discuss how it is used in regression analysis, define, distinguish between, and interpret the R^2 and adjusted R^2 in multiple regression, and infer how well a regression model explains the dependent variable by analyzing the output of the regression equation and an ANOVA table.

THE *F*-STATISTIC

An *F*-test assesses how well the set of independent variables, as a group, explains the variation in the dependent variable. That is, the *F*-statistic is used to test whether *at least one* of the independent variables explains a significant portion of the variation of the dependent variable.

For example, if there are four independent variables in the model, the hypotheses are structured as:

$$H_0: b_1 = b_2 = b_3 = b_4 = 0 \text{ versus } H_a: \text{at least one } b_j \neq 0$$

The *F*-statistic, *which is always a one-tailed test*, is calculated as:

$$F = \frac{MSR}{MSE} = \frac{RSS/k}{SSE/n-k-1}$$

where:
RSS = regression sum of squares
SSE = sum of squared errors
MSR = mean regression sum of squares
MSE = mean squared error

Professor's Note: Recall from the previous topic review that the regression sum of squares and the sum of squared errors are found in an ANOVA table. We analyze an ANOVA table from a multiple regression later in this LOS.

To determine whether at least one of the coefficients is statistically significant, the calculated *F*-statistic is compared with the **one-tailed** critical *F*-value, F_c, at the appropriate level of significance. The degrees of freedom for the numerator and denominator are:

$$df_{numerator} = k$$

$$df_{denominator} = n - k - 1$$

where:
n = number of observations
k = number of independent variables

The decision rule for the *F*-test is:

Decision rule: reject H_0 if F (test-statistic) > F_c (critical value)

Rejection of the null hypothesis at a stated level of significance indicates that at least one of the coefficients is significantly different than zero, which is interpreted to mean that at least one of the independent variables in the regression model makes a significant contribution to the explanation of the dependent variable.

Professor's Note: It may have occurred to you that an easier way to test all of the coefficients simultaneously is to just conduct all of the individual t-tests and see how many of them you can reject. This is the wrong approach, however, because if you set the significance level for each t-test at 5%, for example, the significance level from testing them all simultaneously is NOT 5%, but rather some higher percentage. Just remember to use the F-test on the exam if you are asked to test all of the coefficients simultaneously.

Example: Calculating and interpreting the F-statistic

An analyst runs a regression of monthly value-stock returns on five independent variables over 60 months. The total sum of squares is 460, and the sum of squared errors is 170. Test the null hypothesis at the 5% significance level that all five of the independent variables are equal to zero.

Answer:

The null and alternative hypotheses are:

H_0: $b_1 = b_2 = b_3 = b_4 = b_5 = 0$ versus H_a: at least one $b_j \neq 0$

$$RSS = SST - SSE = 460 - 170 = 290$$

$$MSR = \frac{290}{5} = 58.0$$

$$MSE = \frac{170}{60 - 5 - 1} = 3.15$$

$$F = \frac{58.0}{3.15} = 18.41$$

The critical F-value for 5 and 54 degrees of freedom at a 5% significance level is approximately 2.40. Remember, it's a **one-tailed** test, so we use the 5% F-table! Therefore we can reject the null hypothesis and conclude that at least one of the five independent variables is significantly different than zero.

Professor's Note: When testing the hypothesis that all the regression coefficients are simultaneously equal to zero, the F-test is always a one-tailed test, despite the fact that it looks like it should be a two-tailed test because there is an equal sign in the null hypothesis. This is a common source of confusion among Level 2 candidates; make sure you don't make that mistake on the exam.

COEFFICIENT OF DETERMINATION, R^2

In addition to an F-test, the multiple coefficient of determination, R^2, can be used to test the overall effectiveness of the entire set of independent variables in explaining the dependent variable. Its interpretation is similar to that for simple linear regression: the percentage of variation in the dependent variable that is *collectively* explained by all of the independent variables. For example, an R^2 of 0.63 indicates that the model, as a whole, explains 63% of the variation in the dependent variable.

R^2 is also calculated the same way as in simple linear regression.

$$R^2 = \frac{\text{total variation} - \text{unexplained variation}}{\text{total variation}} = \frac{\text{SST} - \text{SSE}}{\text{SST}} = \frac{\text{explained variation}}{\text{total variation}} = \frac{\text{RSS}}{\text{SST}}$$

Adjusted R^2

Unfortunately, R^2 by itself *may not be a reliable measure of the explanatory power of the multiple regression model*. This is because R^2 almost always increases as variables are added to the model, even if the marginal contribution of the new variables is not statistically significant. Consequently, a relatively high R^2 may reflect the impact of a large set of independent variables rather than how well the set explains the dependent variable. This problem is often referred to as overestimating the regression.

To overcome the problem of overestimating the impact of additional variables on the explanatory power of a regression model, many researchers recommend adjusting R^2 for the number of independent variables. The *adjusted R^2* value is expressed as:

$$R_a^2 = 1 - \left[\left(\frac{n-1}{n-k-1} \right) \times (1 - R^2) \right]$$

where:
n = number of observations
k = number of independent variables
R_a^2 = adjusted R^2

Whenever there is more than one independent variable, R_a^2 is less than or equal to R^2. So while adding a new independent variable to the model will increase R^2, it may either *increase or decrease* the R_a^2. If the new variable has only a small effect on R^2, the value of R_a^2 may decrease. In addition, R_a^2 may be less than zero if the R^2 is low enough.

Example: Calculating R^2 and adjusted R^2

An analyst runs a regression of monthly value-stock returns on five independent variables over 60 months. The total sum of squares for the regression is 460, and the sum of squared errors is 170. Calculate the R^2 and adjusted R^2.

Answer:

$$R^2 = \frac{460 - 170}{460} = 0.630 = 63.0\%$$

$$R_a^2 = 1 - \left[\left(\frac{60-1}{60-5-1} \right) \times (1 - 0.63) \right] = 0.596 = 59.6\%$$

The R^2 of 63% suggests that the five independent variables together explain 63% of the variation in monthly value-stock returns.

Example: Interpreting adjusted R^2

Suppose the analyst now adds four more independent variables to the regression, and the R^2 increases to 65.0%. Identify which model the analyst would most likely prefer.

Answer:

With nine independent variables, even though the R^2 has increased, from 63% to 65%, the adjusted R^2 has decreased from 59.6% to 58.7%:

$$R_a^2 = 1 - \left[\left(\frac{60-1}{60-9-1} \right) \times (1-0.65) \right] = 0.587 = 58.7\%$$

The analyst would prefer the first model because the adjusted R^2 is higher and the model has five independent variables as opposed to nine.

ANOVA TABLES

Analysis of variance (ANOVA) is a statistical procedure that provides information on the explanatory power of a regression. We first discussed the use of ANOVA tables in the previous topic review of simple linear regression. Once again, the interpretation is the same in multiple regression.

The results of the ANOVA procedure are presented in an ANOVA table, which accompanies the output of a multiple regression program. An example of a generic ANOVA table is presented in Figure 3.

Figure 3: ANOVA Table

Source	df (Degrees of Freedom)	SS (Sum of Squares)	MS (Mean Square= SS/df)
Regression	k	RSS	MSR
Error	n – k –1	SSE	MSE
Total	n – 1	SST	

The information in an ANOVA table is used to attribute the total variation of the dependent variable to one of two sources: the regression model or the residuals. This is indicated in the first column in the table, where the "source" of the variation is listed.

The information in an ANOVA table can be used to calculate R^2, the F-statistic, and the standard error of estimate (SEE). That is:

$$R^2 = \frac{RSS}{SST}$$

$$F = \frac{MSR}{MSE} \text{ with k and } n - k - 1 \text{ degrees of freedom}$$

$$SEE = \sqrt{MSE}$$

 Professor's Note: R^2, F, and SEE are provided along with the standard ANOVA table produced by most statistical software packages. On the exam, be prepared to fill in "missing data" from an ANOVA output.

Let's look at an example to tie all of this together.

Example: Using an ANOVA table with regression output

In an attempt to estimate a regression equation that can be used to forecast BuildCo's future sales, 22 years of BuildCo's annual sales were regressed against two independent variables:

GDP = the level of gross domestic product

ΔI = changes in 30-year mortgage interest rates (expressed in percentage terms)

The output from a common statistical software package is contained in the following table.

Regression Results for BuildCo Sales Data

	Coefficient	Standard Error	t-Statistic	p-Value
Intercept	6.000	4.520	1.327	0.20
Level of gross domestic product (GDP)	0.004	0.003	?	0.20
Changes in 30-year mortgage rates (ΔI)	−20.500	3.560	?	< 0.001

ANOVA	df	SS	MS	F	Significance F
Regression	?	236.30	? 118.15	?	p < 0.005
Error	? SSE 116.11		? 6.11		
Total	? SST ?				
R^2	?				
R_a^2	?				

Based on the output in the table, the regression equation can be stated as:

$$\overline{\text{BuildCo Sales}} = 6.000 + 0.004(\text{GDP}) - 20.500(\Delta I)$$

Fill in the missing data and interpret the results of the regression at a 5% level of significance with respect to:

- The significance of the individual independent variables.
- The utility of the model as a whole.

Answer:

Step 1: Fill in the missing data.

The computed test statistics for the regression coefficients are:

$$t_{\text{GDP}} = \frac{0.004}{0.003} = 1.333$$

$$t_{\Delta I} = \frac{-20.500}{3.560} = -5.758$$

Degrees of freedom are:

$$df_{\text{regression}} = k = 2$$
$$df_{\text{error}} = n - k - 1 = 22 - 2 - 1 = 19$$
$$df_{\text{total}} = n - 1 = 22 - 1 = 21$$

Other calculations:

$$\text{SST} = \text{RSS} + \text{SSE} = 236.30 + 116.11 = 352.41$$

$$\text{MSR} = \frac{\text{RSS}}{k} = \frac{236.30}{2} = 118.15$$

$$\text{MSE} = \frac{\text{SSE}}{n - k - 1} = \frac{116.11}{19} = 6.11$$

$$\text{F} = \frac{\text{MSR}}{\text{MSE}} = \frac{118.15}{6.11} = 19.34$$

$$\text{R}^2 = \frac{\text{RSS}}{\text{SST}} = \frac{236.30}{352.41} = 67.05\%$$

$$\text{R}_a^2 = 1 - \left(\frac{n-1}{n-k-1}\right)(1 - \text{R}^2) = 1 - \left(\frac{21}{19}\right)(1 - 0.6705) = 63.58\%$$

The following table shows what the complete ANOVA table looks like:

Regression Results for BuildCo Sales Data

	Coefficient	Standard Error	t-Statistic	p-Value
Intercept	6.000	4.520	1.327	0.20
Level of gross domestic product (GDP)	0.004	0.003	1.333	0.20
Changes in 30-year mortgage rates (ΔI)	−20.500	3.560	−5.758	< 0.001

only P less than 5%

ANOVA	df	SS	MS	F	Significance F
Regression	2	236.30	118.15	19.34	p < 0.005
Error	19	116.11	6.11		
Total	21	352.41			

R^2	67.05%
R_a^2	63.58%

Step 2: Determine the significance of the individual independent variables.

The contribution of the individual variables, as indicated by the significance of their slope coefficients, can be tested using *t*-tests. However, since the *p*-values are included with the regression output, as is usually the case, the level of significance can be observed directly. Just for practice, let's test for significance of the individual coefficients using *t*-tests *and* p-values.

- Using *p*-values. Only the *p*-value of the coefficient for ΔI is less than the 5% level of significance, so we conclude that only ΔI contributes significantly to the level of BuildCo's annual sales.
- Using *t*-statistics. The hypothesis test structure is:

$$H_0: b_j = 0 \text{ versus } H_a: b \neq 0$$

The critical two-tailed *t*-values with df = 19 are ±2.093.

The decision rule is reject H_0 if t_{b_j} is greater than 2.093 or less than −2.093.

Since $t_{GDP} = 1.33$ does not fall in the rejection region, we cannot reject the null for GDP, and we conclude that the level of GDP does not make a statistically significant contribution to the variation in sales at the 5% level.

Since $(t_{\Delta I} = -5.758) < (t_c = -2.093)$, we conclude that changes in mortgage rates make a significant contribution to the variation in sales at the 5% level.

Professor's Note: The use of p-values or t-tests will always result in the same conclusions about the statistical significance of the slope estimate (i.e., coefficients on the independent variables). On the exam, use the p-value if it is provided!

Step 3: Determine the utility of the model as a whole.

The overall utility of the model can be generally assessed with the coefficient of determination, R^2. The R^2 value indicates that GDP and ΔI explain 67.05% of the variation in BuildCo's annual sales.

Tests of significance for the set of independent variables should be performed using the *F*-test. The hypotheses for the one-sided *F*-test can be structured as:

$$H_0: b_{\Delta I} = b_{GDP} = 0 \text{ versus } H_a: b_{\Delta I} \neq 0, \text{ or } b_{GDP} \neq 0$$

F_c at the 5% significance level with $df_{numerator} = 2$ and $df_{denominator} = 19$ is 3.52. Remember, this is a one-tailed test.

The decision rule is reject H_0 if F is greater than 3.52.

Since F > 3.52, the null hypothesis can be rejected and we can conclude that at least one of the independent variables significantly contributes to the dependent variable. That is, changes in mortgage rates *and* the level of GDP together explain a significant amount of the variation in BuildCo's annual sales at the 5% significance level. Notice that we could have reached this conclusion by observing that the ANOVA table reports that *F* is significant at a level less than 5%.

DUMMY VARIABLES

LOS 12.f: Formulate a multiple regression equation using dummy variables to represent qualitative factors, and interpret the coefficients and regression results.

Observations for most independent variables (e.g., firm size, level of GDP, and interest rates) can take on a wide range of values. However, there are occasions when the independent variable is binary in nature—it is either "on" or "off." Independent variables that fall into this category are called *dummy variables* and are often used to quantify the impact of qualitative events.

Dummy variables are assigned a value of "0" or "1." For example, in a time series regression of monthly stock returns, you could employ a "January" dummy variable that would take on the value of "1" if a stock return occurred in January and "0" if it occurred in any other month. The purpose of including the January dummy variable would be to see if stock returns in January were significantly different than stock returns in all other months of the year. Many "January Effect" anomaly studies employ this type of regression methodology.

The estimated regression coefficient for dummy variables indicates the difference in the dependent variable for the category represented by the dummy variable and the average value of the dependent variable for all classes except the dummy variable class. For example, testing the slope coefficient for the January dummy variable would indicate whether, and by how much, security returns are different in January as compared to the other months.

An *important consideration* when performing multiple regression with dummy variables is the choice of the number of dummy variables to include in the model. Whenever we want to distinguish between *n* classes, we must use n – 1 dummy variables. Otherwise, the regression assumption of no exact linear relationship between independent variables would be violated.

Interpreting the Coefficients in a Dummy Variable Regression

Consider the following regression equation for explaining quarterly EPS in terms of the quarter of their occurrence:

$$EPS_t = b_0 + b_1 Q_{1t} + b_2 Q_{2t} + b_3 Q_{3t} + \varepsilon_t$$

where:
EPS_t = a quarterly observation of earnings per share
Q_{1t} = 1 if period t is the first quarter, Q_{1t} = 0 otherwise
Q_{2t} = 1 if period t is the second quarter, Q_{2t} = 0 otherwise
Q_{3t} = 1 if period t is the third quarter, Q_{3t} = 0 otherwise

The intercept term, b_0, represents the average value of *EPS* for the fourth quarter. The slope coefficient on each dummy variable estimates the *difference* in earnings per share (on average) between the respective quarter (i.e., quarter 1, 2, or 3) and the omitted quarter (the fourth quarter in this case). *Think of the omitted class as the reference point.*

For example, suppose we estimate the quarterly EPS regression model with ten years of data (40 quarterly observations) and find that b_0 = 1.25, b_1 = 0.75, b_2 = –0.20, and b_3 = 0.10:

$$\widehat{EPS}_t = 1.25 + 0.75 Q_{1t} - 0.20 Q_{2t} + 0.10 Q_{3t}$$

We can use the equation to determine the average EPS in each quarter over the past ten years:

average fourth quarter EPS = 1.25

average first quarter EPS = 1.25 + 0.75 = 2.00

average second quarter EPS = 1.25 – 0.20 = 1.05

average third quarter EPS = 1.25 + 0.10 = 1.35

These are also the model's predictions of future EPS in each quarter of the following year. For example, to use the model to predict EPS in the first quarter of the next year, set $\hat{Q}_1 = 1$, $\hat{Q}_2 = 0$, and $\hat{Q}_3 = 0$. Then $\widehat{EPS}_{2009} = 1.25 + 0.75(1) - 0.20(0) + 0.10(0)$ = 2.00. This simple model uses average EPS for any specific quarter over the past ten years as the forecast of EPS in its respective quarter of the following year.

As with all multiple regression results, the *F*-statistic for the set of coefficients and the R^2 should be evaluated to determine if the quarters, individually or collectively, contribute to the explanation of quarterly EPS.

We can also test whether the average EPS in each of the first three quarters is equal to the fourth quarter EPS (the omitted quarter) by testing the individual slope coefficients using the following null hypotheses:

H_0: b_1 = 0 tests whether fourth quarter EPS = first quarter EPS
H_0: b_2 = 0 tests whether fourth quarter EPS = second quarter EPS
H_0: b_3 = 0 tests whether fourth quarter EPS = third quarter EPS

The t-statistic for each test is equal to the coefficient divided by its standard error, and the critical t-value is a two-tailed value with $n - k - 1 = 40 - 3 - 1 = 36$ degrees of freedom.

Example: Hypothesis testing with dummy variables

The standard error of the coefficient b_1 is equal to 0.15 from the EPS regression model. Test whether first quarter EPS is equal to fourth quarter EPS at the 5% significance level.

Answer:

We are testing the following hypothesis:

$$H_0 : b_1 = 0 \text{ vs. } H_A : b_1 \neq 0$$

The t-statistic is $0.75/0.15 = 5.0$ and the two-tail 5% critical value with 36 degrees of freedom is approximately 2.03. Therefore we should reject the null and conclude that first quarter EPS is statistically significantly different than fourth quarter EPS at the 5% significance level.

Example of Regression Application with Dummy Variables

Mazumdar and Sengupta (2005)[2] provide a more complex example of an investment application of multiple regression using dummy variables. They determine that loan spreads relative to LIBOR on private debt contracts are negatively associated with measures of the quality of the company's financial disclosures.

The dependent variable (SPREAD) is the quoted spread in basis points over LIBOR on the first year of the loan. The independent variables include a number of quantitative variables, including, for example, average total disclosure score (DISC), standard deviation of daily stock returns (STDRETN), current ratio (CRATIO), and market to book ratio (MKBK). The authors also include three dummy variables in the regression:

*   SECURE, which is equal to one if the loan is collateralized, and equal to zero otherwise.
*   BID, which is equal to one if the loan contained the option to price the loan relative to a different index, and equal to zero otherwise.
*   RESTRUC, which is equal to one if the loan was a result of corporate restructuring, and equal to zero otherwise.

---

2. Mazumdar, S. and P. Sengupta. 2005. "Disclosure of the Loan Spread on Private Debt." *Financial Analysts Journal*, vol. 61, no. 3 (May/June): 83–95.

In the model both SECURE and RESTRUC are positive and statistically significantly different from zero, while BID is not. The proper interpretation is that the loan spreads on private debt contracts are higher for collateralized loans than for uncollateralized loans, and higher for loans used for corporate restructuring than for loans used for other purposes, *after controlling for the other independent variables in the model.*

WARM-UP: WHY MULTIPLE REGRESSION ISN'T AS EASY AS IT LOOKS

Regression analysis relies on the assumptions listed in LOS 12.d. When these assumptions are violated, the inferences drawn from the model are questionable. There are three primary assumption violations that you will encounter: (1) heteroskedasticity, (2) serial correlation (i.e., autocorrelation), and (3) multicollinearity.

On exam day, you must be able to answer the following four questions about each of the three assumption violations:

- What is it?
- What is its effect on regression analysis?
- How do we detect it?
- How do we correct for it?

Recall that the calculated test statistic for the estimated regression coefficient on the jth independent variable is:

$$t = \frac{\hat{b}_j - b_j}{s_{\hat{b}_j}}$$

Note that the denominator in the test statistic equation above, $s_{\hat{b}_j}$, is the standard error for coefficient j. Without getting into the math, suffice it to say that the coefficient standard error is calculated using the standard error of estimate (SEE), which is the standard deviation of the error term. Any violation of an assumption that affects the error term will ultimately affect the coefficient standard error. Consequently, this will affect the t-statistic and F-statistic and any conclusions drawn from hypothesis tests involving these statistics.

LOS 12.g: Discuss the types of heteroskedasticity and the effects of heteroskedasticity and serial correlation on statistical inference.

WHAT IS HETEROSKEDASTICITY?

Recall from LOS 12.d that one of the assumptions of multiple regression is that the variance of the residuals is constant across observations. **Heteroskedasticity** occurs when the variance of the residuals is not the same across all observations in the sample. This happens when there are subsamples that are more spread out than the rest of the sample.

Unconditional heteroskedasticity occurs when the heteroskedasticity is not related to the level of the independent variables, which means that it doesn't systematically increase or decrease with changes in the value of the independent variable(s). While this is a violation of the equal variance assumption, *it usually causes no major problems with the regression.*

Conditional heteroskedasticity is heteroskedasticity that is related to the level of (i.e., conditional on) the independent variables. For example, conditional heteroskedasticity exists if the variance of the residual term increases as the value of the independent variable increases, as shown in Figure 4. Notice in this figure that the residual variance associated with the larger values of the independent variable, *X*, is larger than the residual variance associated with the smaller values of *X*. Conditional heteroskedasticity *does create significant problems for statistical inference.*

Figure 4: Conditional Heteroskedasticity

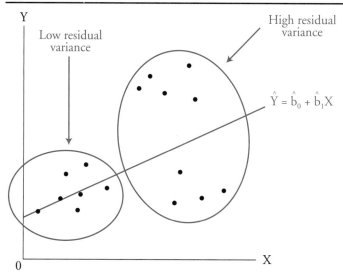

Effect of Heteroskedasticity on Regression Analysis

There are four effects of heteroskedasticity you need to be aware of:

- The standard errors are usually unreliable estimates.
- The coefficient estimates (the $\hat{b}_j$) aren't affected.
- If the standard errors are too small, but the coefficient estimates themselves are not affected, the *t*-statistics will be too large and the null hypothesis of no statistical significance is rejected too often. The opposite will be true if the standard errors are too large.
- The *F*-test is also unreliable.

Detecting Heteroskedasticity

There are two methods to detect heteroskedasticity: examining scatter plots of the residuals and using the Breusch-Pagan chi-square test. A scatter plot of the residuals versus one or more of the independent variables can reveal patterns among observations.

Example: Detecting heteroskedasticity with a residual plot

You have been studying the monthly returns of a mutual fund over the past five years, hoping to draw conclusions about the fund's average performance. You calculate the mean return, the standard deviation, and the portfolio's beta by regressing the fund's returns on S&P 500 index returns (the independent variable). The standard deviation of returns and the fund's beta don't seem to fit the firm's stated risk profile. For your analysis, you have prepared a scatter plot of the error terms (actual return – predicted return) for the regression using five years of returns, as shown in the following figure. Determine whether the residual plot indicates that there may be a problem with the data.

Residual Plot

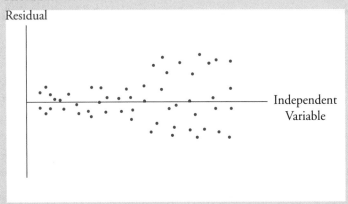

Answer:

The residual plot in the previous figure indicates the presence of conditional heteroskedasticity. Notice how the variation in the regression residuals increases as the independent variable increases. This indicates that the variance of the fund's returns about the mean is related to the level of the independent variable.

The more common way to detect conditional heteroskedasticity is the *Breusch-Pagan test*, which calls for the regression of the squared residuals on the independent variables. If conditional heteroskedasticity is present, the independent variables will significantly contribute to the explanation of the squared residuals. The test statistic for the Breusch-Pagan test, which has a chi-square distribution, is calculated as:

BP chi-square test $= n \times R^2_{resid}$ with k degrees of freedom

where:

n = the number of observations

R^2_{resid} = R^2 from a second regression of the squared residuals
from the first regression on the independent variables

k = the number of independent variables

Professor's Note: The R^2 used in the BP test is the R^2 from a second regression, NOT the original regression.

This is a one-tailed test because heteroskedasticity is only a problem if the R^2 and the BP test statistic are too large.

Example: The Breusch-Pagan test

The residual plot of mutual fund returns over time shows evidence of heteroskedasticity. To confirm your suspicions, you regress the squared residuals from the original regression on the independent variable, S&P 500 index returns. The R^2 from that regression is 8%. Use the Breusch-Pagan test to determine whether heteroskedasticity is present at the 5% significance level.

Answer:

With five years of monthly observations, n is equal to 60. The test statistic is:

$$n \times R^2 = 60 \times 0.08 = 4.8$$

The one-tailed critical value for a chi-square distribution with one degree of freedom and α equal to 5% is 3.841. Therefore you should reject the null hypothesis and conclude that you have a problem with conditional heteroskedasticity.

Correcting Heteroskedasticity

Heteroskedasticity is not easy to correct, and the details of the available techniques are beyond the scope of the CFA curriculum (which means you don't need to know the details for the exam!).

- The most common remedy and the one recommended in the CFA curriculum is to calculate *robust standard errors* (also called White-corrected standard errors or heteroskedasticity-consistent standard errors). These robust standard errors are then used to recalculate the *t*-statistics using the original regression coefficients. On the exam, use robust standard errors to calculate *t*-statistics if there is evidence of heteroskedasticity.

Example: Using White-corrected standard errors

An analyst runs a regression of annualized Treasury bill rates (the dependent variable) on annual inflation rates (the independent variable) using monthly data for ten years. The results of the regression are shown in the following table.

Regression of T-Bill Rates on Inflation Rates

Variable	Coefficient	Standard Error	t-Statistic	p-Value
Intercept	4.82	0.85	5.67	< 0.0001
Inflation	0.60	0.28	2.14	0.0340

He determines using the Breusch-Pagan test that heteroskedasticity is present, so he also estimates the White-corrected standard error for the coefficient on inflation to be 0.31. The critical two-tail 5% t-value for 118 degrees of freedom is 1.98. Is inflation statistically significant at the 5% level?

Answer:

The t-statistic should be recalculated using the White-corrected standard error as:

$$t = \frac{0.60}{0.31} = 1.94$$

This is less than the critical t-value of 1.98, which means after correcting for heteroskedasticity, the null hypothesis that the inflation coefficient is zero cannot be rejected. Therefore, inflation is not statistically significant. Notice that because the coefficient estimate of 0.60 was not affected by heteroskedasticity, but the original standard error of 0.28 was too low, the original t-statistic of 2.14 was too high. After using the higher White-corrected standard error of 0.31, the t-statistic fell to 1.94.

WHAT IS SERIAL CORRELATION?

Serial correlation, also known as **autocorrelation**, refers to the situation in which the residual terms are correlated with one another. Serial correlation is a relatively common problem with time series data.

- *Positive serial correlation* exists when a positive regression error in one time period increases the probability of observing a positive regression error for the next time period.
- *Negative serial correlation* occurs when a positive error in one period increases the probability of observing a negative error in the next period.

Effect of Serial Correlation on Regression Analysis

Because of the tendency of the data to cluster together from observation to observation, positive serial correlation typically results in coefficient standard errors that are too small, even though the estimated coefficients are accurate. These small standard error terms will cause the computed t-statistics to be larger than they should be, which will cause too many Type I errors: the rejection of the null hypothesis when it is actually true. The F-test will also be unreliable.

Because of the tendency of the data to diverge from observation to observation, negative serial correlation typically causes the standard errors to be too large, which leads to *t*-statistics that are too small. This will cause us to fail to reject the null hypothesis when it is actually false, resulting in too many Type II errors.

 Professor's Note: Positive serial correlation is much more common in economic and financial data, so focus your attention on its effects.

Detecting Serial Correlation

There are two methods that are commonly used to detect the presence of serial correlation: residual plots and the Durbin-Watson statistic.

A scatter plot of residuals versus time, like those shown in Figure 5, can reveal the presence of serial correlation. Figure 5 illustrates examples of positive and negative serial correlation.

Figure 5: Residual Plots for Serial Correlation

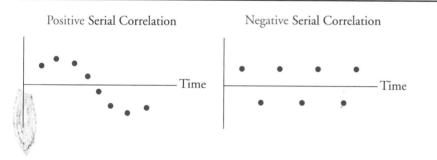

The more common method is to use the **Durbin-Watson statistic** (DW) to detect the presence of serial correlation. It is calculated as:

$$DW = \frac{\sum_{t=2}^{T}(\hat{\varepsilon}_t - \hat{\varepsilon}_{t-1})^2}{\sum_{t=1}^{T}\hat{\varepsilon}_t^2}$$

where:
$\hat{\varepsilon}_t$ = residual for period t

If the sample size is very large:

$$DW \approx 2(1 - r)$$

where:
r = correlation coefficient between residuals from one period and those from the previous period

You can see from the approximation that the Durbin-Watson test statistic is approximately equal to 2 if the error terms are homoskedastic and not serially correlated ($r = 0$). DW < 2 if the error terms are positively serially correlated ($r > 0$), and DW > 2 if the error terms are negatively serially correlated ($r < 0$). But how much above or below the magic number 2 is statistically significant enough to reject the null hypothesis of no serial correlation?

There are tables of DW statistics that provide upper and lower critical DW-values (d_u and d_l, respectively) for various sample sizes, levels of significance, and numbers of degrees of freedom against which the computed DW test statistic can be compared. The DW-test procedure for serial correlation is as follows:

H_0: the regression has *no* serial correlation

The decision rules are rather complicated because they allow for rejecting the null in favor of either positive or negative correlation. The test can also be inconclusive, which means we don't accept or reject (See Figure 6).

- If DW < d_l, the error terms are *positively* serially correlated (i.e., reject the null hypothesis of no serial correlation).
- If d_l < DW < d_u, the test is inconclusive.
- If d_u < DW < 4 − d_u, there is no serial correlation (i.e., do not reject the null).
- If 4 − d_u < DW < 4 − d_l, the test is inconclusive.
- If 4 − d_l < DW < 4, the error terms are *negatively* serially correlated (i.e., reject the null hypothesis of no serial correlation).

Figure 6: **Durbin-Watson Decision Rule**

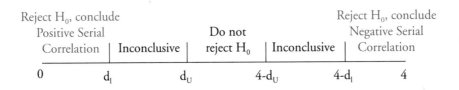

(H_0: No serial correlation)

Reject H_0, conclude Positive Serial Correlation	Inconclusive	Do not reject H_0	Inconclusive	Reject H_0, conclude Negative Serial Correlation
0	d_l	d_U	4-d_U	4-d_l 4

Example: The Durbin-Watson test for serial correlation

Suppose you have a regression output which includes three independent variables that provide you with a DW statistic of 1.23. Also suppose that the sample size is 40. At a 5% significance level, determine if the error terms are serially correlated.

Answer:

From a 5% DW table with n = 40 and k = 3, the upper and lower critical DW values are found to be d_l = 1.34 and d_u = 1.66, respectively. Since DW < d_l (i.e., 1.23 < 1.34), you should reject the null hypothesis and conclude that the regression has positive serial correlation among the error terms.

Correcting Serial Correlation

Possible remedies for serial correlation include:

- *Adjust the coefficient standard errors*, which is the method recommended in the CFA curriculum, using the Hansen method. The Hansen method also corrects for conditional heteroskedasticity. These adjusted standard errors, which are sometimes called serial correlation consistent standard errors or Hansen-White standard errors, are then used in hypothesis testing of the regression coefficients. Only use the Hansen method if serial correlation is a problem. The White-corrected standard errors are preferred if only heteroskedasticity is a problem. If both conditions are present, use the Hansen method.

- *Improve the specification of the model.* The best way to do this is to explicitly incorporate the time-series nature of the data (e.g., include a seasonal term). This can be tricky.

WHAT IS MULTICOLLINEARITY?

LOS 12.h: Describe multicollinearity and discuss its causes and effects in regression analysis.

Multicollinearity refers to the condition when two or more of the independent variables, or linear combinations of the independent variables, in a multiple regression are highly correlated with each other. This condition distorts the standard error of estimate and the coefficient standard errors, leading to problems when conducting t-tests for statistical significance of parameters.

Effect of Multicollinearity on Regression Analysis

As a result of multicollinearity, there is a *greater probability that we will incorrectly conclude that a variable is not statistically significant* (e.g., a Type II error). Multicollinearity is likely to be present to some extent in most economic models. The issue is whether the multicollinearity has a significant effect on the regression results.

Detecting Multicollinearity

The most common way to detect multicollinearity is the situation where t-tests indicate that none of the individual coefficients is significantly different than zero, while the F-test is statistically significant and the R^2 is high. This suggests that the variables together explain much of the variation in the dependent variable, but the individual independent variables don't. The only way this can happen is when the independent variables are highly correlated with each other, so while their common source of variation is explaining the dependent variable, the high degree of correlation also "washes out" the individual effects.

High correlation among independent variables is sometimes suggested as a sign of multicollinearity. In fact, answers to some old CFA questions suggest the following general rule of thumb: If the absolute value of the sample correlation between any two independent variables in the regression is greater than 0.7, multicollinearity is a potential problem.

However, this only works if there are exactly two independent variables. If there are more than two independent variables, while individual variables may not be highly correlated, linear combinations might be, leading to multicollinearity. High correlation among the independent variables suggests the possibility of multicollinearity, but low correlation among the independent variables *does not necessarily* indicate multicollinearity is *not* present.

Example: Detecting multicollinearity

Bob Watson, CFA, runs a regression of mutual fund returns on average P/B, average P/E, and average market capitalization, with the following results:

Variable	Coefficient	p-Value
Average P/B	3.52	0.15
Average P/E	2.78	0.21
Market Cap	4.03	0.11
F-test	34.6	< 0.001
R^2	89.6%	

Determine whether or not multicollinearity is a problem in this regression.

Answer:

The R^2 is high and the F-test is statistically significant, which suggest that the three variables as a group do an excellent job of explaining the variation in mutual fund returns. However, none of the independent variables individually is statistically significant to any reasonable degree, since the p-values are larger than 10%. This is a classic indication of multicollinearity.

Correcting Multicollinearity

The most common method to correct for multicollinearity is to omit one or more of the correlated independent variables. Unfortunately, it is not always an easy task to identify the variable(s) that are the source of the multicollinearity. There are statistical procedures that may help in this effort, like stepwise regression, which systematically remove variables from the regression until multicollinearity is minimized.

WARM-UP: MODEL SPECIFICATION

Regression model specification is the selection of the explanatory (independent) variables to be included in the regression and the transformations, if any, of those explanatory variables.

For example, suppose we're trying to predict a P/E ratio using a cross-sectional regression with fundamental variables that are related to P/E. Valuation theory tells us that the stock's dividend payout ratio (DPO), growth rate (G), and beta (B) are associated with P/E. One specification of the model would be:

Specification 1: $P/E = b_0 + b_1 DPO + b_2 G + b_3 B + \varepsilon$

If we also decide that market capitalization (M) is related to P/E ratio, we would create a second specification of the model by including M as an independent variable:

Specification 2: $P/E = a_0 + a_1 DPO + a_2 G + a_3 B + a_4 M + \varepsilon$

Finally, suppose we conclude that market cap is not linearly related to P/E, but the natural log of market cap is linearly related to P/E. Then we would transform M by taking its natural log and creating a new variable lnM. Thus our third specification would be:

Specification 3: $P/E = c_0 + c_1 DPO + c_2 G + c_3 B + c_4 lnM + \varepsilon$

> *Professor's Note: Notice that we used "a" instead of "b" in Specification 2 and "c" in Specification 3. We must do that to recognize that when we change the specifications of the model, the regression parameters change. For example, we wouldn't expect the intercept in Specification 1 (b_0) to be the same as in Specification 2 (a_0) or the same as Specification 3 (c_0).*

MODEL MISSPECIFICATION

LOS 12.i: Discuss the effects of model misspecification on the results of a regression analysis, and explain how to avoid the common forms of misspecification.

There are three broad categories of *model misspecification*, or ways in which the regression model can be specified incorrectly, each with several subcategories:

1. The functional form can be misspecified.
   - Important variables are omitted.
   - Variables should be transformed.
   - Data is improperly pooled.

2. Explanatory variables are correlated with the error term in time series models.
   - A lagged dependent variable is used as an independent variable.
   - A function of the dependent variable is used as an independent variable ("forecasting the past").
   - Independent variables are measured with error.

3. Other time-series misspecifications that result in nonstationarity.

 Professor's Note: We'll focus on the first two categories because nonstationarity in time series regressions is covered in the next topic review.

The *effects of the model misspecification on the regression results*, as shown in Figure 7, are basically the same for all of the misspecifications we will discuss: regression coefficients are often biased and/or inconsistent, which means we can't have any confidence in our hypothesis tests of the coefficients or in the predictions of the model.

Figure 7: Effects of Model Misspecification

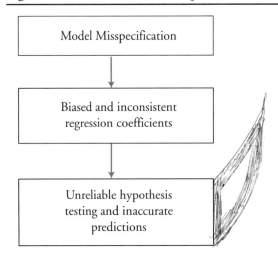

 Professor's Note: Recall the definitions of unbiased and consistent estimators from the Level 1 curriculum:

- *An unbiased estimator is one for which the expected value of the estimator is equal to the parameter you are trying to estimate. For example, because the expected value of the sample mean is equal to the population mean, the sample mean is an unbiased estimator of the population mean.*

- *A consistent estimator is one for which the accuracy of the parameter estimate increases as the sample size increases. As the sample size increases, the standard error of the sample mean falls, and the sampling distribution bunches more closely around the population mean. In fact, as the sample size approaches infinity, the standard error approaches zero.*

EXAMPLES OF MISSPECIFICATION OF FUNCTIONAL FORM

Let's start with a regression in which we're trying to predict monthly returns on portfolios of Chinese stocks (R) using four independent variables: portfolio beta (B), the natural log of market capitalization (lnM), the natural log of the price-to-book ratio ln(PB), and free float (FF). Free float is equal to the ratio of shares available to be traded by the investing public to total company shares. The regression is estimated with 72 monthly observations from July 1996 to June 2002. The correct specification of the model is as follows:

$$R = b_0 + b_1B + b_2lnM + b_3lnPB + b_4FF + \varepsilon$$

Suppose we determine in this specification that both lnM and FF are statistically significant at the 1% level.

Professor's Note: The correct regression model specification is based on a study by Wang and Xu (2004).[3] The incorrect specifications that follow are designed to illustrate examples of common misspecifications, but they are not included in the Wang and Xu study.

Misspecification #1: Omitting a Variable

Suppose we do not include lnM in the regression model:

$$R = a_0 + a_1B + a_2lnPB + a_3FF + \varepsilon$$

If lnM is correlated with any of the remaining independent variables (B, lnPB, or FF), then the error term is also correlated with the same independent variables and the resulting regression coefficients (the estimates of a_0, a_1, and a_2) are biased and inconsistent. That means our hypothesis tests and predictions using the model are unreliable.

Misspecification #2: Variable Should Be Transformed

Regression assumes that the dependent variable is linearly related to each of the independent variables. Typically, however, market capitalization is not linearly related to portfolio returns, but the natural log of market cap is linearly related. If we include market cap in the regression without transforming it by taking the natural log—if we use M and not ln(M)—we've misspecified the model.

$$R = c_0 + c_1B + c_2M + c_3lnPB + c_4FF + \varepsilon$$

Other examples of transformations include squaring the variable or taking the square root of the variable. If financial statement data are included in the regression model, a

3. Fenghua Wang and Yexiao Xu. "What Determines Chinese Stock Returns." *Financial Analysts Journal* 6 (November/December 2004): 65–77.

common transformation is to standardize the variables by dividing by sales (for income statement or cash flow items) or total assets (for balance sheet items). You should recognize these as items from *common-size financial statements*.

Misspecification #3: Incorrectly Pooling Data

Suppose the relationship between returns and the independent variables during the first three years is actually different than relationship in the second three-year period (i.e., the regression coefficients are different from one period to the next). By pooling the data and estimating one regression over the entire period, rather than estimating two separate regressions over each of the subperiods, we have misspecified the model and our hypothesis tests and predictions of portfolio returns will be misleading.

Misspecification #4: Using Lagged Dependent Variable as Independent Variable

A lagged variable in a time series regression is the value of a variable from a prior period. In our example, the dependent variable is portfolio return in month t, so a lagged dependent variable would be the portfolio return in the previous period, month $t - 1$ (which is denoted as R_{t-1}).

$$R = d_0 + d_1B + d_2\ln M + d_3\ln PB + d_4FF + d_5R_{t-1} + \varepsilon$$

If the error terms in the regression model are also serially correlated (which is common in time series regressions), then this model misspecification will result in biased and inconsistent regression estimates and unreliable hypothesis tests and return predictions.

Misspecification #5: Forecasting the Past

The proper specification of the model is to measure the dependent variable as returns during a particular month (say July 1996), and the independent variable $\ln(M)$ as the natural log of market capitalization *at the beginning* of July. Remember that market cap is equal to shares outstanding times price per share. If we measure market cap *at the end* of July and use it in our regression, we're naturally going to conclude that stocks with higher market cap at the end of July had higher returns during July. In other words, our model is misspecified because it is forecasting the past: we're using variables measured at the end of July to predict a variable measured during July.

Misspecification #6: Measuring Independent Variables with Error

The free float (FF) independent variable is actually trying to capture the relationship between corporate governance quality and portfolio returns. However, because we can't actually measure "corporate governance quality," we have to use a proxy variable. Wang and Xu used free float to proxy for corporate governance quality. The presumption is that the higher the level of free float, the more influence the capital markets have on management's decision making process and the more effective the corporate governance structure. However, because we're using free float as a proxy, we're actually measuring the variable we want to include in our regression—corporate governance quality—with error. Once again our regression estimates will be biased and inconsistent and our hypothesis testing and predictions unreliable.

Professor's Note: For more information on corporate governance and the valuation implications of effective corporate governance practices, see the topic review of corporate governance in Study Session 9.

Another common example when an independent variable is measured with error is when we want to use expected inflation in our regression but use actual inflation as a proxy.

QUALITATIVE DEPENDENT VARIABLES

LOS 12.j: Discuss models with qualitative dependent variables.

Financial analysis often calls for the use of a model that has a **qualitative dependent variable**, a dummy variable that takes on a value of either zero or one. An example of an application requiring the use of a qualitative dependent variable is a model that attempts to predict when a bond issuer will default. In this case, the dependent variable may take on a value of one in the event of default and zero in the event of no default. An ordinary regression model is not appropriate for situations that require a qualitative dependent variable. However, there are several different types of models that use a qualitative dependent variable.

- **Probit and logit models.** A probit model is based on the normal distribution, while a logit model is based on the logistic distribution. Application of these models results in estimates of the probability that the event occurs (e.g., probability of default). The maximum likelihood methodology is used to estimate coefficients for probit and logit models. These coefficients relate the independent variables to the likelihood of an event occurring, such as a merger, bankruptcy, or default.
- **Discriminant models.** Discriminant models are similar to probit and logit models but make different assumptions regarding the independent variables. Discriminant analysis results in a linear function similar to an ordinary regression which generates an overall score, or ranking, for an observation. The scores can then be used to rank or classify observations. A popular application of a discriminant model makes use of financial ratios as the independent variables to predict the qualitative dependent variable bankruptcy. A linear relationship among the independent variables produces a value for the dependent variable that places a company in a bankrupt or not bankrupt class.

The analysis of regression models with qualitative dependent variables is the same as we have been discussing all through this topic review. Examine the individual coefficients using t-tests, determine the validity of the model with the F-test and the R^2, and look out for heteroskedasticity, serial correlation, and multicollinearity.

INTERPRETING REGRESSION RESULTS

LOS 12.k: Interpret the economic meaning of the results of multiple regression analysis, and critique a regression model and its results.

The economic meaning of the results of a regression estimation focuses primarily on the slope coefficients. For example, suppose that we run a regression using a cross section of stock returns (in percent) as the dependent variable, and the stock betas (CAPM) and market capitalizations (in $ billions) as our independent variables. The slope coefficients indicate the expected change in the stock returns for a one unit change in beta or market capitalization. The estimated regression equation is:

$$\text{Return} = 5.0 + 4.2\ \text{Beta} - 0.05\ \text{Mkt.Cap.} + \varepsilon$$

Furthermore, assume that these coefficient estimates are significantly different from zero in a statistical sense. The economic meaning of these results is that, on average, a one unit increase in beta risk is associated with a 4.2% *increase* in return, while a $1 billion increase in market capitalization implies a 0.05% *decrease* in return.

As is always the case with statistical inferences, it is possible to identify a relationship that has statistical significance without having any economic significance. For instance, a study of dividend announcements may identify a statistically significant abnormal return following the announcement, but these returns may not be sufficient to cover transactions costs.

ASSESSING A MULTIPLE REGRESSION MODEL—PUTTING IT ALL TOGETHER

The flow chart in Figure 8 will help you evaluate a multiple regression model and grasp the "big picture" in preparation for the exam.

Figure 8: Assessment of a Multiple Regression Model

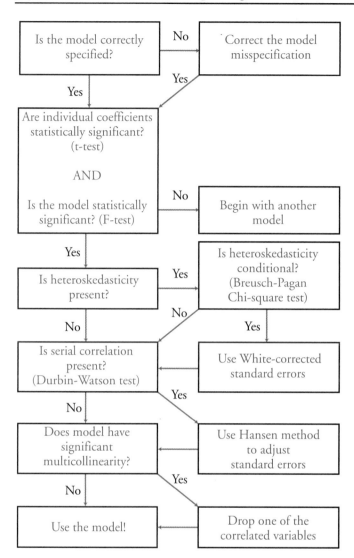

KEY CONCEPTS

LOS 12.a

The multiple regression equation specifies a dependent variable as a linear function of two or more independent variables:

$$Y_i = b_0 + b_1X_{1i} + b_2X_{2i} + \dots + b_kX_{ki} + \varepsilon_i$$

The intercept term is the value of the dependent variable when the independent variables are equal to zero. Each slope coefficient is the estimated change in the dependent variable for a one-unit change in that independent variable, holding the other independent variables constant.

LOS 12.b

A *t*-test is used for hypothesis testing of regression parameter estimates:

$$t_{bj} = \frac{\hat{b}_j - b_j}{s_{\hat{b}_j}}, \text{ with } n - k - 1 \text{ degrees of freedom}$$

Testing for statistical significance means testing $H_0: b_j = 0$ vs. $H_a: b_j \neq 0$.

LOS 12.c

The confidence interval for regression coefficient is:

estimated regression coefficient $\pm$ (critical *t*-value)(coefficient standard error)

The value of dependent variable Y is predicted as:

$$\hat{Y} = \hat{b}_0 + \hat{b}_1X_1 + \hat{b}_2X_2 + \dots + \hat{b}_kX_k$$

LOS 12.d

Assumptions of multiple regression mostly pertain to the error term, ε_i.
- A linear relationship exists between the dependent and independent variables.
- The independent variables are not random, and there is no exact linear relation between any two or more independent variables.
- The expected value of the error term is zero.
- The variance of the error terms is constant.
- The error for one observation is not correlated with that of another observation.
- The error term is normally distributed.

LOS 12.e
The *F*-distributed test statistic can be used to test the significance of all (or any subset of) the independent variables (i.e., the overall fit of the model) using a one-tailed test:

$$F = \frac{MSR}{MSE} = \frac{RSS/k}{SSE/[n-k-1]} \text{ with k and n} - k - 1 \text{ degrees of freedom}$$

The coefficient of determination, R^2, is the percentage of the variation in Y that is explained by the set of independent variables.
- R^2 increases as the number of independent variables increases—this can be a problem.
- The adjusted R^2 adjusts the R^2 for the number of independent variables.

An ANOVA table is used to assess the usefulness of a regression model's independent variable(s) in explaining the dependent variable:

Source	*df* *(Degrees of Freedom)*	*SS* *(Sum of Squares)*	*MS* *Mean Square = (SS/df)*
Regression	k	RSS	MSR
Error	n – k – 1	SSE	MSE
Total	n – 1	SST	

$$MSE = \frac{SSE}{n-k-1}; \ MSR = \frac{RSS}{k}; \ R^2 = \frac{RSS}{SST}; \ F = \frac{MSR}{MSE}; \ SEE = \sqrt{MSE}$$

LOS 12.f
Qualitative independent variables (dummy variables) capture the effect of a binary independent variable:
- Slope coefficient is interpreted as the change in the dependent variable for the case when the dummy variable is one.
- Use one less dummy variable than the number of categories.

LOS 12.g,h
Summary of what you need to know regarding violations of the assumptions of multiple regression:

Violation	Conditional Heteroskedasticity	Serial Correlation	Multicollinearity
What is it?	Residual variance related to level of independent variables	Residuals are correlated	Two or more independent variables are correlated
Effect?	Too many Type I errors	Too many Type I errors (positive correlation)	Too many Type II errors
Detection?	Breusch-Pagan chi-square test $= n \times R^2$	Durbin-Watson test $\approx 2(1 - r)$	Conflicting t and F statistics; correlations among independent variables if $k = 2$
Correction?	Use White-corrected standard errors	Use Hansen method to adjust standard errors	Drop one of the correlated variables

LOS 12.i
There are six common misspecifications of the regression model that you should be aware of and able to recognize:
- Omitting a variable.
- Variable should be transformed.
- Incorrectly pooling data.
- Using lagged dependent variable as independent variable.
- Forecasting the past.
- Measuring independent variables with error.

The effects of the model misspecification on the regression results are basically the same for all of the misspecifications: regression coefficients are biased and inconsistent, which means we can't have any confidence in our hypothesis tests of the coefficients or in the predictions of the model.

LOS 12.j
Qualitative dependent variables (e.g., bankrupt versus non-bankrupt) require methods other than ordinary least squares (e.g., probit, logit, or discriminant analysis).

LOS 12.k
The values of the slope coefficients suggest the economic meaning of the relationship between the independent and dependent variables, but it is important for the analyst to keep in mind that a regression may have statistical significance even when there is no practical economic significance in the relationship.

CONCEPT CHECKERS

Use the following ANOVA table for Questions 1 through 4.

Source	Sum of Squares (SS)	Degrees of Freedom
Regression	1,025 RSS	5 =K
Error	925	25 = n-k-1

1. The number of sample observations in the regression estimation is *closest* to:
    A. 29.
    B. 30.
    C. 31.

2. The mean squared error (MSE) is *closest* to:
    A. 37.
    B. 82.
    C. 205.

3. The R^2 statistic is *closest* to:
    A. 53%.   1025
    B. 50%.   1950
    C. 47%.

$$SST = RSS + SSE$$
$$R^2 = \frac{RSS}{SST}$$

4. The *F*-statistic is *closest* to:
    A. 1.1.
    B. 3.3.
    C. 5.5.

$$F = \frac{MSR}{MSE}$$

Use the following information to answer Questions 5 through 9.

Multiple regression was used to explain stock returns using the following variables:

Dependent variable:
    RET   = annual stock returns (%)
Independent variables:
    MKT   = Market capitalization = Market capitalization / $1.0 million
    IND   = Industry quartile ranking (IND = 4 is the highest ranking)
    FORT   = Fortune 500 firm, where {FORT = 1 if the stock is that of a Fortune 500
             firm, FORT = 0 if not a Fortune 500 stock}

The regression results are presented in the tables below.

	Coefficient	Standard Error	t-Statistic	p-Value
Intercept	0.5220	1.2100	0.430	0.681
Market Capitalization	0.0460	0.0150	3.090	0.021
Industry Ranking	0.7102	0.2725	2.610	0.040
Fortune 500	0.9000	0.5281	1.700	0.139

ANOVA	df	SS	MSS	F	Significance F
Regression	3	20.5969	6.8656	12.100	0.006
Error	6	3.4031	0.5672		
Total	9	24.0000			

Test	Test-Statistic
Breusch-Pagan	17.7
Durbin-Watson	1.8

5. Based on the results in the table, which of the following *most accurately* represents the regression equation?
    A. 0.43 + 3.09(MKT) + 2.61(IND) + 1.70(FORT).
    B. 0.681 + 0.021(MKT) + 0.04(IND) + 0.139(FORT).
    C. 0.522 + 0.0460(MKT) + 0.7102(IND) + 0.9(FORT).

6. The expected amount of the stock return attributable to it being a Fortune 500 stock is *closest* to:
    A. 0.522.
    B. 0.139.
    C. 0.900.

7. The expected return on the stock of a firm that is not in the Fortune 500, has a market capitalization of $5 million, and is in an industry with a rank of 3 is *closest* to:
    A. 2.88%.
    B. 3.98%.
    C. 1.42%.

8. Does being a Fortune 500 stock contribute significantly to stock returns?
    A. Yes, at a 10% level of significance.
    B. Yes, at a 5% level of significance.
    C. No, not at a reasonable level of significance.

9.   The *p*-value of the Breusch-Pagan test is 0.0005. The lower and upper limits for the Durbin-Watson test are 0.40 and 1.90, respectively. Based on this data and the information in the tables, there is evidence of:
        A. only serial correlation.
        B. serial correlation and heteroskedasticity.
        C. only heteroskedasticity.

Use the following information to answer Questions 10 through 11.

An analyst evaluates the sum of squared error and total sum of squares from a multiple regression with four independent variables to be 4,320 and 9,105 respectively. There are 65 observations in the sample.

[handwritten: SSE = 4320 SST = 9105 RSS = 4785]
[handwritten: n = 65 K = 4]

10.   The *F*-statistic is *closest* to:
        A. 13.54.
        B. 13.77.
        C. 16.61.

[handwritten: $F = \dfrac{MSR}{MSE} = \dfrac{1196.25}{72} =$]

11.   The critical *F*-value for testing $H_0 = b_1 = b_2 = b_3 = b_4 = 0$ vs. H_a: at least one $b_j \neq 0$ at the 5% significance level is *closest* to:
        A. 2.37.
        B. 2.53.
        C. 2.76.

[handwritten: 2.50   F(test stat) > F(test value) = reject null!]

12.   Which of the following situations is *least likely* to result in the misspecification of a regression model with monthly returns as the dependent variable?
        A. Failing to include an independent variable that is related to monthly returns.
        B. Using leading P/E from the previous period as an independent variable.
        C. Using actual inflation as an independent variable to proxy for expected inflation.

13.   The *least likely* result of regression model misspecification is:
        A. unreliable hypothesis tests of the regression coefficients.
        B. inconsistent regression coefficients.
        C. unbiased regression coefficients.

CHALLENGE PROBLEMS

14. Phil Ohlmer is developing a regression model to predict returns on a hedge fund composite index using several different independent variables. Which of the following list of independent variables, if included in the model, is *most likely* to lead to biased and inconsistent regression coefficients and why?
    A. Small-cap index returns, high-yield bond index returns, and emerging market index returns; because small-cap returns and hedge fund index returns are likely to be correlated.
    B. Small-cap index returns, high-yield bond index returns, and emerging market index returns; because small-cap returns and emerging market index returns are likely to be correlated.
    C. Small-cap index returns, previous period hedge fund composite index returns, high-yield bond index returns, and emerging market index returns; because the regression model is likely to be misspecified.

15. What condition is the Durbin-Watson statistic designed to detect in multiple regression, and what is the *most appropriate* remedy to correct for that condition?

	Condition	Remedy
A.	Serial correlation	Use robust standard errors
B.	Autocorrelation	Use generalized least squares
C.	Heteroskedasticity	Use generalized least squares

16. Which of the following situations is *least likely* the result of a multiple regression analysis with more than 50 observations?

	R^2	Adjusted R^2
A.	71%	69%
B.	83%	86%
C.	10%	−2%

Use the following information for Questions 17 and 18.

Phil Ohlmer estimates a cross sectional regression in order to predict price to earnings ratios (P/E) with fundamental variables that are related to P/E, including dividend payout ratio (DPO), growth rate (G), and beta (B). In addition, all 50 stocks in the sample come from two industries, electric utilities or biotechnology. He defines the following dummy variable:

IND = 0 if the stock is in the electric utilities industry, or
= 1 if the stock is in the biotechnology industry

The results of his regression are shown in the following table.

Variable	Coefficient	t-Statistic
Intercept	6.75	3.89*
IND	8.00	4.50* *tests the null that industry returns are equal*
DPO	4.00	1.86
G	12.35	2.43*
B	−0.50	1.46

*significant at the 5% level

17. Based on these results, it would be *most appropriate* to conclude that:
   A. biotechnology industry returns are statistically significantly larger than electric utilities industry returns.
   B. electric utilities returns are statistically significantly larger than biotechnology industry returns, holding DPO, G, and B constant.
   C. biotechnology industry returns are statistically significantly larger than electric utilities industry returns, holding DPO, G, and B constant.

18. Ohlmer is valuing a biotechnology stock with a dividend payout ratio of 0.00, a beta of 1.50, and an expected earnings growth rate of 0.14. The predicted P/E on the basis of the values of the explanatory variables for the company is *closest* to:
   A. 7.7.
   B. 15.7.
   C. 17.2.

19. Assumptions underlying a multiple regression are *most likely* to include:
   A. The expected value of the error term is 0.00 < i < 1.00.
   B. Linear and non-linear relationships exist between the dependent and independent variables.
   C. The error for one observation is not correlated with that of another observation.

20. Qualitative dependent variables should be verified using:
   A. a dummy variable based on the logistic distribution.
   B. a discriminant model using a linear function for ranked observations.
   C. tests for heteroskedasticity, serial correlation, and multicollinearity.

ANSWERS – CONCEPT CHECKERS

1. **C** $k = 5$ and $n - 5 - 1 = 25$, so $n = 31$

2. **A** $MSE = \dfrac{SSE}{df_{error}} = \dfrac{925}{25} = 37$

3. **A** $R^2 = \dfrac{SSR}{SST} = \dfrac{1,025}{1,950} = 53\%$

4. **C** $F = \dfrac{MSR}{MSE} = \dfrac{\dfrac{SSR}{df_{regression}}}{\dfrac{SSE}{df_{error}}} = \dfrac{\dfrac{1,025}{5}}{\dfrac{925}{25}} = \dfrac{205}{37} = 5.5$

5. **C** The coefficients column contains the regression parameters.

6. **C** The regression equation is $0.522 + 0.0460(MKT) + 0.7102(IND) + 0.9(FORT)$. The coefficient on FORT is the amount of the return attributable to the stock of a Fortune 500 firm.

7. **A** The regression equation is $0.522 + 0.0460(MKT) + 0.7102(IND) + 0.9(FORT)$, so $RET = 0.522 + 0.0460(5) + 0.7102(3) + 0.900(0) = 2.88\%$.

8. **C** The p-value = 0.139, or 13.9%, which is not a reasonable level of significance.

9. **C** The Breusch-Pagan test is statistically significant, which indicates heteroskedasticity. The Durbin-Watson statistic is greater than the lower limit, but less than the upper limit, which places it in the "inconclusive" area. Thus, we are unable to reject the null hypothesis that there is no serial correlation present.

10. **C** $SSR = 9,105 - 4,320 = 4,785$

    $F = \dfrac{\dfrac{4,785}{4}}{\dfrac{4,320}{65 - 4 - 1}} = \dfrac{1,196.25}{72} = 16.61$

11. **B** This is a one-tailed test, so the critical F-value at the 5% significance level with 4 and 60 degrees of freedom is approximately 2.53.

12. **B** Using leading P/E from a prior period as an independent variable in the regression is unlikely to result in misspecification because it is not related to any of the six types of misspecifications previously discussed. We're not forecasting the past because leading P/E is calculated using beginning-of-period stock price and a forecast of earnings for the next period. Omitting a relevant independent variable from the regression and using actual instead of expected inflation (measuring the independent variable in error) are likely to result in model misspecification.

13. **C** The effects of the model misspecification on the regression results are basically the same for all of the misspecifications: regression coefficients are biased and inconsistent, which means we can't have any confidence in our hypothesis tests of the coefficients or in the predictions of the model. Notice that choice C states that model misspecification will result in "unbiased" regression coefficients, while in fact model misspecification is most likely to result in "biased" regression coefficients.

ANSWERS – CHALLENGE PROBLEMS

14. **C** Including a lagged dependent variable (previous period hedge fund composite index returns) in the list of independent variables is likely to lead to model misspecification and biased and inconsistent regression coefficients.

The fact that an independent variable (small-cap returns) and the dependent variable (hedge fund index returns) are correlated is not a problem for the regression model; we would expect that if the model has predictive power the dependent variable would be correlated with the independent variables. The fact that two independent variables (small-cap returns and emerging market index returns) are correlated is not a problem of model misspecification, but potentially one of multicollinearity, but without additional information we can't draw any conclusions concerning whether multicollinearity is a problem (remember "most likely").

15. **A** The Durbin-Watson statistic tests for serial correlation of the residuals. The appropriate remedy if serial correlation is detected is to use robust standard errors to calculate the *t*-statistics.

16. **B** Adjusted R^2 must be less than or equal to R^2. However, if R^2 is low enough and the number of independent variables is large, adjusted R^2 may be negative.

17. **C** The *t*-statistic tests the null that industry returns are equal. The dummy variable is significant and positive, and the dummy variable is defined as being equal to one for biotechnology stocks, which means that biotechnology stock returns are statistically significantly larger than electric utility stock returns. Remember, however, this is only accurate if we hold the other independent variables in the model constant.

18. **B** Note that IND = 1 because the stock is in the biotech industry. Predicted P/E = 6.75 + (8.00×1) + (4.00×0.00) + (12.35×0.14) − (0.50×1.5) = 15.7.

19. **C** Assumptions underlying a multiple regression include: the error for one observation is not correlated with that of another observation; the expected value of the error term is zero; a linear relationship exists between the dependent and independent variables; the variance of the error terms is constant.

20. **C** All qualitative dependent variable models must be tested for heteroskedasticity, serial correlation, and multicollinearity. Each of the alternatives are potential examples of a qualitative dependent variable model, but none are universal elements of all qualitative dependent variable models.

TIME-SERIES ANALYSIS

EXAM FOCUS

This topic review builds on the previous review on multiple regression, only here the focus is on time series analysis. A time series is a set of observations of a random variable spaced evenly through time (e.g., quarterly sales revenue for a company over the past 60 quarters). For the exam, identifying and correcting regression violations, such as heteroskedasticity, nonstationarity, serial correlation, etc., will be important, as well as being able to calculate a value when a time-series model is provided. Know why a log-linear model is sometimes used; understand the implications of seasonality and how to detect and correct it, as well as the root mean squared error (RMSE) criterion. Be sure you can look at a plot of data to detect nonstationarity or use the output from a regression analysis to analyze a time-series model.

TREND MODELS

LOS 13.a: Calculate and evaluate the predicted trend value for a time series, modeled as either a linear trend or a log-linear trend, given the estimated trend coefficients.

A **time series** is a set of observations for a variable over successive periods of time (e.g., monthly stock market returns for the past ten years). The series has a **trend** if a consistent pattern can be seen by plotting the data (i.e., the individual observations) on a graph. For example, a seasonal trend in sales data is easily detected by plotting the data and noting the significant jump in sales during the same month(s) each year.

Linear Trend Model

A **linear trend** is a time series pattern that can be graphed using a straight line. A downward sloping line indicates a negative trend, while an upward-sloping line indicates a positive trend.

The simplest form of a linear trend is represented by the following linear trend model:

$$y_t = b_0 + b_1(t) + \varepsilon_t$$

where:
y_t = the value of the time series (the dependent variable) at time t
b_0 = intercept at the vertical axis (y-axis)
b_1 = slope coefficient (or trend coefficient)
ε_t = error term (or residual term or disturbance term)
t = time (the independent variable); t = 1, 2, 3…T

Ordinary least squares (OLS) regression (simple linear regression) is used to estimate the coefficient in the trend line, which provides the following prediction equation:

$$\hat{y}_t = \hat{b}_0 + \hat{b}_1(t)$$

where :
$\hat{y}_t$ = the predicted value of y (the dependent variable) at time t
$\hat{b}_0$ = the estimated value of the intercept term
$\hat{b}_1$ = the estimated value of the slope coefficient

> *Professor's Note: Don't let this model confuse you. It's very similar to the simple linear regression model we covered previously; only here, (t) takes on the value of the time period. For example, in period 2, the equation becomes:*

$$\hat{y}_2 = \hat{b}_0 + \hat{b}_1(2)$$

> *And, likewise, in period 3:*

$$\hat{y}_3 = \hat{b}_0 + \hat{b}_1(3)$$

> *This means $\hat{y}$ increases by the value of $\hat{b}_1$ each period.*

Example: Using a Linear Trend Model

Assume you are given a linear trend model with $\hat{b}_0$ = 1.70 and $\hat{b}_1$ = 3.0.

Calculate $\hat{y}_t$ for t = 1 and t = 2.

Answer:

When t = 1, $\hat{y}_1 = 1.70 + 3.0(1) = 4.70$

When t = 2, $\hat{y}_2 = 1.70 + 3.0(2) = 7.70$

Note that the difference between $\hat{y}_1$ and $\hat{y}_2$ is 3.0, or the value of the trend coefficient b_1.

Example: Trend Analysis

Consider hypothetical time series data for manufacturing capacity utilization.

Manufacturing Capacity Utilization

Quarter	Time (t)	Manufacturing Capacity Utilization (in %)	Quarter	Time (t)	Manufacturing Capacity Utilization (in %)
2004.1	1	82.4	2005.4	8	80.9
2004.2	2	81.5	2006.1	9	81.3
2004.3	3	80.8	2006.2	10	81.9
2004.4	4	80.5	2006.3	11	81.7
2005.1	5	80.2	2006.4	12	80.3
2005.2	6	80.2	2007.1	13	77.9
2005.3	7	80.5	2007.2	14	76.4

Applying the OLS methodology to fit the linear trend model to the data produces the results shown below.

Time Series Regression Results for Manufacturing Capacity Utilization

Regression model: $y_t = b_0 + b_1 t + \varepsilon_t$

R square	0.346		
Adjusted R square	0.292		
Standard error	1.334		
Observations	14		

	Coefficients	Standard Error	t-Statistic
Intercept	82.137	0.753	109.066
Manufacturing utilization	−0.223	0.088	−2.534

Based on this information, predict the projected capacity utilization for the time period involved in the study (i.e., in-sample estimates).

Answer:

As shown in the regression output, the estimated intercept and slope parameters for our manufacturing capacity utilization model are $\hat{b}_0 = 82.137$ and $\hat{b}_1 = -0.223$, respectively. This means that the prediction equation for capacity utilization can be expressed as:

$$\hat{y}_t = 82.137 - 0.223t$$

With this equation, we can generate estimated values for capacity utilization, $\hat{y}_t$, for each of the 14 quarters in the time series. For example, using the model capacity utilization for the first quarter of 2004 is estimated at 81.914:

$$\hat{y}_t = 82.137 - 0.223(1) = 82.137 - 0.223 = 81.914$$

Note that the estimated value of capacity utilization in that quarter (using the model) is not exactly the same as the actual, measured capacity utilization for that quarter (82.4). The difference between the two is the error or residual term associated with that observation:

$$\text{Residual (error)} = \text{actual value} - \text{predicted value} \approx 82.4 - 81.9 = 0.5$$

Note that since the actual, measured value is greater than the predicted value of y for 2004.1, the error term is positive. Had the actual, measured value been less than the predicted value, the error term would have been negative.

The projections (i.e., values generated by the model) for all quarters are compared to the actual values below.

Projected Versus Actual Capacity Utilization

Quarter	Time	$\hat{y}_t$	y_t	Quarter	Time	$\hat{y}_t$	y_t
2004.1	1	81.914	82.4	2005.4	8	80.353	80.9
2004.2	2	81.691	81.5	2006.1	9	80.130	81.3
2004.3	3	81.468	80.8	2006.2	10	79.907	81.9
2004.4	4	81.245	80.5	2006.3	11	79.684	81.7
2005.1	5	81.022	80.2	2006.4	12	79.460	80.3
2005.2	6	80.799	80.2	2007.1	13	79.237	77.9
2005.3	7	80.576	80.5	2007.2	14	79.014	76.4

The following graph shows visually how the predicted values compare to the actual values, which were used to generate the regression equation. The **residuals**, or **error terms**, are represented by the distance between the predicted (straight) regression line and the actual data plotted in blue. For example, the residual for t = 10 is 81.9 – 79.907 = 2.0

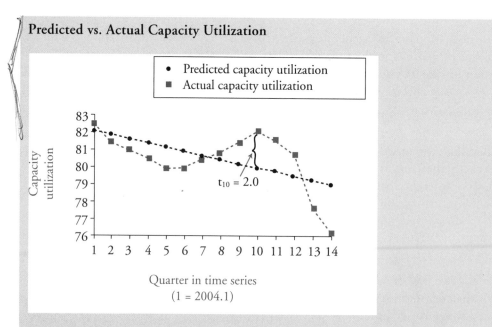

Predicted vs. Actual Capacity Utilization

Since we utilized a linear regression model, the predicted values will by definition fall on a straight line. Since the raw data does not display a linear relationship, the model will not do a good job of predicting future values.

Notice that the error terms appear to be positively correlated: six of the first seven are negative, the next five are positive, and the last two are negative. This is also an indication that the model is not appropriate for the data, as we will discuss in LOS 13.c.

Log-Linear Trend Models

Time series data, particularly financial time series, often display *exponential growth*. Positive exponential growth means that the data (i.e., the time series) tends to increase at some continuously compounded rate of growth. If we plot the data, the observations will form a convex (i.e., non-linear) curve. Negative exponential growth means that the data tends to decrease at some continuously compounded rate of growth, and the plotted time series will show a concave curve.

When a series exhibits exponential growth, each successive value of the series can be defined as:

$$y_t = e^{b_0 + b_1(t)}$$

where :
y_t = the value of the dependent variable at time t
b_0 = the intercept term
b_1 = the constant rate of growth
e = the base of the natural logarithm
t = time = 1, 2, 3...T

This model defines y, the dependent variable, as an *exponential* function of time, the independent variable. Rather than try to fit the curved nature of the data with a linear (straight line) regression, we take the natural log of both sides of the equation and arrive at the *log-linear* model. This is frequently used when time series data exhibit exponential growth.

$$\ln(y_t) = \ln\left(e^{b_0 + b_1(t)}\right) \Rightarrow \ln(y_t) = b_0 + b_1(t)$$

Notice that in the original equation, the exponent of e, the base of the natural logs, is itself a linear function. When you take the natural log of both sides of the equation, you arrive at a model which describes the *natural log* of y (i.e., the original dependent variable that showed exponential growth) as a *linear* function of time.

Now that the equation has been transformed from an exponential to a linear function, we can use a linear regression technique to model the series. The use of the transformed data produces a *linear* trend line with a better fit for the data and increases the predictive ability of the model. Because the log-linear model more accurately captures the behavior of the time series, the impact of *serial correlation* (discussed below) in the error terms is minimized.

Example: Log-Linear Trend Model

An analyst estimates a log-linear trend model using quarterly revenue data (in millions of $) from the first quarter of 1996 to the fourth quarter of 2007 for JP Northfield, Inc.:

$$\ln \text{revenue}_t = b_0 + b_1(t) + \varepsilon_t \qquad t = 1, 2, \dots 48$$

The results are shown in the following table.

	Coefficient	Standard Error	t-statistic
Intercept	4.00	0.05	80.0
Trend	0.09	0.01	9.0

Calculate JP Northfield's predicted revenues in the first quarter of 2008.

Answer:

In the first quarter of 2008, t is equal to 49 because the sample has 48 observations.

$$\ln \text{revenue}_{49} = 4.00 + 0.09(49) = 8.41$$

$$\text{revenue}_{49} = e^{\ln \text{revenue}_{49}} = e^{8.41} = \$4,492 \text{ million}$$

The first answer you get in this calculation is the natural log of the revenue forecast. In order to turn the natural log into a revenue figure, you use the 2nd function of the LN key (e^x) on your BA II Plus: enter 8.41 and press [2nd] e^x = 4,492 million.

LOS 13.b: Discuss the factors that determine whether a linear or log-linear trend should be used with a particular time series, and evaluate the limitations of trend models.

Factors that Determine Which Model is Best

To determine if a linear or log-linear trend model should be used, the analyst should plot the data. A *linear trend model* may be appropriate if the data points appear to be equally distributed above and below the regression line. Inflation rate data can often be modeled with a linear trend model.

If, on the other hand, the data plots with a non-linear (curved) shape, then the residuals from a linear trend model will be persistently positive or negative for a period of time. In this case, the *log-linear model* may be more appropriate. By taking the log of the y variable, a regression line can better fit the data. Financial data (e.g., stock indices and stock prices) and company sales data are often best modeled with a log-linear model.

Figure 1 shows a time series that is best modeled with a log-linear trend model rather than a linear trend model.

Figure 1: Linear vs. Log-Linear Trend Models

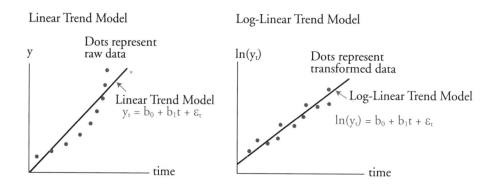

The left panel is a plot of data that exhibits exponential growth (e.g., compound growth) along with a linear trend line. The panel on the right is a plot of the natural logs of the original data and a representative log-linear trend line. The log-linear model fits the transformed data better than the linear trend model fits the original data and would, therefore, yield more accurate forecasts.

The bottom line is that growth at a constant *rate* calls for a log-linear model, so the raw data needs to be transformed. When the data grows by a constant *amount*, a linear trend model is more appropriate.

Limitations of Trend Models

Recall from the previous two topic reviews that one of the assumptions underlying linear regression is that the residual term is independently distributed and the residuals are uncorrelated with each other. A violation of this assumption is referred to as autocorrelation (which is covered in LOS 13.d). In this case, the residuals are persistently positive or negative for a period of time and it is said that the data exhibit serial correlation. This is a significant limitation, as it means that the model is not appropriate for the time series and that we should not use it to predict future performance.

In the preceding discussion, we suggested that a log-linear trend model would be better than a linear trend model when there is serial correlation in the data. However, it may be the case that even a log-linear model is not appropriate in the presence of serial correlation. In this case, we will want to turn to the autoregressive models discussed below.

 Professor's Note: Recall from the previous topic review that the Durbin Watson statistic (DW) is used to detect autocorrelation. For a time series model without serial correlation DW should be approximately equal to 2.0. A DW significantly less than 2.0 suggests that the residual terms are positively correlated. Please see LOS 12.g from the previous topic review for more detail on implementing the DW test.

AUTOREGRESSIVE MODELS

LOS 13.d: Discuss the structure of an autoregressive model of order p, calculate one- and two-period-ahead forecasts given the estimated coefficients, and explain how autocorrelations of the residuals can be used to test whether the autoregressive model fits the time series.

 Professor's Note: In the material that follows, we discuss the LOS in the order that we believe is best suited for effective learning.

Using a lagged dependent variable as an independent variable does not automatically mean that the regression is misspecified. In this section, we turn our attention to **autoregressive models** (AR), in which the dependent variable is regressed against one or more lagged values of itself. For example, the sales for a firm in March could be regressed against the sales for the firm in the two previous months of January and February.

The following model illustrates how variable x would be regressed on itself with a lag of one and two periods:

$$x_t = b_0 + b_1 x_{t-1} + b_2 x_{t-2} + \varepsilon_t$$

A model with two lags is referred to as a *second-order* autoregressive model, or an AR(2) model (i.e., autoregressive model using two lagged values of the dependent variable). In general, an AR model of order p, AR(p), is expressed as:

$$x_t = b_0 + b_1 x_{t-1} + b_2 x_{t-2} + \ldots + b_p x_{t-p} + \varepsilon_t$$

where p indicates the number of lagged values that the autoregressive model will include.

Forecasting With an Autoregressive Model

Autoregressive time series multi-period forecasts are calculated in the same manner as those for other regression models, but since the independent variable is a lagged value of the dependent variable, it is necessary to calculate a one-step-ahead forecast before a two-step-ahead forecast can be calculated. The calculation of successive forecasts in this manner is referred to as the **chain rule of forecasting**.

A one-period-ahead forecast for an AR(1) model is determined in the following manner:

$$\hat{x}_{t+1} = \hat{b}_0 + \hat{b}_1 x_t$$

Likewise, a two-step-ahead forecast for an AR(1) model is calculated as:

$$\hat{x}_{t+2} = \hat{b}_0 + \hat{b}_1 \hat{x}_{t+1}$$

Note that the ^ symbol above the variables in the equations indicates that the inputs used in multi-period forecasts are actually forecasts (estimates) themselves. This implies that multi-period forecasts are more uncertain than single period forecasts. For example, for a two-step-ahead model, there is the usual uncertainty associated with forecasting x_{t+1} using x_t, plus the additional uncertainty of forecasting x_{t+2} using the forecast value for x_{t+1}.

Example: Forecasting

Suppose that an AR(1) model has been estimated and has produced the following prediction equation: $x_t = 1.2 + 0.45x_{t-1}$. Calculate a two-step-ahead forecast if the current value of x is 5.0.

Answer:

One-step-ahead forecast: If $x_t = 5$, then $\hat{x}_{t+1} = 1.2 + 0.45(5) = 3.45$.

Two-step-ahead forecast: If $\hat{x}_{t+1} = 3.45$, then $\hat{x}_{t+2} = 1.2 + 0.45(3.45) = 2.75$.

Autocorrelation & Model Fit

When an AR model is correctly specified, the residual terms will not exhibit *serial correlation*. Serial correlation (or autocorrelation) means the error terms are correlated. When the error terms are correlated, standard errors are unreliable and *t*-tests of individual coefficients can incorrectly show statistical significance or insignificance.

If the residuals possess some degree of serial correlation, the AR model that produced the residuals is not the best model for the time series being analyzed. The procedure to test whether an AR time series model is correctly specified involves three steps:

Step 1: **Estimate** the AR model being evaluated using linear regression:

Start with a first-order AR model [i.e., AR(1)] using $x_t = b_0 + b_1 x_{t-1} + \varepsilon_t$.

Step 2: **Calculate** the autocorrelations of the model's residuals (i.e., the level of correlation between the forecast errors from one period to the next).

Step 3: **Test** whether the autocorrelations are significant:

If the model is correctly specified, none of the correlations will be statistically significant. To test for significance, a *t*-test is used to test the hypothesis that the correlations of the residuals are zero. The *t*-statistic is the estimated autocorrelation divided by the standard error. The standard error is $1/\sqrt{T}$, where T is the number of observations, so the test statistic for each autocorrelation is $t = \dfrac{\rho_{\varepsilon_t,\varepsilon_{t-k}}}{1/\sqrt{T}}$ with $(T-2)$ degrees of freedom, where k is the number of lagged terms and $\rho_{\varepsilon_t,\varepsilon_{t-k}}$ is the correlation of error term t with the kth lagged error term.

Professor's Note: The Durbin-Watson test that we used with trend models is not appropriate for testing for serial correlation of the error terms in an autoregressive model. Use this t-test instead.

Example: Testing an AR model for proper specification

The correlations of the error terms from the estimation of an AR(1) model using a sample with 102 observations are presented in the following figure. Determine whether the model is correctly specified.

Autocorrelation Analysis

Model: $y_t = b_0 + b_1 y_{t-1} + \varepsilon_t$

Lag	Autocorrelation	t-Statistic	Lag	Autocorrelation	t-Statistic
1	0.0616114	0.622245	7	−0.010146	−0.102470
2	0.0843368	0.851760	8	0.0211711	0.213818
3	0.0258823	0.261398	9	−0.0959502	−0.969050
4	0.0188928	0.190808	10	0.0389730	0.393608
5	0.1001404	1.011368	11	−0.0677132	−0.683870
6	−0.0638219	−0.644570	12	−0.0122798	−0.124020

Answer:

The critical two-tail *t*-value at the 5% significance level and 100 degrees of freedom is 1.98. The *t*-statistics indicate that none of the autocorrelations of the residuals in the previous figure is statistically different from zero because their absolute values are less than 1.98. Thus, there is sufficient reason to believe that the error terms from the AR(1) model are not serially correlated.

If the t-tests indicate that any of the correlations computed in Step 2 are statistically significant (i.e., $t \geq 1.98$), the AR model is not specified correctly. Lags corresponding to the significant correlations are included in the model and the correlations of the residuals (error terms) are checked again. This procedure will be followed until all autocorrelations are insignificant.

SEASONALITY

LOS 13.k: Discuss how to test and correct for seasonality in a time-series model, and calculate and interpret a forecasted value using an AR model with a seasonal lag.

Seasonality in a time-series is a pattern that tends to repeat from year to year. One example is monthly sales data for a retailer. Given that sales data normally vary according to the time of year, we might expect this month's sales to be related to sales for the same month last year.

When seasonality is present, modeling the associated time series data would be incomplete unless the regression model incorporates the effects of the seasonality.

Example: Detecting seasonality

You are interested in predicting occupancy levels for a resort hotel chain and have acquired the chain's quarterly occupancy levels for the most recent 40 quarters (ten years). You decide to model the quarterly occupancy time-series using the AR(1) model:

$$\ln y_t = b_0 + b_1 \ln y_{t-1} + \varepsilon_t$$

Determine whether seasonality exists using the results presented in the following example.

Autoregression Output for Log-Quarterly Hotel Occupancy

Resort Occupancy Levels

AR(1) Model $\ln y_t = b_0 + b_1 \ln y_{t-1} + \varepsilon_t$

R^2	0.7929		
Standard error	0.1952		
Observations	39		
	Coefficients	Standard Error	*t*-Statistic
Intercept	0.0375	0.0274	1.369
Lag 1	0.5318	0.1635	3.2526

Autocorrelation of Residuals

Residual Lag	Autocorrelation	Standard Error	*t*-Statistic
1	−0.0615	0.1601	−0.3841
2	−0.0121	0.1601	−0.0756
3	−0.0212	0.1601	−0.1324
4	0.8719	0.1601	5.4460

Answer:

The bottom part of the table contains the residual autocorrelations for the first four lags of the time series. What stands out is the relatively large correlation and *t*-statistic for the fourth lag. With 39 observations and two parameters, (b_0 and b_1), there are 37 degrees of freedom. At a significance level of 5%, the critical *t*-value is 2.026.

The t-statistics indicate that none of the first three lagged autocorrelations is significantly different from zero. However, the *t*-statistic at Lag 4 is 5.4460, which means that we must reject the null hypothesis that the Lag 4 correlation is zero and conclude that seasonality is present in the time-series. Thus, we conclude that this model is misspecified and will be unreliable for forecasting purposes. We need to include a seasonality term to make the model useable.

 Professor's Note: With an AR(1) model, we lose one observation (i.e., we go from 40 to 39 observations). With an AR(2) model, we lose two observations, and so on.

Correcting seasonality. The interpretation of seasonality in the above example is that occupancy in any quarter is related to occupancy in the previous quarter and the same quarter in the previous year. For example, fourth quarter 2008 occupancy is related to third quarter 2008 occupancy as well as fourth quarter 2007 occupancy.

To adjust for seasonality in an AR model, an additional lag of the *dependent* variable (corresponding to the same season in the previous year) is added to the original model as another *independent* variable. For example, if quarterly data are used, the seasonal lag is 4; if monthly data are used the seasonal lag is 12; and so on.

Example: Correcting for seasonality in a time-series model

We continue with our resort occupancy level example, where the significant residual correlation at Lag 4 indicates seasonality in the quarterly time series. By testing the correlations of the error terms, it appears that occupancy levels in each quarter are related not only to the previous quarter, but also to the corresponding quarter in the previous year. To adjust for this problem, we add a lagged value of the dependent variable to the original model that corresponds to the seasonal pattern.

To model the autocorrelation of the same quarters from year to year, we use an AR(1) model with a seasonal lag: $\ln y_t = b_0 + b_1(\ln y_{t-1}) + b_2(\ln y_{t-4}) + \varepsilon_t$. Note that this specification, the inclusion of a seasonal lag, does not result in an AR(2) model. It results in an AR(1) model incorporating a seasonal lag term.

The results obtained when this model is fit to the natural logarithm of the time series are presented below. Determine whether the model is specified correctly and if we can use it to predict resort occupancy levels.

Log-Resort Hotel Occupancy

AR(1) Model with a Seasonal Lag: $\ln y_t = b_0 + b_1(\ln y_{t-1}) + b_2(\ln y_{t-4}) + \varepsilon_t$

R^2	0.948983874		
Standard error	0.3754		
Observations	38		
	Coefficients	Standard Error	*t*-Statistic
Intercept	0.0085	0.0049	1.7347
Lag 1	0.2598	0.0527	4.9298
Lag 4	0.7921	0.2166	3.6570

Autocorrelation of Residuals			
Residual Lag	Autocorrelation	Standard Error	*t*-Statistic
1	−0.0526	0.1622	−0.3243
2	0.0715	0.1622	0.4408
3	−0.0241	0.1622	−0.1486
4	−0.0435	0.1622	−0.2682

Answer:

Notice in the bottom of the table that the fourth-lag residual autocorrelation has dropped substantially and is, in fact, no longer statistically significant. Also notable in these results is the improvement in the R-square for the adjusted model (94.9%) compared to the R-square from the original model (79.3%). The results shown in the figure indicate that, by incorporating a seasonal lag term, the model is now specified correctly.

FORECASTING WITH AN AR MODEL WITH A SEASONAL LAG

Example: Forecasting with an Autoregressive Model

Based on the regression results from the previous example and the occupancy levels over the past year (presented below), forecast the level of hotel occupancy for the first quarter of 2003.

Quarterly Hotel Occupancy Levels

Quarter	2002.1	2002.2	2002.3	2002.4
Occupancy Level	250,000	750,000	450,000	600,000

Answer:

We express the seasonally adjusted forecasting equation as:

$\ln y_t = 0.0085 + 0.2598(\ln y_{t-1}) + 0.7921(\ln y_{t-4})$

where y_t is the occupancy level for the tth quarter (t = first, second, third, or fourth quarter).

To forecast the occupancy level for the hotel chain for the first quarter of 2003 (i.e., 2003.1), the following computation is made:

$\ln y_{2003.1} = 0.0085 + 0.2598(\ln y_{2002.4}) + 0.7921(\ln y_{2002.1})$

$\ln y_{2003.1} = 0.0085 + 0.2598(\ln 600,000) + 0.7921(\ln 250,000)$

$\ln y_{2003.1} = 0.0085 + 0.2598(13.3047) + 0.7921(12.4292)$

$\ln y_{2003.1} = 13.3103$

Since $y = e^{\ln(y)}$, $y_{2003.1} = e^{13.3103} = 603,378.52$

The forecasted level of hotel occupancy for the first quarter of 2003 is 603,379, a significant increase over the same quarter the previous year. With such a significant increase in forecasted occupancy, the analyst should re-examine the model and it's inputs. Forecasting is always fraught with uncertainty, even when the model being used seems to fit the data well.

Professor's Note: Once again, the first answer you get in this calculation is the natural log of the occupancy forecast. In order to turn the natural log into an occupancy figure, you use the 2nd function of the LN key (e^x) on your BA II Plus: enter 13.3103 and press [2nd] e^x = 603,378.52.

IN-SAMPLE AND OUT-OF-SAMPLE FORECASTING

LOS 13.f: Contrast in-sample forecasts and out-of-sample forecasts, and compare the forecasting accuracy of different time-series models based on the root mean squared error criterion.

In-sample forecasts are *within* the range of data (i.e., time period) used to estimate the model, which for a time series is known as the sample or test period. In-sample forecast errors are $(y_t - \hat{y}_t)$, where t is an observation within the sample period. In other words, we are comparing how accurate our model is in forecasting the actual data we used to develop the model. If the predicted value is greater than the actual value the error or residual term is negative. If the predicted value is less than the actual value the error or residual term is positive. The Predicted vs. Actual Capacity Utilization figure in our Trend Analysis example shows an example of values predicted by the model compared to the values used to generate the model.

Out-of-sample forecasts are made *outside* of the sample period. In other words, we compare how accurate a model is in forecasting the y variable value for a time period outside the period used to develop the model. Out-of-sample forecasts are important because they provide a test of whether the model adequately describes the time series and whether it has relevance (i.e., predictive power) in the real world. Nonetheless, an analyst should be aware that most published research employs in-sample forecasts only.

The **root mean squared error** criterion (RMSE) is used to compare the accuracy of autoregressive models in forecasting out-of-sample values. For example, a researcher may have two autoregressive (AR) models: an AR(1) model and an AR(2) model. To determine which model will more accurately forecast future values, we calculate the RMSE (the square root of the average of the squared errors) for the out-of-sample data. Note that the model with the lowest RMSE for in-sample data may not be the model with the lowest RMSE for out-of-sample data.

For example, assume we have 60 months of historical unemployment data. We estimate both models over the first 36 of 60 months. To determine which model will produce better (i.e., more accurate) forecasts, we then forecast the values for the last 24 of 60 months of historical data. Using the actual values for the last 24 months as well as the values predicted by the models, we can calculate the RMSE for each model.

The model with the lower RMSE for the out-of-sample data will have lower forecast error and will be expected to have better predictive power in the future.

 In addition to examining the RMSE criteria for a model, we will also want to examine the stability of regression coefficients, which we discuss below.

REGRESSION COEFFICIENT INSTABILITY

LOS 13.g: Discuss the instability of coefficients of time-series models.

Financial and economic time series inherently exhibit some form of *instability* or *nonstationarity*. This is because financial and economic conditions are dynamic, and the estimated regression coefficients in one period may be quite different from those estimated during another period.

Models estimated with shorter time series are usually more stable than those with longer time series because a longer sample period increases the chance that the underlying economic process has changed. Thus, there is a tradeoff between the increased statistical reliability when using longer time periods and the increased stability of the estimates when using shorter periods.

The primary concern when selecting a time series sample period is the underlying economic processes. Have there been regulatory changes? Has there been a dramatic change in the underlying economic environment?

If the answer is yes, then the historical data may not provide a reliable model. Merely examining the significance of the autocorrelation of the residuals will not indicate whether the model is valid. We must also examine whether the data is covariance stationary.

COVARIANCE STATIONARITY

LOS 13.c: Explain the requirement for a time series to be covariance stationary, and discuss the significance of a series not being stationary.

Statistical inferences based on OLS estimates for an AR time series model may be invalid unless the time series being modeled is **covariance stationary.**

A time series is covariance stationary if it satisfies the following three conditions:

1. *Constant and finite expected value.* The expected value of the time series is constant over time. (In the next section, we will refer to this value as the mean-reverting level.)

2. *Constant and finite variance.* The time series' volatility around its mean (i.e., the distribution of the individual observations around the mean) does not change over time.

3. *Constant and finite covariance with leading or lagged values.* The covariance of the time series with leading or lagged values of itself is constant.

To determine if the first two requirements are satisfied, one can examine a plot of the data over time. If it appears that the mean or variance changes over time, then the data is not covariance stationary. It is often the case that financial or economic data are not covariance stationary. For example, if the data exhibit seasonality or trends over time (e.g. sales or consumption data), the mean will not be constant. Note also that data that were stationary in the past may not be stationary in the future if economic processes change.

To understand the concept behind the third requirement, consider the data in Figure 2. The first two columns contain original data from our manufacturing capacity utilization example. Columns three and four contain the corresponding lagged variables, with a lag of one quarter. Note that column one begins with the second quarter's observation while column three begins with the first quarter's observation. The third condition states that regardless of the lag or lead used (e.g., one quarter, two quarters), the covariance between the two series must be the same. In other words, the covariance between values from different time periods must always be the same, regardless of the length of the lead or lag that is employed.

Figure 2: Lagged Data for Manufacturing Capacity Utilization

Quarter	Manufacturing Capacity Utilization t	Lagged Quarter	Manufacturing Capacity Utilization t-1
2004.2	81.5	2004.1	82.4
2004.3	80.8	2004.2	81.5
2004.4	80.5	2004.3	80.8
2005.1	80.2	2004.4	80.5
2005.2	80.2	2005.1	80.2
2005.3	80.5	2005.2	80.2
2005.4	80.9	2005.3	80.5
2006.1	81.3	2005.4	80.9
2006.2	81.9	2006.1	81.3
2006.3	81.7	2006.2	81.9
2006.4	80.3	2006.3	81.7
2007.1	77.9	2006.4	80.3
2007.2	76.4	2007.1	77.9

MEAN REVERSION

LOS 13.e: Explain mean reversion, and calculate a mean-reverting level.

A time series exhibits **mean reversion** if it has a tendency to move toward its mean. In other words, the time series has a tendency to decline when the current value is above the mean and rise when the current value is below the mean. If a time series is at its mean-reverting level, the model predicts that the next value of the time series will be the same as its current value (i.e., $\hat{x}_t = x_{t-1}$ when a time series is at its mean-reverting level).

For an AR(1) model, $x_t = b_0 + b_1 x_{t-1}$, the above equality implies that $x_t = b_0 + b_1 x_t$. Solving for x_t, the mean-reverting level is expressed as $x_t = \dfrac{b_0}{(1 - b_1)}$.

So, if $x_t > \dfrac{b_0}{(1-b_1)}$, the AR(1) model predicts that x_{t+1} will be lower than x_t, and if

$x_t < \dfrac{b_0}{1-b_1}$, the model predicts that x_{t+1} will be higher than x_t.

Example: Mean-reverting time series

Calculate the mean-reverting level for the manufacturing capacity utilization time series using the following regression results:

Time Series Regression Results for Manufacturing Capacity Utilization

Regression model: $x_t = b_0 + b_1 x_{t-1}$			
R square	0.346508		
Adjusted R square	0.29205		
Standard error	1.333885		
Observations	14		
	Coefficients	*Standard Error*	*t-Statistic*
Intercept	82.137	0.753	109.080
Manufacturing utilization	−0.223	0.0884	−2.522

Answer:

$b_0 = 82.137$ and $b_1 = -0.223$, so the mean-reverting level, $b_0 / (1 - b_1)$, is

computed as: mean-reverting level $= \dfrac{82.137}{\left[1-\left(-0.223\right)\right]} = 67.16$

This means that if the current level of manufacturing capacity utilization is above 67.16, it is expected to fall in the next period, and if manufacturing capacity utilization is below 67.16 in the current period, it is expected to rise in the next period.

There are some data that do not have a tendency to move toward the mean. These data are not covariance stationary and follow a random walk.

RANDOM WALKS

LOS 13.h: Describe the characteristics of random walk processes, and contrast them to covariance stationary processes.

Random walk. If a time series follows a random walk process, the predicted value of the series (i.e., the value of the dependent variable) in one period is equal to the value of the series in the previous period plus a random error term. Since the only change in the time

---

series from one period to the next is a totally random value, it cannot be modeled unless the data are transformed in some way.

A time series that follows a simple random walk process is described in equation form as $x_t = x_{t-1} + \varepsilon_t$, where the best forecast of x_t is x_{t-1} and:

1. $E(\varepsilon_t) = 0$: The expected value of each error term is zero.

2. $E(\varepsilon_t^2) = \sigma^2$: The variance of the error terms is homoskedastic (i.e., constant).

3. $E(\varepsilon_i, \varepsilon_j) = 0$; if $i \neq j$: There is no serial correlation in the error terms.

Random Walk with a Drift. If a time series follows a random walk *with a drift*, the intercept term is not equal to zero. That is, in addition to a random error term, the time series is expected to increase or decrease by a constant amount from period to period. A random walk with a drift can be described as:

$$x_t = b_0 + b_1 x_{t-1} + \varepsilon_t$$

where:
b_0 = the constant drift
b_1 = 1

Covariance Stationarity. Neither a random walk nor a random walk with a drift exhibits covariance stationarity. To show this, let's start by expressing a random walk as:

$$x_t = b_0 + b_1 x_{t-1} + \varepsilon_t$$

where:
$b_0 = 0$ (for a random walk without a drift)
$b_0 \neq 0$ (for a random walk with a drift)
$b_1 = 1$ (for a random walk with or without a drift)

In either case (with or without a drift), the mean-reverting level is $\dfrac{b_0}{1 - b_1} = \dfrac{b_0}{0}$ (the

division of any number by zero is undefined), and as we stated earlier, a time series must have a **finite mean-reverting level** to be covariance stationary. Thus, a random walk, with or without a drift, is not covariance stationary, and exhibits what is known as a unit root. The presence of a unit root means that the least squares regression procedure that we have been using to estimate an AR(1) model will not work without transforming the data. We discuss unit roots and how they are handled in the next section.

Unit Roots

LOS 13.i: Discuss the implications of unit roots for time-series analysis, explain when unit roots are likely to occur and how to test them, and demonstrate how a time series with a unit root can be transformed so that it can be analyzed with an autoregressive model.

LOS 13.j: Discuss the steps of the unit root test for nonstationarity, and explain the relation of the test to autoregressive time series models.

Professor's Note: For purposes of clarity, we discuss LOS 13.j and the first two parts of LOS 13.i together. We then return to the final part of LOS 13.i, when we discuss the transformation of time series data under the title of "First Differencing."

As we discussed in the previous LOS, if the coefficient on the lag variable is 1.0, the series is not covariance stationary. If the value of the lag coefficient is equal to one, the time series is said to have a **unit root** and will follow a random walk process. Since a time series that follows a random walk is not covariance stationary, modeling such a time series in an AR model can lead to incorrect statistical conclusions, and decisions made on the basis of these conclusions may be wrong. Unit roots are most likely to occur in time series that trend over time or have a seasonal element.

Unit Root Test for Nonstationarity

Nonstationarity means that the time series is not covariance stationary. To determine whether a time series is covariance stationary, we can (1) plot the data, (2) run an AR model and examine autocorrelations, and/or (3) perform the Dickey Fuller test.

First, as discussed above, we can **plot the raw data** to see if the mean and variance appear constant. If the pattern of the plotted points (i.e., the individual dots on the graph) seems to expand or contract, the variance of the data is probably expanding or contracting (i.e., it is not constant). Also, if the plotted points seem to trend upward or downward, the mean is not constant.

An example of how plotted data can reveal nonstationarity can be found in retail sales. Plotting retail sales will usually indicate significantly different sales at the end of the year compared to the rest of the year. Likewise, a store that specializes in summer wear will typically realize the majority of its sales in the early part of the year.

This seasonality is an example of nonstationarity and can be detected using an **autoregressive** (AR) model. Thus, in the second method, an AR model is run and the significance of the autocorrelations is examined. A stationary process will usually have autocorrelations insignificantly different from zero at all lags or autocorrelations that decay to zero as the lag increases.

The third method utilizes the Dickey Fuller test. For statistical reasons, you cannot directly test whether the coefficient on the independent variable in an AR time series is equal to 1.0. To compensate, **Dickey and Fuller** created a rather ingenious test for a unit root. Remember, if an AR(1) model has a coefficient of 1.0, it has a unit root and no finite mean reverting level (i.e., it is not covariance stationary). Dickey and Fuller (DF) transform the AR(1) model to run a simple regression. To transform the model, they (1) start with the basic form of the AR(1) model and (2) subtract x_{t-1} from both sides:

(1) $\qquad x_t = b_0 + b_1 x_{t-1} + \varepsilon$

(2) $\qquad x_t - x_{t-1} = b_0 + b_1 x_{t-1} - x_{t-1} + \varepsilon \quad \rightarrow$

$$x_t - x_{t-1} = b_0 + (b_1 - 1)x_{t-1} + \varepsilon$$

Then, rather than directly testing whether the original coefficient is different from 1.0, they test whether the new, transformed coefficient $(b_1 - 1)$ is different from zero using a modified *t*-test. If $(b_1 - 1)$ is not significantly different from zero, they say that b_1 must be equal to 1.0 and, therefore, the series must have a unit root.

Professor's Note: In their actual test, DF use the variable g, which equals $(b_1 - 1)$. The null hypothesis is g = 0, i.e. the time series has a unit root. Note that the DF test is used because a standard t-test cannot be used to test directly whether the coefficient of the AR(1) model is equal to 1.0. Also note that the LOS does not ask you to actually perform the DF test, so for the exam, understand how the test is conducted and be able to interpret its results. For example, if on the exam you are told the null cannot be rejected, your answer is that the time series has a unit root. If the null is rejected, the time series does not have a unit root.

FIRST DIFFERENCING

If we believe a time series is a random walk (i.e., has a unit root), we can transform the data to a covariance stationary time series using a procedure called **first differencing**. The first differencing process involves subtracting the value of the time series (i.e., the dependent variable) in the immediately preceding period from the current value of the time series to define a new dependent variable, *y*. Note that by taking first differences, you model the **change** in the value of the dependent variable rather than the value of the dependent variable.

So, if the original time series of *x* has a unit root, the change in *x*, $x_t - x_{t-1} = \varepsilon_t$, is just the error term. This means we can define y_t as:

$$y_t = x_t - x_{t-1} \Rightarrow y_t = \varepsilon_t$$

Then, stating *y* in the form of an AR(1) model:

$$y_t = b_0 + b_1 y_{t-1} + \varepsilon$$

where :
$$b_0 = b_1 = 0$$

This transformed time series has a finite mean-reverting level of $\dfrac{0}{1-0} = 0$ and is, therefore, covariance stationary.

Example: Unit root

Suppose we decide to model the lagged capacity utilization data in Figure 2. Using an AR(1) model the results indicate that the capacity utilization time series probably contains a unit root and is, therefore, not covariance stationary. Discuss how this model can be transformed into a viable prediction model that is covariance stationary.

Answer:

Covariance stationarity can often be achieved by transforming the data using first differencing and modeling the first-differenced time series as an autoregressive time series.

Example: First differencing

The next figure contains the first-differences of our manufacturing capacity utilization time series for the period 2004.1 through 2007.3. The first two columns contain the original time series. The first differences of the original series are contained in the third column of the table, and the one-period lagged values on the first-differences are presented in the fourth column of the table. Note that the first differences in this example represent the *change* in manufacturing capacity from the preceding period and are designated as y_t and y_{t-1}.

First-Differenced Manufacturing Capacity Utilization Data

Quarter	Capacity	Change in Capacity $y_t = x_t - x_{t-1}$	Lagged Change in Capacity $y_{t-1} = x_{t-1} - x_{t-2}$
2004.1	82.4		
2004.2	81.5	−0.9	
2004.3	80.8	−0.7	−0.9
2004.4	80.5	−0.3	−0.7
2005.1	80.2	−0.3	−0.3
2005.2	80.2	0.0	−0.3
2005.3	80.5	0.3	0.0
2005.4	80.9	0.4	0.3
2006.1	81.3	0.4	0.4
2006.2	81.9	0.6	0.4
2006.3	81.7	−0.2	0.6
2006.4	80.3	−1.4	−0.2
2007.1	77.9	−2.4	−1.4
2007.2	76.4	−1.5	−2.4
2007.3	76.4	0.0	−1.5

After this transformation, it is appropriate to regress the AR(1) model,
$y_t = b_0 + b_1 y_{t-1}$. The regression results for the first-differenced time series are presented in the next figure, where it can be seen that the estimated coefficient on the lag variable is less than one (0.655).

Regression Output for First-Differenced Manufacturing Capacity

AR(1) Model $y_t = b_0 + b_1 y_{t-1} + \varepsilon_t$	*Change in Capacity Utilization*		
R^2	0.430869388		
Adjusted R^2	0.379130241		
Standard error	0.699210366		
Observations	13		
	Coefficients	*Standard Error*	*t-Statistic*	*p-Value*
Intercept	–0.090014589	0.220409703	–0.4084	0.69082
Lag 1	0.65496839	0.226964091	2.885780	0.0148

USING TWO TIME SERIES

LOS 13.m: Explain how time-series variables should be analyzed for nonstationarity and/or cointegration before use in a linear regression.

Occasionally an analyst will run a regression using two time series (i.e., time series utilizing two different variables). For example, using the market model to estimate the equity beta for a stock, an analyst regresses a time series of the stock's returns on a time series of returns for the market. Notice that now we are faced with two different time series, either or both of which could be subject to nonstationarity.

To test whether the two time series have unit roots, the analyst first runs separate DF tests with five possible results:

1. Both time series are covariance stationary (i.e., neither has a unit root).

2. Only the dependent variable time series is covariance stationary (i.e., the independent variable time series has a unit root).

3. Only the independent variable time series is covariance stationary (i.e., the dependent variable time series has a unit root).

4. Neither time series is covariance stationary (i.e., they both have unit roots) and the two series *are not* cointegrated.

5. Neither time series is covariance stationary (i.e., they both have unit roots) and the two series *are* cointegrated.

In scenario 1 the analyst can use linear regression, and the coefficients should be statistically reliable, but regressions in scenarios 2 and 3 will not be reliable. Whether linear regression can be used in scenarios 4 and 5 depends upon whether the two time series are *cointegrated*.

Cointegration

Cointegration means that two time series are economically linked (related to the same macro variables) or follow the same trend and that relationship is not expected to change. If two time series are cointegrated, the error term from regressing one on the other is covariance stationary and the *t*-tests are reliable. This means that scenario 5 will produce reliable regression estimates, whereas scenario 4 will not.

To test whether two time series are cointegrated, we regress one variable on the other using the following model:

$y_t = b_0 + b_1 x_t + \varepsilon$
where:
y_t = value of time series y at time t
x_t = value of time series x at time t

The residuals are tested for a unit root using the Dickey Fuller test with critical t-values calculated by Engle and Granger (i.e., the DF–EG test). If the test rejects the null hypothesis of a unit root, we say the error terms generated by the two time series are covariance stationary and the two series are cointegrated. If the two series are cointegrated, we can use the regression to model their relationship.

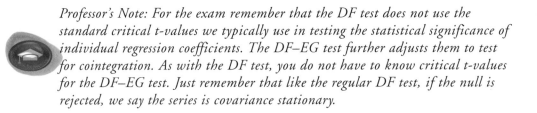

Professor's Note: For the exam remember that the DF test does not use the standard critical t-values we typically use in testing the statistical significance of individual regression coefficients. The DF–EG test further adjusts them to test for cointegration. As with the DF test, you do not have to know critical t-values for the DF–EG test. Just remember that like the regular DF test, if the null is rejected, we say the series is covariance stationary.

Figure 3: Using Regressions with More than One Time Series

Independent Variable Unit Root?	Dependent Variable Unit Root?	Cointegrated?	Covariance Stationary?	Use Linear Regression?
no	no	n/a	yes	yes
yes	no	n/a	no	no
no	yes	n/a	no	no
yes	yes	no	no	no
yes	yes	yes	yes	yes

AUTOREGRESSIVE CONDITIONAL HETEROSKEDASTICITY

LOS 13.l: Explain autoregressive conditional heteroskedasticity (ARCH), and discuss how ARCH models can be applied to predict the variance of a time series.

When examining a single time series, such as an AR model, **autoregressive conditional heteroskedasticity (ARCH)** exists if the variance of the residuals in one period is *dependent* on the variance of the residuals in a previous period. When this condition exists, the standard errors of the regression coefficients in AR models and the hypothesis tests of these coefficients are invalid.

Using ARCH Models

An ARCH model is used to test for autoregressive conditional heteroskedasticity. Within the ARCH framework, an ARCH(1) time series is one for which the variance of the residuals in one period is dependent on (i.e., a function of) the variance of the residuals in the preceding period. To test whether a time series is ARCH(1), the squared residuals from an estimated time-series model, $\hat{\varepsilon}_t^2$, are regressed on the first lag of the squared residuals $\hat{\varepsilon}_{t-1}^2$.

The ARCH(1) regression model is expressed as:

$$\hat{\varepsilon}_t^2 = a_0 + a_1\hat{\varepsilon}_{t-1}^2 + \mu_t$$

where a_0 is the constant and μ_t is an error term.

If the coefficient, a_1, is statistically different from zero, the time series is ARCH(1).

If a time-series model has been determined to contain ARCH errors, regression procedures that correct for heteroskedasticity, such as *generalized least squares*, must be used in order to develop a predictive model. Otherwise, the standard errors of the model's coefficients will be incorrect, leading to invalid conclusions.

Predicting the Variance of a Time Series

However, if a time series has ARCH errors, an ARCH model can be used to predict the variance of the residuals in future periods. For example, if the data exhibit an ARCH(1) pattern, the ARCH(1) model can be used in period t to predict the variance of the residuals in period t + 1:

$$\hat{\sigma}_{t+1}^2 = \hat{a}_0 + \hat{a}_1\hat{\varepsilon}_t^2$$

Example: ARCH(1) time series

The next figure contains the results from the regression of an ARCH(1) model. The squared errors for periods t through T are regressed on the squared errors for periods $t - 1$ through $T - 1$. (μ_t is the error term for the model.) Determine whether the results indicate autoregressive conditional heteroskedasticity (ARCH), and if so, calculate the predicted variance of the error terms in the next period if the current period squared error is 0.5625

ARCH (1) Regression Results

Model: $\hat{\varepsilon}_t^2 = a_0 + a_1\hat{\varepsilon}_{t-1}^2 + \mu_t$	Coefficients	Standard Error	t-Statistic	p-Value
Constant	5.9068	1.08631	5.4375	< 0.001
Lag 1	0.4515	0.09558	4.7238	< 0.001

Answer:

Since the p-value for the coefficient on the lagged variable indicates statistical significance, we can conclude that the time series is ARCH(1). As such, the variance of the error term in the next period can be computed as:

$$\hat{\sigma}_{t+1}^2 = \hat{a}_0 + \hat{a}_1\hat{\varepsilon}_t^2 = 5.9068 + 0.4515(0.5625) = 6.1608$$

Professor's Note: If the coefficient a_1 is zero, the variance is constant from period to period. If a_1 is greater than (less than) zero, the variance increases (decreases) over time (i.e., the error terms exhibit heteroskedasticity).

CHOOSING THE CORRECT MODEL

LOS 13.n: Select and justify the choice of a particular time-series model from a group of models.

To determine what type of model is best suited to meet your needs, follow these guidelines:

1. Determine your goal.
   - Are you attempting to model the relationship of a variable to other variables (e.g., cointegrated time series, cross-sectional multiple regression)?
   - Are you trying to model the variable over time (e.g., trend model)?

2. If you have decided on using a time series analysis for an individual variable, plot the values of the variable over time and look for characteristics that would indicate nonstationarity, such as non-constant variance (heteroskedasticity), non-constant mean, seasonality, or structural change.

A **structural change** is indicated by a significant *shift* in the plotted data at a point in time that seems to divide the data into two distinct patterns. (Figure 4 shows a data plot that indicates a structural shift in the time series at Point a.) When this is the case you have to run two different models, one incorporating the data before and one after that date, and test whether the time series has actually shifted. If the time series has shifted significantly, a single time series encompassing the entire period (i.e., both patterns) will likely produce unreliable results, so the most recent model may be more appropriate.

Figure 4: A Structural Shift in a Time Series

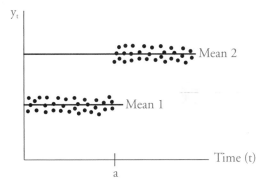

3. If there is no seasonality or structural shift, use a trend model.
   - If the data plot on a straight line with an upward or downward slope, use a linear trend model.
   - If the data plot in a curve, use a log-linear trend model.

4. Run the trend analysis, compute the residuals, and test for serial correlation using the Durbin Watson test.
   - If you detect no serial correlation, *you can use the model.*
   - If you detect serial correlation, you must use another model (e.g., AR).

5. If the data has serial correlation, reexamine the data for stationarity before running an AR model. If it is not stationary, treat the data for use in an AR model as follows:
   - If the data has a linear trend, first-difference the data.
   - If the data has an exponential trend, first-difference the natural log of the data.
   - If there is a structural shift in the data, run two separate models as discussed above.
   - If the data has a seasonal component, incorporate the seasonality in the AR model as discussed below.

6. After the series is covariance stationary, run an AR(1) model and test for serial correlation and seasonality.
   - If there is no remaining serial correlation, *you can use the model.*
   - If you still detect serial correlation, incorporate lagged values of the variable (possibly including one for seasonality—e.g., for monthly data, add the 12th lag of the time series) into the AR model until you have removed (i.e., modeled) any serial correlation.

7. Test for ARCH. Regress the square of the residuals on squares of lagged values of the residuals and test whether the resulting coefficient is significantly different from zero.
   - If the coefficient is not significantly different from zero, *you can use the model.*
   - If the coefficient is significantly different from zero, ARCH is present. Correct using generalized least squares.

8. If you have developed two statistically reliable models and want to determine which is better at forecasting, calculate their out-of-sample RMSE.

KEY CONCEPTS

LOS 13.a
A time series is a set of observations for a variable over successive periods of time. A time series model captures the time series pattern and allows us to make predictions about the variable in the future.

LOS 13.b
A simple linear trend model is: $y_t = b_0 + b_1 t + \varepsilon_t$, estimated for t = 1, 2, ..., T.

A log-linear trend model, $\ln(y_t) = b_0\, b_1 t + \varepsilon_t$, is appropriate for exponential data.

A plot of the data should be used to determine whether a linear or log-linear trend model should be used.

The primary limitation of trend models is that they are not useful if the residuals exhibit serial correlation.

LOS 13.c
A time series is covariance stationary if its mean, variance, and covariances with lagged and leading values do not change over time. Covariance stationarity is a requirement for AR models.

LOS 13.d
An autoregressive model is one in which the independent variable is a lagged value of the dependent variable. An AR model with p lags is referred to as an AR(p) model:

$$x_t = b_0 + b_1 x_{t-1} + b_2 x_{t-2} + ... + b_p x_{t-p} + \varepsilon_t$$

An AR(p) model is specified correctly if the autocorrelation of residuals is not significant.

Multiperiod forecasting with AR models is done one period at a time, where uncertainty increases with each successive forecast because it is based on previously forecasted values.

LOS 13.e
A time series is mean reverting if it tends towards its mean over time. The mean reverting level for an AR(1) model is $\dfrac{b_0}{(1-b_1)}$.

LOS 13.f
In-sample forecasts predict y values for the time period used to estimate the model. Out-of-sample forecasts predict y values for periods outside the sample used to estimate the model. Out-of-sample forecasts are most relevant to analysts.

LOS 13.g
Most economic and financial time series data are not stationary. The degree of the nonstationarity depends on the length of the series and the underlying economic environment.

LOS 13.h
A random walk time series is one for which the value in one period is equal to the value in another period, plus a random error. A random walk process does not have a mean reverting level and is not stationary.

LOS 13.i
A time series has a unit root if the coefficient on the lagged dependent variable is equal to one. A series with a unit root is not covariance stationary. Economic and finance time series frequently have unit roots. Data with a unit root must be first differenced before being used in a time series model.

LOS 13.j
To determine whether a time series is covariance stationary, we can (1) plot the data, (2) run an AR model, and/or (3) perform the Dickey Fuller test.

LOS 13.k
Seasonality in a time series is tested by calculating the autocorrelations of error terms. A statistically significant lagged error term corresponding to the periodicity of the data indicates seasonality. Seasonality can be corrected by incorporating the appropriate seasonal lag term in an AR model.

If a seasonal lag coefficient is appropriate and corrects the seasonality, the AR model with the seasonal terms will have no statistically significant autocorrelations of error terms.

LOS 13.l
ARCH is present if the variance of the residuals from an AR model are correlated across time. ARCH is detected by estimating $\hat{\varepsilon}_t^2 = a_0 + a_1\hat{\varepsilon}_{t-1}^2 + \mu_t$. If a_1 is significant, ARCH exists and the variance of errors can be predicted using: $\hat{\sigma}_{t+1}^2 = \hat{a}_0 + \hat{a}_1\hat{\varepsilon}_t^2$.

LOS 13.m
When working with two time series in a regression: 1) if neither time series has a unit root then the regression can be used; 2) if only one series has a unit root, the regression results will be invalid; 3) if both time series have a unit root and are cointegrated, then the regression can be used; 4) if both time series have a unit root but are not cointegrated, the regression results will be invalid.

The Dickey Fuller test with critical t-values calculated by Engle and Granger is used to determine whether two times series are cointegrated.

LOS 13.n
The RMSE criterion is used to determine which forecasting model will produce the most accurate forecasts. The RMSE equals the square root of the average squared error.

CONCEPT CHECKERS

Use the following data to answer Questions 1 and 2.

The results of the estimation of monthly revolving credit outstanding (RCO) on the one-period lagged values for RCO from January 2006 through December 2008 are presented in the following table.

Regression Results for Outstanding Revolving Credit Study

Model: $RCO_t = b_0 + b_1 RCO_{t-1} + \varepsilon_t$

R^2	0.952643	
Adjusted R^2	0.951208	
Standard error	9.261452	
Observations	35	

	Coefficients	Standard Error	t-Statistic	p-Value
Intercept	−34.0019	24.19417	−1.40537	0.169255
Lag 1	1.065697	0.041362	25.76512	< 0.0001

1. What type of time-series model was used to produce the regression results in the table?
   A. An AR model.
   B. A heteroskedasticity (H) model.
   C. A trend model with a drift.

2. An approach that may work in the case of modeling a time series that has a unit root is to:
   A. use an ARCH model.
   B. use a trend model.
   C. model the first differences of the time series.

Use the following data to answer Questions 3 through 7.

Consider the results of the regression of monthly real estate loans (RE) in billions of dollars by commercial banks over the period January 2005 through September 2008 in the following table:

Time Series Regression Results for Real Estate Loans

Model: $RE_t = b_0 + b_1 t + \varepsilon_t$	$t = 1, 2, ..., 45$
R^2	0.967908
Adjusted R^2	0.9671617
Standard error	29.587649
Observations	45
Durbin-Watson	0.601

— tests serial corr.

	Coefficients	Standard Error
Intercept	1195.6241	8.9704362
b_1	12.230448	0.3396171

← t-stat = $\frac{1195}{8.97}$ 133.?? 36.0125

3. The regression of real estate loans against time is a(an):
    A. trend line model.
    B. AR model.
    C. ARCH model.

4. The results of the estimation indicate a(an):
    A. upward trend.
    B. AR(2) model.
    C. ARCH system.

5. Are the intercept and slope coefficient significantly different from zero at the 5% level?
    A. Both are statistically significant.
    B. One is, but the other is not.
    C. Neither of them is statistically significant.

6. The forecasted value of real estate loans for October 2008 is *closest* to:
    A. $1,733.764 billion.
    B. $1,745.990 billion.
    C. $1,758.225 billion.

handwritten: t A. t = 133.227 / b1 t = 36.012 / CI = 1195

handwritten: y = b₀ - b₁ / linear trend model equation

7. Based on the time series regression results, is there evidence of serial correlation of the residuals?
    A. Yes positive, but not negative serial correlation.
    B. Yes negative, but not positive serial correlation.
    C. Neither positive nor negative serial correlation.

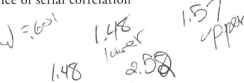

8. An analyst has determined that monthly sport utility vehicle (SUV) sales in the United States have been increasing over the last ten years, but the growth rate over that period has been relatively constant. Which model is *most appropriate* to predict future SUV sales?
    A. $SUVsales_t = b_0 + b_1(t) + e_t$.
    B. $lnSUVsales_t = b_0 + b_1(t) + e_t$.
    C. $lnSUVsales_t = b_0 + b_1(SUVsales_{t-1}) + e_t$.

9. Are the two time series shown in the following figures likely to be covariance stationary?

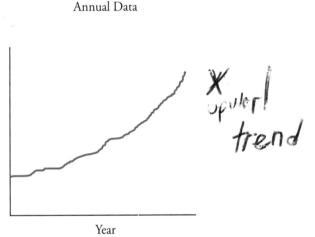

(a) Time Series Y: Quarterly Data

(b) Time Series Z: Annual Data

4th quarter observations

Quarter

Year

    A. Y is, but Z is not covariance stationary.
    B. Z is, but Y is not covariance stationary.
    C. Neither is covariance stationary.

10. Given the prediction equation: $\hat{x}_t = 5 + 1.75x_{t-1}$, what is the forecast value of x_{t+2} if x_{t-1} is 16.5?
    A. 64.28.
    B. 117.49.
    C. 210.61.

11. Which of the following AR models is *most appropriate* for a time series with annual seasonality using quarterly observations?
    A. $b_1x_{t-1} + b_2x_{t-12} + \varepsilon_t$.
    B. $b_0 + b_1x_{t-1} + b_2x_{t-4} + \varepsilon_t$.
    C. $b_0 + b_1x_{t-4} + b_2x_{t-12} + \varepsilon_t$.

Use the following data to answer Questions 12 through 14.

Regression Results for Monthly Cash Flow Study

	Coefficients	Standard Error	t-Statistic	p-Value
Intercept	26.8625	12.15146	2.210639	0.035719
Lag 1	0.7196	0.042584	16.89837	< 0.0001

Autocorrelation of the Residual

Lag	Autocorrelation	Standard Error	t-Statistic	p-Value
12	−0.0254	0.0632	-0.4019	0.5612

12. The number of observations in the time series used to estimate the model represented in the table above is *closest* to:
    A. 16.
    B. 50.
    C. 250.

$0.0632 = \dfrac{1}{\sqrt{T}}$

13. Based on the information given, what type of model was used?
    A. AR(1).
    B. AR(2).
    C. AR(12).

14. Does the information indicate the presence of seasonality?
    A. No, because the lag-12 autocorrelation of the residual is not significant.
    B. Yes, because the lag-12 autocorrelation of the residual is significantly different than one.
    C. There is not enough information provided; the autocorrelation for the first lag is also needed to detect seasonality.

Use the following data to answer Questions 15 through 18.

A monthly time series of changes in payroll expenses (in millions of $) at a major retail chain was regressed with an AR(1) model from January 2000 to June 2008 (102 months). The results of the regression, and the first 12 lagged residual autocorrelations are shown in the next two tables.

Regression Results for Payroll Changes

Model: $y_t = b_0 + b_1 y_{t-1} + \varepsilon_t$

	Coefficients	Standard Error	t-Statistic
Intercept	1.2304	0.00923135	133.28495
Lag 1	0.1717	0.00476779	36.01249

Lagged Residual Autocorrelation Analysis

Lag	Autocorrelation	t-Statistic	Lag	Autocorrelation	t-Statistic
1	−0.105	?	7	0.017	0.17170
2	−0.140	−1.4139	8	−0.036	−0.36360
3	−0.044	−0.4444	9	0.163	1.64620
4	−0.032	−0.3232	10	−0.066	−0.66660
5	−0.170	−1.7169	11	0.115	1.16140
6	0.109	1.1008	12	0.021	0.21209

15. The mean reverting level for this time series is *closest* to:
    A. 1.050.
    B. 1.342.
    C. 1.485.

16. The *t*-statistic for testing the hypothesis that the first order autocorrelation is zero is *closest* to:
    A. −1.0604.
    B. −10.710.
    C. −36.012.

17. If payroll expense in June 2008 was $1 million, the forecast for payroll expense in August 2008 is *closest* to:
    A. $1.402 million.
    B. $1.471 million.
    C. $1.511 million.

18.   Assuming a 5% level of significance, does the model appear to be properly specified?
A. Yes, because the lag coefficient is significant.
B. No, because most of the autocorrelations are negative.
C. Yes, because none of the autocorrelations are significant.

ANSWERS – CONCEPT CHECKERS

1. **A**   The independent variable is the dependent variable lagged one period, so the model is an AR(1) model.

2. **C**   The first-differenced series usually does not have a unit root and is, therefore, covariance stationary.

3. **A**   With a trend model, the independent variable is time, t.

4. **A**   The slope is positive and significantly different from zero indicating an upward trend.

5. **A**   The t-statistic to test the statistical significance of the intercept and slope coefficient is the parameter estimate divided by its standard error. We reject the null hypothesis and conclude the coefficients are statistically significant if the absolute value of the t-statistic is greater than the two-tail 5% critical t-value with 43 degrees of freedom, which is 2.02.

    $$t_{b_0} = \frac{1,195.6241}{8.9704362} = 133.3$$

    $$t_{b_1} = \frac{12.230448}{0.3396171} = 36.0$$

    Both the intercept term and the slope coefficient are significantly different from zero at the 5% level because both t-statistics are greater than the critical t-value of 2.02.

6. **C** $\hat{Y}_{46}$ = \$1,195.6241 + \$12.230448(46) = \$1,758.225 billion.

7. **A**   The Durbin-Watson statistic is used to detect serial correlation in the residuals. The lower critical value for a DW test with one independent variable and 45 observations is 1.48 and the upper critical value is 1.57. The actual DW-statistic is 0.601, which is less than the lower critical value. This indicates the residuals are positively serially correlated. The DW-statistic would have to be greater than 4 − 1.48 = 2.52 in order to conclude that negative serial correlation is present. See the previous topic review for details on implementing the Durbin-Watson test.

8. **B**   A log-linear model (choice B) is most appropriate for a time series that grows at a relatively constant growth rate. Neither a linear trend model (choice A), nor an AR(1) model (choice C) are appropriate in this case.

9. **C**   Time series Y has a seasonal pattern because the fourth quarter observations are significantly higher than the other quarters. This suggests that the expected value of time series Y is not constant, and therefore it is not covariance stationary.

    Time series Z has a definite upward trend, which once again suggests the expected value of the time series Z is not constant, and therefore it is not covariance stationary.

10. **B**   Given x_{t-1} = 16.5, $\hat{x}_t$ = 5 + 1.75(16.5) = 33.875. So, $\hat{x}_{t+1}$ = 5 + 1.75$\hat{x}_t$ = 5 + 1.75(33.875) = 64.28. So, $\hat{x}_{t+2}$ = 5 + 1.75$\hat{x}_{t+1}$ = 5 + 1.75(64.28) = 117.49.

11. **B**   The seasonal (annual) lag occurs on a quarterly basis, so the appropriate model is $b_0 + b_1 x_{t-1} + b_2 x_{t-4} + \varepsilon_t$. The intercept b_0 should be included in the model.

12. **C** The standard error of the estimated autocorrelations is $1/\sqrt{T}$, where T is the number of observations (periods). So, if the standard error is given as 0.0632, the number of observations, T, in the time series must be $(1/0.0632)^2 \approx 250$.

13. **A** The results in the table indicate that the prediction equation is $x_t = 26.8625 + 0.7196x_{t-1}$, which is estimated from an AR(1) model.

14. **A** The autocorrelation in the twelfth month is not statistically different from zero. Thus, there appears to be no seasonality.

15. **C** The mean-reverting level is $b_0 / (1 - b_1) = 1.2304 / (1 - 0.1717) = 1.48545$.

16. **A** $t = \dfrac{-0.105}{1/\sqrt{102}} = -1.0604$

17. **B** $y_{\text{July 2008}} = 1.2304 + 0.1717(\$1) = \$1.402$ million

   $y_{\text{August 2008}} = 1.2304 + 0.1717(\$1.402) = \$1.471$ million

18. **C** The critical t-value at a 5% level of significance with 100 degrees of freedom is approximately 1.98. At this level, none of the residual autocorrelations is significant, indicating that the model is properly specified. The presence of an ARCH process, however, should also be tested.

SELF-TEST: QUANTITATIVE METHODS

Professor's Note: We've included the following item set to give you a head start on practicing exam-like questions. Remember that the Level 2 exam consists of all item set format questions; that is, a vignette presenting the relevant information followed by six multiple choice questions on that topic. In addition to the three full-length practice exams included with the Study Notes pack, we also offer six more full-length Level 2 practice exams. Practice Exams Volume 2 contains three full 120-question (20 item sets, 6-hour) exams, and three more complete exams are available online. Each book contains the answers for self-grading, and explanations are available online for all questions.

Use the following information to answer Questions 1 through 6.

Theresa Miller is attempting to forecast sales for Alton Industries based on a multiple regression model. The model Miller estimates is:

$$\text{sales} = b_0 + (b_1 \times \text{DOL}) + (b_2 \times \text{IP}) + (b_3 \times \text{GDP}) + \varepsilon_t$$

where:
sales = change in sales adjusted for inflation
DOL = change in the real value of the \$ (rates measured in €/\$)
IP   = change in industrial production adjusted for inflation (millions of \$)
GDP = change in inflation-adjusted GDP (millions of \$)

All changes in variables are in percentage terms.

Miller runs the regression using monthly data for the prior 180 months. The model estimates (with coefficient standard errors in parentheses) are:

$$\text{sales} = 10.2 + (5.6 \times \text{DOL}) + (6.3 \times \text{IP}) + (9.2 \times \text{GDP})$$
$$\quad\quad (5.4)\quad (3.5)\quad\quad\quad (4.2)\quad\quad\quad (5.3)$$

The sum of squared errors is 145.6 and the total sum of squares is 357.2.

Miller is concerned that one or more of the assumptions underlying multiple regression has been violated in her analysis. In a conversation with Watson Crick, CFA, a colleague who is considered by many in the firm to be a quant specialist, Miller says, "Two of the key assumptions of multiple regression are:"

Assumption 1: The independent variables are not random, and there is no correlation between any two of the independent variables.

Assumption 2: The variance of the residuals is constant and not related to the level of the independent variables.

Miller tests and fails to reject each of the following two null hypotheses at the 99% confidence interval:

Hypothesis 1: A 2% increase in DOL will result in an increase in sales of more than 12%.

Hypothesis 2: A 1% increase in industrial production will result in a 1% decrease in sales.

Figure 1: Partial table of the Student's t-distribution (One-tailed probabilities)

Df	p = 0.10	p = 0.05	p = 0.025	p = 0.01	p = 0.005
170	1.287	1.654	1.974	2.348	2.605
176	1.286	1.654	1.974	2.348	2.604
180	1.286	1.653	1.973	2.347	2.603

Figure 2: Partial F-Table critical values for right-hand tail area equal to 0.05

	df 1 = 1	df 1 = 3	df 1 = 5
df 2 = 170	3.90	2.66	2.27
df 2 = 176	3.89	2.66	2.27
df 2 = 180	3.89	2.65	2.26

Figure 3: Partial F-Table critical values for right-hand tail area equal to 0.025

	df 1 = 1	df 1 = 3	df 1 = 5
df 2 = 170	5.11	3.19	2.64
df 2 = 176	5.11	3.19	2.64
df 2 = 180	5.11	3.19	2.64

1.   Are the two multiple regression assumptions proposed by Crick stated correctly?

	Assumption 1	Assumption 2
A.	Yes	No
B.	No	Yes
C.	No	No

2.   Did Miller *correctly* interpret the results of the tests in making her reject or fail-to-reject decisions for Hypothesis 1 and Hypothesis 2?

	Hypothesis 1	Hypothesis 2
A.	Yes	Yes
B.	Yes	No
C.	No	Yes

3. The appropriate decision with regard to the *F*-statistic for testing the null hypothesis that all of the independent variables are simultaneously equal to zero at the 5% significance level is to:
    A. reject the null hypothesis because the *F*-statistic is larger than the critical *F*-value of 3.19.
    B. fail to reject the null hypothesis because the *F*-statistic is smaller than the critical *F*-value of 3.19.
    C. reject the null hypothesis because the *F*-statistic is larger than the critical *F*-value of 2.66.

4. The unadjusted R^2 and the standard error of the estimate (SEE) are *closest* to:

	Unadjusted R^2	SEE
A.	59.2%	1.425
B.	59.2%	0.910
C.	40.8%	0.910

5. The multiple regression, as specified, *most likely* suffers from:
    A. heteroskedasticity.
    B. multicollinearity.
    C. positive serial correlation of the error terms.

6. What is the width of the 99% confidence interval for GDP, and is zero in that 99% confidence interval?

	Width of 99% CI	Zero in interval
A.	13.8	Yes
B.	13.8	No
C.	27.6	Yes

SELF-TEST ANSWERS: QUANTITATIVE METHODS

1. **B** Assumption 1 is stated incorrectly. Some correlation between independent variables is unavoidable; high correlation results in multicollinearity. An exact linear relationship between linear combinations of two or more independent variables should not exist.

   Assumption 2 is stated correctly. The assumption is that neither conditional nor unconditional heteroskestasticity is present in the residuals; in other words, the variance of the residuals is constant. Conditional heteroskedasticity occurs when the residual variance is related to the level of one or more of the independent variables.

2. **A** The critical values at the 1% level of significance (99% confidence) are 2.348 for a one-tailed test and 2.604 for a two-tailed test (df = 176).

   Hypothesis 1: This hypothesis is asking whether a 2% increase in DOL will increase sales by more than 12%. This will only happen if the value of the coefficient is greater than 6, since 2 × 6 = 12. Since the regression estimate for this coefficient is 5.6, the t-statistic for this test is (6 − 5.6) / 3.5 = 0.114. This is a one-tailed test, so the critical value is 2.348. Miller is correct in failing to reject the null.

   Hypothesis 2: This hypothesis is asking whether the value of the coefficient is equal to −1.0, since that is the value that would correspond with a 1% increase in industrial production resulting in a 1% decrease in sales. Since the regression estimate for this coefficient is 6.3, the t-statistic for this test is [6.3 − (−1)] / 4.2 = 1.74. This is a two-tailed test, so the critical value is 2.604. Miller is correct in failing to reject the null.

3. **C** SSR = 357.2 − 145.6 = 211.6, F-statistic = (211.6 / 3) / (145.6 / 176) = 85.3. The critical value for a one-tailed 5% F-test with 3 and 176 degrees of freedom is 2.66. Because the F-statistic is greater than the critical F-value, the null hypothesis that all of the independent variables are simultaneously equal to zero should be rejected.

4. **B** $$SEE = \sqrt{\frac{145.6}{180 - 3 - 1}} = 0.910$$

   $$\text{unadjusted } R^2 = \frac{357.2 - 145.6}{357.2} = 0.592$$

5. **B** The regression is highly significant (based on the F-stat in Question 3), but the individual coefficients are not. This is a result of a regression with significant multicollinearity problems. The t-stats for the significance of the regression coefficients are, respectively, 1.89, 1.6, 1.5, 1.74. None of these are high enough to reject the hypothesis that the coefficient is zero at the 5% level of significance (two-tailed critical value of 1.974 from t-table). There is no evidence in the vignette of heteroskedasticity or serial correlation (also known as autocorrelation).

6. **C** The confidence interval is 9.2 +/− (5.3 × 2.604), where 2.604 is the two-tailed 1% t-statistic with 176 degrees of freedom (which is the same as a one-tailed 0.5% t-statistic with 176 degrees of freedom). The interval is −4.6 to 23.0, which has a width of 27.6 and zero is in that interval.

FORMULAS

STUDY SESSION 3: QUANTITATIVE METHODS

Covariance and Correlation

sample covariance: $\text{cov}_{XY} = \dfrac{\sum\limits_{i=1}^{n}(X_i - \overline{X})(Y_i - \overline{Y})}{n-1}$

sample correlation coefficient: $r_{XY} = \dfrac{\text{cov}_{XY}}{(s_X)(s_Y)}$

t-test for correlation coefficient: $t = \dfrac{r\sqrt{n-2}}{\sqrt{1-r^2}}$ with $n-2$ df

Simple Linear Regression

slope coefficient: $\hat{b}_1 = \dfrac{\text{cov}_{XY}}{\sigma_X^2}$

intercept term: $\hat{b}_0 = \overline{Y} - \hat{b}_1\overline{X}$

confidence interval for coefficient:

$$\hat{b}_1 \pm \left(t_c \times s_{\hat{b}_1}\right),\ \text{or}\ \left[\hat{b}_1 - \left(t_c \times s_{\hat{b}_1}\right) < b_1 < \hat{b}_1 + \left(t_c \times s_{\hat{b}_1}\right)\right]$$

coefficient *t*-test: $t_{b_1} = \dfrac{\hat{b}_1 - b_1}{s_{\hat{b}_1}}$ with $n-2$ df

predicted value of the dependent variable: $\hat{Y} = \hat{b}_0 + \hat{b}_1 X_p$

confidence interval for a predicted value (simple linear regression only):

$$\hat{Y} \pm \left(t_c \times s_f\right) \Rightarrow \left[\hat{Y} - \left(t_c \times s_f\right) < Y < \hat{Y} + \left(t_c \times s_f\right)\right]$$

ANOVA Table Information (Simple Linear Regression)

total sum of squares (SST): $\mathrm{SST} = \sum_{i=1}^{n}(Y_i - \overline{Y})^2$

regression sum of squares (RSS): $\mathrm{RSS} = \sum_{i=1}^{n}(\hat{Y}_i - \overline{Y})^2$

sum of squared errors (SSE): $\mathrm{SSE} = \sum_{i=1}^{n}(Y_i - \hat{Y}_i)^2$

coefficient of determination: $R^2 = \dfrac{\text{total variation} - \text{unexplained variation}}{\text{total variation}} = \dfrac{\mathrm{SST} - \mathrm{SSE}}{\mathrm{SST}}$

standard error of estimate (SEE): $\sqrt{\dfrac{\mathrm{SSE}}{n-2}} = \sqrt{\mathrm{MSE}}$

F-statistic: $F = \dfrac{\mathrm{MSR}}{\mathrm{MSE}} = \dfrac{\mathrm{RSS}/k}{\mathrm{SSE}/n-k-1}$ with $n - 2$ df

Multiple Regression

predicted y-value: $\hat{Y}_i = \hat{b}_0 + \hat{b}_1 X_{1i} + \hat{b}_2 X_{2i} + \ldots + \hat{b}_k X_{ki}$

t-test for regression coefficient: $t = \dfrac{\hat{b}_j - b_j}{s_{\hat{b}_j}}$ with $n - k - 1$ df

confidence interval for regression coefficient:

$$\hat{b}_1 \pm \left(t_c \times s_{\hat{b}_1}\right), \text{ or } \left[\hat{b}_1 - \left(t_c \times s_{\hat{b}_1}\right) < b_1 < \hat{b}_1 + \left(t_c \times s_{\hat{b}_1}\right)\right]$$

ANOVA: total variation (SST) = explained variation (RSS) + unexplained variation (SSE)

mean squared error: $\mathrm{MSE} = \dfrac{\mathrm{SSE}}{n-k-1}$

mean regression sum of squares: $\text{MSR} = \dfrac{\text{RSS}}{k}$

F-**test for multiple regression:** $F = \dfrac{\text{MSR}}{\text{MSE}} = \dfrac{\text{RSS}/k}{\text{SSE}/[n-k-1]}$, with k and n – k – 1 df

adjusted R²: $R_a^2 = 1 - \left[\left(\dfrac{n-1}{n-k-1}\right) \times (1-R^2)\right]$

Breusch-Pagan Chi-square test for heteroskedasticity:

$BP = n \times R_{resid}^2$ with k degrees of freedom

Durbin-Watson test for serial correlation: $DW = \dfrac{\sum\limits_{t=2}^{T}(\hat{\varepsilon}_t - \hat{\varepsilon}_{t-1})^2}{\sum\limits_{t=1}^{T}\hat{\varepsilon}_t^2} \approx 2(1-r)$

Time-Series Analysis

AR model of order *p*, AR(*p*): $x_t = b_0 + b_1 x_{t-1} + b_2 x_{t-2} + \ldots + b_p x_{t-p} + \varepsilon_t$

Mean reverting level of AR(1): $x_t = \dfrac{b_0}{(1-b_1)}$

ARCH(1) model: $\hat{\varepsilon}_t^2 = a_0 + a_1\hat{\varepsilon}_{t-1}^2 + \mu_t$

APPENDIX A:
AREAS UNDER THE NORMAL CURVE

Most of the examples in this book have used the Student's t-distribution (which is found in Appendix B) to check for statistical significance. CFA Level 2 candidates should also know how to use the z-table to find the area under the normal curve. Here we present some examples of how to use the cumulative z-table.

Probability Example

Assume that the annual earnings per share (EPS) for a large sample of firms is normally distributed with a mean of $5.00 and a standard deviation of $1.50. What is the approximate probability of an observed EPS value falling between $3.00 and $7.25?

If $EPS = x = \$7.25$, then $z = (x - \mu)/\sigma = (\$7.25 - \$5.00)/\$1.50 = +1.50$

If $EPS = x = \$3.00$, then $z = (x - \mu)/\sigma = (\$3.00 - \$5.00)/\$1.50 = -1.33$

Solving Using The Cumulative Z-Table

For z-value of 1.50: Use the row headed 1.5 and the column headed 0 to find the value 0.9332. This represents the area under the curve to the left of the critical value 1.50.

For z-value of –1.33: Use the row headed 1.3 and the column headed 3 to find the value 0.9082. This represents the area under the curve to the left of the critical value +1.33. The area to the left of –1.33 is $1 - 0.9082 = 0.0918$.

The area between these critical values is $0.9332 - 0.0918 = 0.8414$, or 84.14%.

Hypothesis Testing – One-Tailed Test Example

A sample of a stock's returns on 36 non-consecutive days results in a mean return of 2.0%. Assume the population standard deviation is 20.0%. Can we say with 95% confidence that the mean return is greater than 0%?

$H_0: \mu \leq 0.0\%$, $H_A: \mu > 0.0\%$. The test statistic = z-statistic = $\dfrac{\bar{x} - \mu_0}{\sigma/\sqrt{n}}$ = $(2.0 - 0.0) / (20.0 / 6) = 0.60$.

The significance level = $1.0 - 0.95 = 0.05$, or 5%. Since we are interested in a return greater than 0.0%, this is a one-tailed test.

Using The Cumulative Z-Table

Since this is a one-tailed test with an alpha of 0.05, we need to find the value 0.95 in the cumulative z-table. The closest value is 0.9505, with a corresponding critical z-value of 1.65. Since the test statistic is less than the critical value, we fail to reject H_0.

Hypothesis Testing – Two-Tailed Test Example

Using the same assumptions as before, suppose that the analyst now wants to determine if he can say with 99% confidence that the stock's return is not equal to 0.0%.

H_0: μ = 0.0%, H_A: $\mu \neq$ 0.0%. The test statistic (z-value) = (2.0 – 0.0) / (20.0 / 6) = 0.60. The significance level = 1.0 – 0.99 = 0.01, or 1%. Since we are interested in whether or not the stock return is nonzero, this is a two-tailed test.

Using The Cumulative Z-Table

Since this is a two-tailed test with an alpha of 0.01, there is a 0.005 rejection region in both tails. Thus, we need to find the value 0.995 (1.0 – 0.005) in the table. The closest value is 0.9951, which corresponds to a critical z-value of 2.58. Since the test statistic is less than the critical value, we fail to reject H_0 and conclude that the stock's return equals 0.0%.

CUMULATIVE Z-TABLE

STANDARD NORMAL DISTRIBUTION

$P(Z \leq z) = N(z)$ FOR $z \geq 0$

z	0.00	0.01	0.02	0.03	0.04	0.05	0.06	0.07	0.08	0.09
0.0	0.5000	0.5040	0.5080	0.5120	0.5160	0.5199	0.5239	0.5279	0.5319	0.5359
0.1	0.5398	0.5438	0.5478	0.5517	0.5557	0.5596	0.5636	0.5675	0.5714	0.5753
0.2	0.5793	0.5832	0.5871	0.5910	0.5948	0.5987	0.6026	0.6064	0.6103	0.6141
0.3	0.6179	0.6217	0.6255	0.6293	0.6331	0.6368	0.6406	0.6443	0.6480	0.6517
0.4	0.6554	0.6591	0.6628	0.6664	0.6700	0.6736	0.6772	0.6808	0.6844	0.6879
0.5	0.6915	0.6950	0.6985	0.7019	0.7054	0.7088	0.7123	0.7157	0.7190	0.7224
0.6	0.7257	0.7291	0.7324	0.7357	0.7389	0.7422	0.7454	0.7486	0.7517	0.7549
0.7	0.7580	0.7611	0.7642	0.7673	0.7704	0.7734	0.7764	0.7794	0.7823	0.7852
0.8	0.7881	0.7910	0.7939	0.7967	0.7995	0.8023	0.8051	0.8078	0.8106	0.8133
0.9	0.8159	0.8186	0.8212	0.8238	0.8264	0.8289	0.8315	0.8340	0.8365	0.8389
1.0	0.8413	0.8438	0.8461	0.8485	0.8508	0.8531	0.8554	0.8577	0.8599	0.8621
1.1	0.8643	0.8665	0.8686	0.8708	0.8729	0.8749	0.8770	0.8790	0.8810	0.8830
1.2	0.8849	0.8869	0.8888	0.8907	0.8925	0.8944	0.8962	0.8980	0.8997	0.9015
1.3	0.9032	0.9049	0.9066	0.9082	0.9099	0.9115	0.9131	0.9147	0.9162	0.9177
1.4	0.9192	0.9207	0.9222	0.9236	0.9251	0.9265	0.9279	0.9292	0.9306	0.9319
1.5	0.9332	0.9345	0.9357	0.9370	0.9382	0.9394	0.9406	0.9418	0.9429	0.9441
1.6	0.9452	0.9463	0.9474	0.9484	0.9495	0.9505	0.9515	0.9525	0.9535	0.9545
1.7	0.9554	0.9564	0.9573	0.9582	0.9591	0.9599	0.9608	0.9616	0.9625	0.9633
1.8	0.9641	0.9649	0.9656	0.9664	0.9671	0.9678	0.9686	0.9693	0.9699	0.9706
1.9	0.9713	0.9719	0.9726	0.9732	0.9738	0.9744	0.9750	0.9756	0.9761	0.9767
2.0	0.9772	0.9778	0.9783	0.9788	0.9793	0.9798	0.9803	0.9808	0.9812	0.9817
2.1	0.9821	0.9826	0.9830	0.9834	0.9838	0.9842	0.9846	0.9850	0.9854	0.9857
2.2	0.9861	0.9864	0.9868	0.9871	0.9875	0.9878	0.9881	0.9884	0.9887	0.9890
2.3	0.9893	0.9896	0.9898	0.9901	0.9904	0.9906	0.9909	0.9911	0.9913	0.9916
2.4	0.9918	0.9920	0.9922	0.9925	0.9927	0.9929	0.9931	0.9932	0.9934	0.9936
2.5	0.9938	0.9940	0.9941	0.9943	0.9945	0.9946	0.9948	0.9949	0.9951	0.9952
2.6	0.9953	0.9955	0.9956	0.9957	0.9959	0.9960	0.9961	0.9962	0.9963	0.9964
2.7	0.9965	0.9966	0.9967	0.9968	0.9969	0.9970	0.9971	0.9972	0.9973	0.9974
2.8	0.9974	0.9975	0.9976	0.9977	0.9977	0.9978	0.9979	0.9979	0.9980	0.9981
2.9	0.9981	0.9982	0.9982	0.9983	0.9984	0.9984	0.9985	0.9985	0.9986	0.9986
3.0	0.9987	0.9987	0.9987	0.9988	0.9988	0.9989	0.9989	0.9989	0.9990	0.9990

CUMULATIVE Z-TABLE (CONT.)

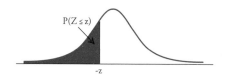

STANDARD NORMAL DISTRIBUTION

$P(Z \le z) = N(z)$ FOR $z \le 0$

z	0.00	0.01	0.02	0.03	0.04	0.05	0.06	0.07	0.08	0.09
0.0	0.5000	0.4960	0.4920	0.4880	0.4840	0.4801	0.4761	0.4721	0.4681	0.4641
-0.1	0.4602	0.4562	0.4522	0.4483	0.4443	0.4404	0.4364	0.4325	0.4286	0.4247
-0.2	0.4207	0.4168	0.4129	0.4090	0.4052	0.4013	0.3974	0.3936	0.3897	0.3859
-0.3	0.3821	0.3783	0.3745	0.3707	0.3669	0.3632	0.3594	0.3557	0.3520	0.3483
-0.4	0.3446	0.3409	0.3372	0.3336	0.3300	0.3264	0.3228	0.3192	0.3156	0.3121
-0.5	0.3085	0.3050	0.3015	0.2981	0.2946	0.2912	0.2877	0.2843	0.2810	0.2776
-0.6	0.2743	0.2709	0.2676	0.2643	0.2611	0.2578	0.2546	0.2514	0.2483	0.2451
-0.7	0.2420	0.2389	0.2358	0.2327	0.2297	0.2266	0.2236	0.2207	0.2177	0.2148
-0.8	0.2119	0.2090	0.2061	0.2033	0.2005	0.1977	0.1949	0.1922	0.1894	0.1867
-0.9	0.1841	0.1814	0.1788	0.1762	0.1736	0.1711	0.1685	0.1660	0.1635	0.1611
-1.0	0.1587	0.1562	0.1539	0.1515	0.1492	0.1469	0.1446	0.1423	0.1401	0.1379
-1.1	0.1357	0.1335	0.1314	0.1292	0.1271	0.1251	0.1230	0.1210	0.1190	0.1170
-1.2	0.1151	0.1131	0.1112	0.1093	0.1075	0.1057	0.1038	0.1020	0.1003	0.0985
-1.3	0.0968	0.0951	0.0934	0.0918	0.0901	0.0885	0.0869	0.0853	0.0838	0.0823
-1.4	0.0808	0.0793	0.0778	0.0764	0.0749	0.0735	0.0721	0.0708	0.0694	0.0681
-1.5	0.0668	0.0655	0.0643	0.0630	0.0618	0.0606	0.0594	0.0582	0.0571	0.0559
-1.6	0.0548	0.0537	0.0526	0.0516	0.0505	0.0495	0.0485	0.0475	0.0465	0.0455
-1.7	0.0446	0.0436	0.0427	0.0418	0.0409	0.0401	0.0392	0.0384	0.0375	0.0367
-1.8	0.0359	0.0351	0.0344	0.0336	0.0329	0.0322	0.0314	0.0307	0.0301	0.0294
-1.9	0.0287	0.0281	0.0274	0.0268	0.0262	0.0256	0.0250	0.0244	0.0239	0.0233
-2.0	0.0228	0.0222	0.0217	0.0212	0.0207	0.0202	0.0197	0.0192	0.0188	0.0183
-2.1	0.0179	0.0174	0.0170	0.0166	0.0162	0.0158	0.0154	0.0150	0.0146	0.0143
-2.2	0.0139	0.0136	0.0132	0.0129	0.0125	0.0122	0.0119	0.0116	0.0113	0.0110
-2.3	0.0107	0.0104	0.0102	0.0099	0.0096	0.0094	0.0091	0.0089	0.0087	0.0084
-2.4	0.0082	0.0080	0.0078	0.0076	0.0073	0.0071	0.0069	0.0068	0.0066	0.0064
-2.5	0.0062	0.0060	0.0059	0.0057	0.0055	0.0054	0.0052	0.0051	0.0049	0.0048
-2.6	0.0047	0.0045	0.0044	0.0043	0.0041	0.0040	0.0039	0.0038	0.0037	0.0036
-2.7	0.0035	0.0034	0.0033	0.0032	0.0031	0.0030	0.0029	0.0028	0.0027	0.0026
-2.8	0.0026	0.0025	0.0024	0.0023	0.0023	0.0022	0.0021	0.0021	0.0020	0.0019
-2.9	0.0019	0.0018	0.0018	0.0017	0.0016	0.0016	0.0015	0.0015	0.0014	0.0014
-3.0	0.0014	0.0013	0.0013	0.0012	0.0012	0.0011	0.0011	0.0011	0.0010	0.0010

APPENDIX B:
STUDENT'S T-DISTRIBUTION

STUDENT'S T-DISTRIBUTION

	Level of Significance for One-Tailed Test					
df	0.100	0.050	0.025	0.01	0.005	0.0005

	Level of Significance for Two-Tailed Test					
df	0.20	0.10	0.05	0.02	0.01	0.001
1	3.078	6.314	12.706	31.821	63.657	636.619
2	1.886	2.920	4.303	6.965	9.925	31.599
3	1.638	2.353	3.182	4.541	5.841	12.294
4	1.533	2.132	2.776	3.747	4.604	8.610
5	1.476	2.015	2.571	3.365	4.032	6.869
6	1.440	1.943	2.447	3.143	3.707	5.959
7	1.415	1.895	2.365	2.998	3.499	5.408
8	1.397	1.860	2.306	2.896	3.355	5.041
9	1.383	1.833	2.262	2.821	3.250	4.781
10	1.372	1.812	2.228	2.764	3.169	4.587
11	1.363	1.796	2.201	2.718	3.106	4.437
12	1.356	1.782	2.179	2.681	3.055	4.318
13	1.350	1.771	2.160	2.650	3.012	4.221
14	1.345	1.761	2.145	2.624	2.977	4.140
15	1.341	1.753	2.131	2.602	2.947	4.073
16	1.337	1.746	2.120	2.583	2.921	4.015
17	1.333	1.740	2.110	2.567	2.898	3.965
18	1.330	1.734	2.101	2.552	2.878	3.922
19	1.328	1.729	2.093	2.539	2.861	3.883
20	1.325	1.725	2.086	2.528	2.845	3.850
21	1.323	1.721	2.080	2.518	2.831	3.819
22	1.321	1.717	2.074	2.508	2.819	3.792
23	1.319	1.714	2.069	2.500	2.807	3.768
24	1.318	1.711	2.064	2.492	2.797	3.745
25	1.316	1.708	2.060	2.485	2.787	3.725
26	1.315	1.706	2.056	2.479	2.779	3.707
27	1.314	1.703	2.052	2.473	2.771	3.690
28	1.313	1.701	2.048	2.467	2.763	3.674
29	1.311	1.699	2.045	2.462	2.756	3.659
30	1.310	1.697	2.042	2.457	2.750	3.646
40	1.303	1.684	2.021	2.423	2.704	3.551
60	1.296	1.671	2.000	2.390	2.660	3.460
120	1.289	1.658	1.980	2.358	2.617	3.373
∞	1.282	1.645	1.960	2.326	2.576	3.291

APPENDIX C:
F-TABLE AT 5 PERCENT (UPPER TAIL)

F-TABLE, CRITICAL VALUES, 5 PERCENT IN UPPER TAIL

Degrees of freedom for the numerator along top row
Degrees of freedom for the denominator along side row

	1	2	3	4	5	6	7	8	9	10	12	15	20	24	30	40
1	161	200	216	225	230	234	237	239	241	242	244	246	248	249	250	251
2	18.5	19.0	19.2	19.2	19.3	19.3	19.4	19.4	19.4	19.4	19.4	19.4	19.4	19.5	19.5	19.5
3	10.1	9.55	9.28	9.12	9.01	8.94	8.89	8.85	8.81	8.79	8.74	8.70	8.66	8.64	8.62	8.59
4	7.71	6.94	6.59	6.39	6.26	6.16	6.09	6.04	6.00	5.96	5.91	5.86	5.80	5.77	5.75	5.72
5	6.61	5.79	5.41	5.19	5.05	4.95	4.88	4.82	4.77	4.74	4.68	4.62	4.56	4.53	4.50	4.46
6	5.99	5.14	4.76	4.53	4.39	4.28	4.21	4.15	4.10	4.06	4.00	3.94	3.87	3.84	3.81	3.77
7	5.59	4.74	4.35	4.12	3.97	3.87	3.79	3.73	3.68	3.64	3.57	3.51	3.44	3.41	3.38	3.34
8	5.32	4.46	4.07	3.84	3.69	3.58	3.50	3.44	3.39	3.35	3.28	3.22	3.15	3.12	3.08	3.04
9	5.12	4.26	3.86	3.63	3.48	3.37	3.29	3.23	3.18	3.14	3.07	6.01	2.94	2.90	2.86	2.83
10	4.96	4.10	3.71	3.48	3.33	3.22	3.14	3.07	3.02	2.98	2.91	2.85	2.77	2.74	2.70	2.66
11	4.84	3.98	3.59	3.36	3.20	3.09	3.01	2.95	2.90	2.85	2.79	2.72	2.65	2.61	2.57	2.53
12	4.75	3.89	3.49	3.26	3.11	3.00	2.91	2.85	2.80	2.75	2.69	2.62	2.54	2.51	2.47	2.43
13	4.67	3.81	3.41	3.18	3.03	2.92	2.83	2.77	2.71	2.67	2.60	2.53	2.46	2.42	2.38	2.34
14	4.60	3.74	3.34	3.11	2.96	2.85	2.76	2.70	2.65	2.60	2.53	2.46	2.39	2.35	2.31	2.27
15	4.54	3.68	3.29	3.06	2.90	2.79	2.71	2.64	2.59	2.54	2.48	2.40	2.33	2.29	2.25	2.20
16	4.49	3.63	3.24	3.01	2.85	2.74	2.66	2.59	2.54	2.49	2.42	2.35	2.28	2.24	2.19	2.15
17	4.45	3.59	3.20	2.96	2.81	2.70	2.61	2.55	2.49	2.45	2.38	2.31	2.23	2.19	2.15	2.10
18	4.41	3.55	3.16	2.93	2.77	2.66	2.58	2.51	2.46	2.41	2.34	2.27	2.19	2.15	2.11	2.06
19	4.38	3.52	3.13	2.90	2.74	2.63	2.54	2.48	2.42	2.38	2.31	2.23	2.16	2.11	2.07	2.03
20	4.35	3.49	3.10	2.87	2.71	2.60	2.51	2.45	2.39	2.35	2.28	2.20	2.12	2.08	2.04	1.99
21	4.32	3.47	3.07	2.84	2.68	2.57	2.49	2.42	2.37	2.32	2.25	2.18	2.10	2.05	2.01	1.96
22	4.30	3.44	3.05	2.82	2.66	2.55	2.46	2.40	2.34	2.30	2.23	2.15	2.07	2.03	1.98	1.94
23	4.28	3.42	3.03	2.80	2.64	2.53	2.44	2.37	2.32	2.27	2.20	2.13	2.05	2.01	1.96	1.91
24	4.26	3.40	3.01	2.78	2.62	2.51	2.42	2.36	2.30	2.25	2.18	2.11	2.03	1.98	1.94	1.89
25	4.24	3.39	2.99	2.76	2.60	2.49	2.40	2.34	2.28	2.24	2.16	2.09	2.01	1.96	1.92	1.87
30	4.17	3.32	2.92	2.69	2.53	2.42	2.33	2.27	2.21	2.16	2.09	2.01	1.93	1.89	1.84	1.79
40	4.08	3.23	2.84	2.61	2.45	2.34	2.25	2.18	2.12	2.08	2.00	1.92	1.84	1.79	1.74	1.69
60	4.00	3.15	2.76	2.53	2.37	2.25	2.17	2.10	2.04	1.99	1.92	1.84	1.75	1.70	1.65	1.59
120	3.92	3.07	2.68	2.45	2.29	2.18	2.09	2.02	1.96	1.91	1.83	1.75	1.66	1.61	1.55	1.50
∞	3.84	3.00	2.60	2.37	2.21	2.10	2.01	1.94	1.88	1.83	1.75	1.67	1.57	1.52	1.46	1.39

APPENDIX D:
F-TABLE AT 2.5 PERCENT (UPPER TAIL)

F-TABLE, CRITICAL VALUES, 2.5 PERCENT IN UPPER TAILS

Degrees of freedom for the numerator along top row
Degrees of freedom for the denominator along side row

	1	2	3	4	5	6	7	8	9	10	12	15	20	24	30	40
1	648	799	864	900	922	937	948	957	963	969	977	985	993	997	1001	1006
2	38.51	39.00	39.17	39.25	39.30	39.33	39.36	39.37	39.39	39.40	39.41	39.43	39.45	39.46	39.46	39.47
3	17.44	16.04	15.44	15.10	14.88	14.73	14.62	14.54	14.47	14.42	14.34	14.25	14.17	14.12	14.08	14.04
4	12.22	10.65	9.98	9.60	9.36	9.20	9.07	8.98	8.90	8.84	8.75	8.66	8.56	8.51	8.46	8.41
5	10.01	8.43	7.76	7.39	7.15	6.98	6.85	6.76	6.68	6.62	6.52	6.43	6.33	6.28	6.23	6.18
6	8.81	7.26	6.60	6.23	5.99	5.82	5.70	5.60	5.52	5.46	5.37	5.27	5.17	5.12	5.07	5.01
7	8.07	6.54	5.89	5.52	5.29	5.12	4.99	4.90	4.82	4.76	4.67	4.57	4.47	4.41	4.36	4.31
8	7.57	6.06	5.42	5.05	4.82	4.65	4.53	4.43	4.36	4.30	4.20	4.10	4.00	3.95	3.89	3.84
9	7.21	5.71	5.08	4.72	4.48	4.32	4.20	4.10	4.03	3.96	3.87	3.77	3.67	3.61	3.56	3.51
10	6.94	5.46	4.83	4.47	4.24	4.07	3.95	3.85	3.78	3.72	3.62	3.52	3.42	3.37	3.31	3.26
11	6.72	5.26	4.63	4.28	4.04	3.88	3.76	3.66	3.59	3.53	3.43	3.33	3.23	3.17	3.12	3.06
12	6.55	5.10	4.47	4.12	3.89	3.73	3.61	3.51	3.44	3.37	3.28	3.18	3.07	3.02	2.96	2.91
13	6.41	4.97	4.35	4.00	3.77	3.60	3.48	3.39	3.31	3.25	3.15	3.05	2.95	2.89	2.84	2.78
14	6.30	4.86	4.24	3.89	3.66	3.50	3.38	3.29	3.21	3.15	3.05	2.95	2.84	2.79	2.73	2.67
15	6.20	4.77	4.15	3.80	3.58	3.41	3.29	3.20	3.12	3.06	2.96	2.86	2.76	2.70	2.64	2.59
16	6.12	4.69	4.08	3.73	3.50	3.34	3.22	3.12	3.05	2.99	2.89	2.79	2.68	2.63	2.57	2.51
17	6.04	4.62	4.01	3.66	3.44	3.28	3.16	3.06	2.98	2.92	2.82	2.72	2.62	2.56	2.50	2.44
18	5.98	4.56	3.95	3.61	3.38	3.22	3.10	3.01	2.93	2.87	2.77	2.67	2.56	2.50	2.44	2.38
19	5.92	4.51	3.90	3.56	3.33	3.17	3.05	2.96	2.88	2.82	2.72	2.62	2.51	2.45	2.39	2.33
20	5.87	4.46	3.86	3.51	3.29	3.13	3.01	2.91	2.84	2.77	2.68	2.57	2.46	2.41	2.35	2.29
21	5.83	4.42	3.82	3.48	3.25	3.09	2.97	2.87	2.80	2.73	2.64	2.53	2.42	2.37	2.31	2.25
22	5.79	4.38	3.78	3.44	3.22	3.05	2.93	2.84	2.76	2.70	2.60	2.50	2.39	2.33	2.27	2.21
23	5.75	4.35	3.75	3.41	3.18	3.02	2.90	2.81	2.73	2.67	2.57	2.47	2.36	2.30	2.24	2.18
24	5.72	4.32	3.72	3.38	3.15	2.99	2.87	2.78	2.70	2.64	2.54	2.44	2.33	2.27	2.21	2.15
25	5.69	4.29	3.69	3.35	3.13	2.97	2.85	2.75	2.68	2.61	2.51	2.41	2.30	2.24	2.18	2.12
30	5.57	4.18	3.59	3.25	3.03	2.87	2.75	2.65	2.57	2.51	2.41	2.31	2.20	2.14	2.07	2.01
40	5.42	4.05	3.46	3.13	2.90	2.74	2.62	2.53	2.45	2.39	2.29	2.18	2.07	2.01	1.94	1.88
60	5.29	3.93	3.34	3.01	2.79	2.63	2.51	2.41	2.33	2.27	2.17	2.06	1.94	1.88	1.82	1.74
120	5.15	3.80	3.23	2.89	2.67	2.52	2.39	2.30	2.22	2.16	2.05	1.94	1.82	1.76	1.69	1.61
∞	5.02	3.69	3.12	2.79	2.57	2.41	2.29	2.19	2.11	2.05	1.94	1.83	1.71	1.64	1.57	1.48

APPENDIX E:
CHI-SQUARED TABLE

Values of χ^2 (Degrees of Freedom, Level of Significance)
Probability in Right Tail

Degrees of Freedom	0.99	0.975	0.95	0.9	0.1	0.05	0.025	0.01	0.005
1	0.000157	0.000982	0.003932	0.0158	2.706	3.841	5.024	6.635	7.879
2	0.020100	0.050636	0.102586	0.2107	4.605	5.991	7.378	9.210	10.597
3	0.1148	0.2158	0.3518	0.5844	6.251	7.815	9.348	11.345	12.838
4	0.297	0.484	0.711	1.064	7.779	9.488	11.143	13.277	14.860
5	0.554	0.831	1.145	1.610	9.236	11.070	12.832	15.086	16.750
6	0.872	1.237	1.635	2.204	10.645	12.592	14.449	16.812	18.548
7	1.239	1.690	2.167	2.833	12.017	14.067	16.013	18.475	20.278
8	1.647	2.180	2.733	3.490	13.362	15.507	17.535	20.090	21.955
9	2.088	2.700	3.325	4.168	14.684	16.919	19.023	21.666	23.589
10	2.558	3.247	3.940	4.865	15.987	18.307	20.483	23.209	25.188
11	3.053	3.816	4.575	5.578	17.275	19.675	21.920	24.725	26.757
12	3.571	4.404	5.226	6.304	18.549	21.026	23.337	26.217	28.300
13	4.107	5.009	5.892	7.041	19.812	22.362	24.736	27.688	29.819
14	4.660	5.629	6.571	7.790	21.064	23.685	26.119	29.141	31.319
15	5.229	6.262	7.261	8.547	22.307	24.996	27.488	30.578	32.801
16	5.812	6.908	7.962	9.312	23.542	26.296	28.845	32.000	34.267
17	6.408	7.564	8.672	10.085	24.769	27.587	30.191	33.409	35.718
18	7.015	8.231	9.390	10.865	25.989	28.869	31.526	34.805	37.156
19	7.633	8.907	10.117	11.651	27.204	30.144	32.852	36.191	38.582
20	8.260	9.591	10.851	12.443	28.412	31.410	34.170	37.566	39.997
21	8.897	10.283	11.591	13.240	29.615	32.671	35.479	38.932	41.401
22	9.542	10.982	12.338	14.041	30.813	33.924	36.781	40.289	42.796
23	10.196	11.689	13.091	14.848	32.007	35.172	38.076	41.638	44.181
24	10.856	12.401	13.848	15.659	33.196	36.415	39.364	42.980	45.558
25	11.524	13.120	14.611	16.473	34.382	37.652	40.646	44.314	46.928
26	12.198	13.844	15.379	17.292	35.563	38.885	41.923	45.642	48.290
27	12.878	14.573	16.151	18.114	36.741	40.113	43.195	46.963	49.645
28	13.565	15.308	16.928	18.939	37.916	41.337	44.461	48.278	50.994
29	14.256	16.047	17.708	19.768	39.087	42.557	45.722	49.588	52.335
30	14.953	16.791	18.493	20.599	40.256	43.773	46.979	50.892	53.672
50	29.707	32.357	34.764	37.689	63.167	67.505	71.420	76.154	79.490
60	37.485	40.482	43.188	46.459	74.397	79.082	83.298	88.379	91.952
80	53.540	57.153	60.391	64.278	96.578	101.879	106.629	112.329	116.321
100	70.065	74.222	77.929	82.358	118.498	124.342	129.561	135.807	140.170

APPENDIX F: CRITICAL VALUES FOR THE DURBIN-WATSON STATISTIC

CRITICAL VALUES FOR THE DURBIN-WATSON STATISTIC ($\alpha = 0.05$)

n	K = 1 D_l	K = 1 Du	K = 2 D_l	K = 2 D_u	K = 3 D_l	K = 3 D_u	K = 4 D_l	K = 4 D_u	K = 5 D_l	K = 5 D_u
15	1.08	1.36	0.95	1.54	0.82	1.75	0.69	1.97	0.56	2.21
16	1.10	1.37	0.98	1.54	0.86	1.73	0.74	1.93	0.62	2.15
17	1.13	1.38	1.02	1.54	0.90	1.71	0.78	1.90	0.67	2.10
18	1.16	1.39	1.05	1.53	0.93	1.69	0.82	1.87	0.71	2.06
19	1.18	1.40	1.08	1.53	0.97	1.68	0.86	1.85	0.75	2.02
20	1.20	1.41	1.10	1.54	1.00	1.68	0.90	1.83	0.79	1.99
21	1.22	1.42	1.13	1.54	1.03	1.67	0.93	1.81	0.83	1.96
22	1.24	1.43	1.15	1.54	1.05	1.66	0.96	1.80	0.86	1.94
23	1.26	1.44	1.17	1.54	1.08	1.66	0.99	1.79	0.90	1.92
24	1.27	1.45	1.19	1.55	1.10	1.66	1.01	1.78	0.93	1.90
25	1.29	1.45	1.21	1.55	1.12	1.66	1.04	1.77	0.95	1.89
26	1.30	1.46	1.22	1.55	1.14	1.65	1.06	1.76	0.98	1.88
27	1.32	1.47	1.24	1.56	1.16	1.65	1.08	1.76	1.01	1.86
28	1.33	1.48	1.26	1.56	1.18	1.65	1.10	1.75	1.03	1.85
29	1.34	1.48	1.27	1.56	1.20	1.65	1.12	1.74	1.05	1.84
30	1.35	1.49	1.28	1.57	1.21	1.65	1.14	1.74	1.07	1.83
31	1.36	1.50	1.30	1.57	1.23	1.65	1.16	1.74	1.09	1.83
32	1.37	1.50	1.31	1.57	1.24	1.65	1.18	1.73	1.11	1.82
33	1.38	1.51	1.32	1.58	1.26	1.65	1.19	1.73	1.13	1.81
34	1.39	1.51	1.33	1.58	1.27	1.65	1.21	1.73	1.15	1.81
35	1.40	1.52	1.34	1.58	1.28	1.65	1.22	1.73	1.16	1.80
36	1.41	1.52	1.35	1.59	1.29	1.65	1.24	1.73	1.18	1.80
37	1.42	1.53	1.36	1.59	1.31	1.66	1.25	1.72	1.19	1.80
38	1.43	1.54	1.37	1.59	1.32	1.66	1.26	1.72	1.21	1.79
39	1.43	1.54	1.38	1.60	1.33	1.66	1.27	1.72	1.22	1.79
40	1.44	1.54	1.39	1.60	1.34	1.66	1.29	1.72	1.23	1.79
45	1.48	1.57	1.43	1.62	1.38	1.67	1.34	1.72	1.29	1.78
50	1.50	1.59	1.46	1.63	1.42	1.67	1.38	1.72	1.34	1.77
55	1.53	1.60	1.49	1.64	1.45	1.68	1.41	1.72	1.38	1.77
60	1.55	1.62	1.51	1.65	1.48	1.69	1.44	1.73	1.41	1.77
65	1.57	1.63	1.54	1.66	1.50	1.70	1.47	1.73	1.44	1.77
70	1.58	1.64	1.55	1.67	1.52	1.70	1.49	1.74	1.46	1.77
75	1.60	1.65	1.57	1.68	1.54	1.71	1.51	1.74	1.49	1.77
80	1.61	1.66	1.59	1.69	1.56	1.72	1.53	1.74	1.51	1.77
85	1.62	1.67	1.60	1.70	1.57	1.72	1.55	1.75	1.52	1.77
90	1.63	1.68	1.61	1.70	1.59	1.73	1.57	1.75	1.54	1.78
95	1.64	1.69	1.62	1.71	1.60	1.73	1.58	1.75	1.56	1.78
100	1.65	1.69	1.63	1.72	1.61	1.74	1.59	1.76	1.57	1.78

INDEX

Notes

Notes

Notes

Notes

Notes

Notes

Notes